THE ARCTIC GOLD RUSH

To Claire P.

The Arctic Gold Rush
The New Race for Tomorrow's Natural Resources

ROGER HOWARD

continuum

Continuum UK   Continuum US
The Tower Building   80 Maiden Lane
11 York Road   Suite 704
London SE1 7NX   New York, NY 10038

www.continuumbooks.com

First published 2009

British Library Cataloguing-in-Publication Data
A catalogue record for this book is available from the British Library.

ISBN 9781441181107

Typeset by Pindar NZ, Auckland, New Zealand
Printed and bound by MPG Books Group, Bodmin and King's Lynn

Contents

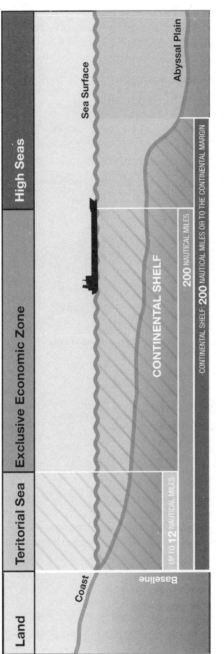

Map 1: Coastal state jurisdiction. The Law of the Sea gives coastal states the right to establish clearly defined zones extending from the coast line (baseline) and along the seabed.

Map 2: Current boundaries of the 'Arctic Five'. Claims can be extended beyond the 200-nautical-mile limit if a country can prove that undersea ridges are part of its continental shelf. The Lomonosov Ridge is thought to be part of the continental shelf of Russia, Denmark and Canada.

Map 3: The Median Line principle. Every point of a median line is equidistant to the nearest point on the shoreline. The UN has given some indications that it is interested in adopting this principle, which favours Canada and Denmark.

Map 4: The Sector Method Principle. The Sector Method principle is based
on straight longitude lines. Russia used this principle in its submission to
the UN Commission on the Limits of the Continental Shelf in 2001. This
principle favours the United States and Norway.

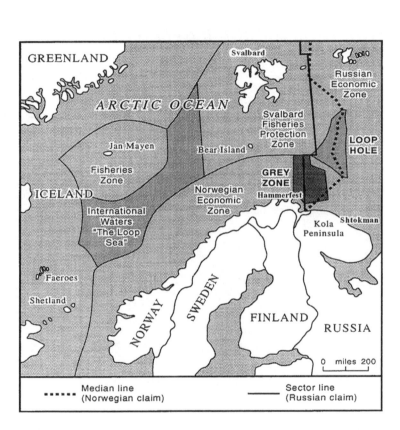

Map 5: The Barents Sea disputes. The Loophole is triangular in shape, bounded on the east by the Russian economic zone, on the south-west by the Grey Zone claimed by both Russia and Norway, and on the north-west by the Svalbard fisheries protection zone.

Acknowledgements

The author is indebted to numerous people for their information and comments but is particularly grateful to Sir Rodric Braithwaite, Dr Lawson Brigham, Tim Daffern, Professor Simon Dixon, Mette Frost, Michael Greenwood, David Jackson, Andrew Latham, Rafiq Latta, Professor Frederic Lasserre, Dr Rob Mandley, Olav Stokke, Claire Pinney (not least for her Russian translations), Professor Don Rothwell and Derek Teevan.

Roger Howard
Oxford, May 2009

Introduction

The place where two Russian explorers hoped to make history and dramatically seize the attention of the outside world was bleak yet utterly compelling. As far as every distant horizon they could see only a frozen, barren landscape that seemed to glow brilliantly beneath the bright sun and the pale blue sky. Nowhere in this icy wasteland was there any form of life or movement, and the silence and sense of isolation were total and overpowering (Map 2).

On that chilled morning of 2 August 2007, as they readied themselves for the journey that lay ahead, the explorers were far too busy to pay much attention to their surroundings. Their mission promised to be difficult, demanding and sometimes dangerous, and even getting this far had not been an easy task. They had arrived after several days of journeying on board a research vessel, *Akademik Fyodorov*, and a nuclear-powered Russian icebreaker, the *Rossiya*, which had smashed a hole through the thick ice below. On board were two miniature submarines, *Mir 1* and *Mir 2*, both of which had been safely lowered and were now ready to be launched. The task for the two men was to descend to the ocean floor that lay nearly 14,000 feet beneath them.

This would be no simple feat. In such extreme temperatures, machinery freezes and vital instruments malfunction, and making their way back to the surface would be even more difficult because of the moving ice floes. If they failed to find the exact spot where they had started then the submarines would be unable to break the ice above them and the crew would face a slow, agonizing death as their air supply slowly ran out.

But the team was ideally qualified to undertake such a hazardous mission. The Captain of *Mir 1*, Anatoly Sagalevich, was a 69-year-old veteran of numerous operations in these tiny vessels. In earlier years he had personally led difficult operations to the ocean's depths to inspect the ghostly underwater graves of sunken ships such as the

Bismarck and *Titanic*. As a departmental head at Moscow's prestigious Institute of Oceanology, he had built up an intricate knowledge of both his vessel and the Arctic's environment, particularly the geology that lay far beneath them.

In the cockpit of *Mir 2* was another distinguished figure whose name was familiar to millions of ordinary Russians. For 68-year-old Artur Chilingarov was not only a deputy chairman in Russia's national Parliament, but also an outstanding polar scientist with a long and impeccable record of exploration and research. Over 20 years before he had been proclaimed as a Hero of the Soviet Union – his country's highest honour – in recognition of the exceptional talents he had shown during a number of expeditions to the South Pole and elsewhere.

Soon the two men were ready to move, and slowly their vessels sank down into the water beneath. From their cockpits they looked up and saw the daylight shine through the ice circle above them until it gradually faded from view and then disappeared altogether. Now, after so much preparation, they started their long journey to the seabed, carefully mapping their path so they could retrace their steps.

Finally, after nearly 4 hours, sonar devices told them that they had, at last, reached the seabed. Sagalevich guided a specially built robotic arm, attached to his vessel's exterior, to collect samples of soil and rocks from the dark waters around them. But this was not the main purpose of the mission. With real skill the veteran explorer now used the exterior arm to plant a Russian flag on the seabed, at a depth of exactly 13,980 feet, in a ceremonial display that he was keen to photograph. Forged from titanium to stave off rust, and anchored by a heavy weight, the flag had been specially made for this great occasion. As Sagalevich wrote proudly in his log shortly afterwards, 'we set the flag of the Russian Federation on the floor of the Arctic Ocean'. The months of preparation had finally paid off.

Back at Moscow's Vnukovo airport, large crowds had gathered, brandishing enormous bottles of champagne and huge national flags, to welcome home the men and women of the Arctic 2007 expedition and fete them as true Russian heroes. As they stepped onto the red carpet and a brass band played, both Sagalevich and Chilingarov prepared to make deeply patriotic statements about their achievement. 'Russia is a great polar empire', Chilingarov exclaimed, adding that this was a victory for every one of his fellow nationals: 'I congratulate all the Russians on reaching the North Pole of the Earth!' Other Russians spoke in equally ecstatic terms. 'This may sound grandiloquent, but for me this is like placing a flag on the moon; this is really a massive scientific achievement', as Sergei Balyasnikov, a spokesman for the Arctic and Antarctic Institute in Moscow, told one international news agency. 'It was the first ever dive of manned vehicles under the Arctic ice. We now know that we can perform this task.'

But unlike the space race of the post-war years, or earlier trips to the North and South Pole, this journey had been more than personal achievement and national prestige. The explorers, and their supporters and unofficial sponsors in the Kremlin, did not just want to be seen to be keeping pace with, or get one step ahead of, any international rival. It was, instead, part of a carefully planned operation to assert Russia's claim over part of a region that seemed to belong to no one. This was why President Vladimir Putin had already described the urgent need for Russia to secure its 'strategic, economic, scientific and defence interests' in the Arctic, and why Chilingarov, a close confidant of the Russian president, has also declared that 'the Arctic is ours and we should manifest our presence'.

The Arctic 2007 expedition was playing an important part in this great game for the Arctic in two distinct ways. On the one hand, the explorers had taken some geological samples from the seabed that they hoped would provide convincing evidence that the region does, after all, belong to Russia. Under international law, Russia, like any other coastal state, has exclusive economic rights over any natural resources found in a zone that extends up to 200 miles from its shores.[1] But it can claim even more if it demonstrates that the 'natural prolongation' of its submerged land mass – its continental shelf – extends beyond that 200-mile limit. In this situation, it can stake a claim over any resources found within that wider area, one that might cover an extra distance of up to 150 miles (Map 1).[2] This area that lies beyond the 200-mile exclusive economic zone is known as the 'outer continental shelf' (OCS).

The crucial treaty on this issue and on many other aspects of international law is the United Nations Convention on the Law of the Sea. First drawn up in December 1982, after years of negotiations involving numerous countries, this extensive agreement seeks to cover almost every aspect of how the seas are governed and used, even though its provisions are often opaque and incomplete. Over the intervening years, this 'Constitution of the Oceans', once heralded by a UN Secretary-General as 'possibly the most significant legal instrument of this century', has been ratified by 158 states, although the single most important player in global politics, the United States, had still not signed up by the summer of 2009.[3]

The 1982 Convention attaches a great deal of importance to the question of how far any piece of land stretches out to sea. Usually a land mass reaches out into the ocean until it drops, often quite sharply, into the much deeper waters of the continental margin. In many cases, this happens quite close to the shores of the coastal state, which is nonetheless still entitled to have a 200-mile exclusive economic zone. But if there is a sudden, discernible drop beyond the 200-mile border, then the coastal country can claim to have an outer continental shelf. Of all the countries that have signed up to the 1982 Convention, perhaps as many as 70 might have this extended shelf, although they need to provide compelling geological evidence of this.[4]

In the Arctic, a great deal of argument revolves around the structure of a massive underwater formation – a submerged mountain range – known as the Lomonosov Ridge. The key question is whether it merges with any country's continental shelf. If it does, then those sections of shelf, instead of dropping suddenly when they reach the continental margin, would stretch far out to sea, reaching well beyond the limits of their respective state's 200-mile zone and in all likelihood well beyond the maximum 350-mile limit.

For some years the Russians have been adamant that their own continental shelf merges with both the Lomonosov and Mendeleev Ridges. This would mean that they could claim economic rights over a much greater area, one that starts at their existing territories in Franz Josef Land, a remote collection of islands in the far north-east of the Barents Sea, and reaches right up as far as the North Pole. It is doubtful that the efforts of Chilingarov and Sagalevich really helped Russia to prove it – some scientists pointed out that the explorers did little besides take photographs and gathered no meaningful geological evidence – but this was at least the ostensible purpose of their trip.[5]

Of course Moscow has certainly never claimed that this gives them sovereignty over more than a very limited share of the Arctic Ocean.[6] To claim any more than a section of such a vast and diverse area would plainly be absurd, for it covers more than 5.4 million square miles and touches the shorelines of four other countries: the United States, Canada, Norway and Denmark, which has claimed Greenland as its own sovereign territory for nearly two centuries. Nor does Russia claim that its continental shelf bestows any special rights over the wider Arctic region, which incorporates not just the Arctic Ocean but much more besides: this wider region covers just over 8 million square miles, comprising around 6 per cent of the earth's surface, and impinges upon the territory of another three countries:

Sweden, Finland and Iceland. And it is home to around four million people, about one-third of whom are indigenous and around half are Russian nationals.

Instead, the Kremlin is seeking to stake its claim over a slice of territory that runs north of its existing borders and into the frozen wasteland that lies above the Arctic. Large parts of this region, the 'High North', have always been a true no man's land, or rather a no man's frozen sea, an area of permanent pack ice that no man has ever bothered to claim as his own, or even shown much interest in, until very recently.

But the difficult issue for the Russians, and for any other country, is to prove it. Again, the 1982 Convention states that a government has to plead its case before a specially designated United Nations body, the Commission on the Limits of the Continental Shelf. Several years before, in December 2001, Moscow had done just that.[7] Six months later, however, the Kremlin had found its advances spurned by the Commission, whose members asked for further data that would make the Russian case more compelling. It was just such geological evidence that the two Russian explorers had been tasked with finding on the ocean floor.

Other members of the 'Arctic Five'[*] are trying just as hard to show that this ridge, and other underground formations, give them their own maritime rights. The Canadian government argues that the Lomonosov Ridge is an extension of the North American land mass and its determination to prove the point became clear in November 2008, when it commissioned two mini submarines that, soon after their planned launch in 2011, will be sent on a series of long-range missions north and west of Ellesmere Island to gather the necessary geological evidence to support the government's case. Canadian scientists hope to soon find what they want, and were encouraged when in late 2008 a joint United States-Canadian mapping mission to the Beaufort Sea produced better than expected results. 'The quality of the data is astonishing', as a Halifax-based scientist told the media. 'We haven't analysed it all, but what we found is that the entire Beaufort Sea – all the way up to the north – is covered with significant amounts of sediments, which makes our case look very promising.'[8]

Some other countries, including Norway, Denmark, Iceland and the United States, have also either pitched their respective claims to an outer continental shelf that reaches beyond the standard 200-mile limit, or look ready to do so. The Danish government is spending

[*] The 'Arctic Five' are Russia, the United States, Canada, Norway and Denmark.

huge sums of money preparing a comprehensive map that it claims
will demonstrate that the Lomonosov Ridge runs from the top of
Greenland all the way to the North Pole. Oslo is also holding high
hopes that the UN Commission will look favourably on its claim for
ownership of areas in the Norwegian Sea, the Barents Sea and the
Arctic Ocean that cover 100,000 square miles. It submitted its own
case to the UN in November 2006, exactly 10 years after signing up
to the 1982 Convention and just within the deadline that the treaty
demands.[9]

But there was also another, more emotive, reason for the Arctic
mission. In a matter of mere hours, dramatic pictures of the Russian
flag being lodged onto the Arctic seabed had been broadcast around
the world, suddenly focusing attention on a region that not many
people knew much about. This was exactly what the leaders in the
Kremlin had hoped for: the Arctic 2007 expedition was all about
expressing and symbolizing Russia's claim to the region, as well
as its resurgent national confidence, before the watching world. 'If
a hundred or a thousand years from now someone goes down to
where we were, they will see the Russian flag', as Chilingarov told
one Russian news agency.

Of course planting a flag in any part of the world doesn't give any
country a right to rule it. As a spokesman in the US State Department,
Tom Casey, pointed out, 'I'm not sure whether they put a metal flag,
a rubber flag or a bedsheet on the ocean floor. Either way, it doesn't
have any legal standing'. Any such 'rights' depend on international
law, and although many countries openly flout it, most are reluctant
to overtly do so for fear of sanctions, military conflict or, in some
cases, frightening off foreign investors. No one is quite sure who owns
large parts of the Arctic, but it was certain that the flag ceremony
did not bestow any special right on Moscow. It did, however, seem
to be symbolic of some people's worst fears about the Russians: that
they would hold few scruples about seizing much of the Arctic for
themselves.

This was why the footage provoked a powerful international
reaction, particularly from those who were closest to hand. To the
Canadians it seemed threatening, reminiscent of a bygone imperial
age when great powers simply seized land by force and then planted
a flag to claim it as their own. Foreign Minister, Peter Mackay,
vigorously protested that 'this isn't the fifteenth century. You can't go
around the world and plant flags', while the European Union's Energy
Commissioner, Andris Piebalgs, later stated simply that he was 'not
at ease with developments in the Arctic' and that 'countries that are

bordering the Arctic should be extremely serious about not making conflictual announcements, because whatever solution is found, it should be between all the countries bordering it'.[10] Newspapers across the world echoed the same message, condemning Moscow's 'stunt' as a sign of its 'Czarist impulses' and claiming that it was just a 'Kremlin-sponsored act of bravado aimed at boosting national pride'.

Back in Moscow, there was little sign of remorse as international tension suddenly heightened. 'We are happy that we placed a Russian flag on the ocean bed, where not a single person has ever been, and I don't give a damn what some foreign individuals think about that', claimed Artur Chilingarov. Making a reference to an expedition led by a Soviet Arctic researcher, Ivan Papanin, on a drifting ice floe in the winter of 1937, he claimed that 'Russia [has] always expanded its territory by northern lands' and that 'seventy years ago, they would say, "Bolsheviks have conquered the Arctic". Now our crew is United Russia. The Russian flag is the point of the North Pole of the Earth. Full stop. If someone doesn't like it, let them dive as deep as 14,000 feet and try and leave something down there'. A short distance away from where he was speaking, some youths from the pro-Kremlin Young Guard movement were showing even less remorse. 'Who has shown the planet what is what?' they chanted, 'it's our Arctic explorer Chilingarov! The Russian people are in the Arctic now!'

Superficially, it is of course surprising that the Arctic should arouse so much attention and interest. Yet, as other parts of the world prove, most obviously the Middle East, some of the world's harshest and most difficult environments can also harbour great natural wealth.

The heart of the issue is climate change. Although local temperatures have always ebbed and flowed, the climatic variations in the region over the past quarter century are far more dramatic than anything it is known to have previously witnessed. Over the past six decades average winter temperatures in western Canada and Alaska have increased by as much as seven degrees Fahrenheit, and as temperatures rise, so too does the speed with which the Arctic ice is melting.

Of course, the Arctic Ocean has never been completely frozen over, because the constant movement (the fracturing and melting of its vast ice packs) often creates open waters. Even then, there are considerable seasonal fluctuations. In September and October, after months of summer sun, the ice packs are confined mostly to the ocean's northern-most regions, and only a small amount floats into some of the constituent waters, such as the Greenland, Kara and Barents Seas and the Canadian archipelago, that lie further south. In February and

March, however, a great deal of ice is usually found in all of these areas, as well as in peripheral waters, such as the Bering Sea, Hudson Bay, the Sea of Okhotsk and Baffin Bay (Map 2).

What has happened in recent years is a drastic alteration of this pattern. Around 41 per cent of permanent ice is estimated to have already completely disappeared from the region over the last quarter century, and every year a further million square miles or so vanishes, shrinking the ice cap to around half of the size it covered in the mid-twentieth century. Data provided by NASA satellites shows that in 1979, perennial sea ice covered an area twice the size of the United States. Twenty-five years later, however, an area equivalent to New York, Georgia and Texas had completely vanished, mostly from the Beaufort, Chukchi, Siberian and Laptev Seas.

The implications of this rapid and drastic climate change are, of course, vast, affecting everyone in the region and many more beyond, in some way or another. This is the subject of numerous specialist studies, most notably a huge research document, the *Arctic Climate Impact Assessment*, published in 2004. This extensive study has argued that a great many people will inevitably lose out from these changes: 'the reduction in sea ice is very likely to have devastating consequences for polar bears, ice-dependent seals, and local people for whom the animals are a primary food source'. But it adds there could also be some benefits too, including the opening of job opportunities for local people and, from an environmental point of view, 'increased areas of tree growth in the Arctic [that] could serve to take up carbon dioxide and supply more wood products and related employment'.[11]

For many governments – not just those whose own territory extends beyond the Arctic Circle – what matters most, at least for the moment, are the region's natural resources and their accessibility to them. Above all, many experts have long been convinced that the Arctic Ocean has resources on a vast scale and recognized that the gradual thaw of its ice is now making them accessible for the first time. A leading American organization, for example, estimates that the region might even hold as much as 13 per cent of the world's remaining deposits of oil and 30 per cent of its gas, while traces of numerous precious metals, including gold, platinum and iron ore, have also been found.[12]

Such revelations have become even more important because by the time that Chilignarov and Sagalevich made their underwater expedition, fears were mounting that the world's natural resources – its supply of oil in particular – were beginning to run out. The market price of crude oil started to climb considerably in early

2004, allowing producers to reap vast earnings. It was a tempting reminder that whoever could claim the Arctic's resources would have an increasingly precious commodity on their hands.

The likely presence of so many natural resources is a vastly more important consideration than any prospect of international shipping routes that might one day traverse the Arctic's waters. In recent years, there have been media reports of two such sea lanes. One of these runs through the Northwest Passage, a series of distinct but connected straits that stretch along the Canadian and Alaskan shores and link the Pacific and Atlantic Oceans. The other is Russia's Northern Sea Route, which runs along across the Barents, Kara, Laptev, East Siberian and Chukchi Seas, through the Bering Straits and then into the northern Pacific (Map 2). Both, it is sometimes said, would create a shorter link between east and west than the Suez and Panama Canals currently offer, and the opening of these new commercial 'highways' would drastically reduce sailing times and slash shipping costs. But many of these reports have been exaggerated; although these trade routes will certainly become more navigable during the summer months, they are most unlikely to become ice-free all year round. As a result, sailing times will remain uncertain and tight schedules could be easily disrupted.

However, in the context of oil, gas and other natural resources the full importance of the outer continental shelf, in the Arctic in particular but also throughout the wider world, becomes clear. A very high proportion of the world's oil and natural gas is estimated to lie offshore and now that the technology to develop these reserves has been developed, coastal states the world over have a greater interest than ever before in demonstrating that they have an outer continental shelf. The economic future of some of the world's developing countries, such as Barbados, Tonga and Palau, could even hinge on this single issue.

No one is quite sure, however, who rules large parts of this region, which has only recently assumed so much importance. There are all sorts of competing claims here, all of which have long been ignored or downplayed, but which are now the focus of intense scrutiny from governments, lawyers, explorers, geologists and military men.

Of course, the same could be said about other regions whose fate has nonetheless been resolved amicably. Disputes over the Antarctic were temporarily settled in 1959 when representatives of 12 countries, including the two superpowers as well as important players on the international stage, such as France, Japan and the United Kingdom, met in Washington to negotiate and sign an agreement to determine the region's future. Under the terms of the deal, each signatory state agreed not to 'recognize, dispute or establish territorial sovereignty claims' to the region for the next 50 years.[13] This was because 'Antarctica shall continue forever to be used exclusively for peaceful purposes and shall not become the scene or object of international discord'. As a result, the signatories decided that 'any measure of a military nature, such as the establishment of military bases and fortifications, the carrying out of military manoeuvres, as well as the testing of any type of weapon' should be prohibited.[14] Since it came into effect in June 1961, a further 38 countries have signed and ratified its provisions.

Unfortunately this is not a helpful analogy. This is not because of the geographical differences between them – many of the Arctic's disputed regions are seas, whereas Antarctica is a land mass – but for another reason. The 1959 treaty has proved enduring essentially because oil and natural gas were discovered in Antarctica only long after it was signed. Since the nineteenth century it had been regarded as a lucrative source of whale and seal stocks, but petroleum was found only in the early 1980s. Now that the technology to exploit these resources has been developed, it is possible that the agreement might break down. In any event, the southern region does not have the Arctic's superb strategic setting.

It is tempting to view the Arctic as the likely setting of a scenario that has become much discussed in recent years and continues to be much feared: the scenario of brutal, bitter and bloody confrontation waged between rival international powers that are desperate to acquire the world's diminishing supply of natural resources. From this viewpoint the provocative journey of Chilingarov and Sagalevich appears, if not quite an opening round, a premonition of the trouble that lies ahead. However, the central argument of this book is that this scenario is even less likely to happen in the Arctic than elsewhere, but there are other dangers that soon could become very real.

Part 1
The Setting

1

A Looming Resource War?

For a few brief weeks in the summer of 2008, it seemed that everyone's worst fears for the future were being realized with an alarming rapidity. The price of oil surged, reaching new heights that just months before would have been unthinkable even to the most reckless Wall Street trader. Across the world demonstrators took to the streets, demanding immediate government action to alleviate the crippling financial burden that the increase imposed. Tens of thousands of Spanish truckers blocked roads, turning back traffic at the French border and creating 12-mile queues outside Madrid and Barcelona while their counterparts in France, Portugal and Italy quickly followed their example. Other protests were much more violent. Eighteen demonstrators were injured in Jakarta when the police used water cannons and truncheons against a furious mob that had gathered outside Parliament, and there were also violent protests in Nepal, Haiti and Malaysia.

At the same time, global stocks of rice were slumping to their lowest levels for 30 years, causing panic, disorder and eventually violence in those parts of the world where rice is a staple food. City streets in places as far apart as Haiti and Morocco, Uzbekistan and Yemen, were thronged with violent mobs protesting about the price rise.[1] Fears over the potential impact of the rice crisis were heightened even more when the UN Food and Agriculture Organization predicted a serious shortfall over the coming years, and the President of the World Bank, Robert Zoellick, estimated that 'thirty-three countries around the world face potential social unrest because of the acute hike in food and energy prices'.[2]

Such scenes may offer a revealing glimpse of tomorrow's world, in which global demand will continue to grow for diminishing resources. In particular, pessimists argue that this is why future 'resource wars' could so easily break out. According to this viewpoint, as fears of future energy shortages grow and commodity prices rise, despite their massive setbacks in the global economic downturn that began in 2008, then so too will the temptation grow for governments to resort to military force and seize the world's diminishing natural resources for themselves. And the bitter civil wars that are being fought in some parts of the world, notably West Africa, are said to illustrate the bloody outcome of such a scenario.

This was the gloomy conclusion of a report, *Climate Change and International Security*, that was published by the European Union in March 2008. Authored at the highest levels of government in Brussels, it argued that 'more disputes over land and maritime borders and other territorial rights are likely' as a result of climate change and in particular claimed that:

> *one of the most significant potential conflicts over resources arises from intensified competition over access to, and control over, energy resources. That in itself is, and will continue to be, a cause of instability. However, because much of the world's hydrocarbon reserves are in regions vulnerable to the impacts of climate change and because many oil and gas producing states already face significant social economic and demographic challenges, instability is likely to increase. This has the potential to feed back into greater energy insecurity and greater competition for resources. A possible wider use of nuclear energy for power generation might raise new concerns about proliferation, in the context of a non-proliferation regime that is already under pressure. As previously inaccessible regions open up due to the effects of climate change, the scramble for resources will intensify.[3]*

The report continues to say that the Arctic presents one real source of tension because its energy resources are 'changing the geo-strategic dynamics of the region with potential consequences for international stability and European security interests'. It added that 'the resulting new strategic interests are illustrated by the recent planting of the Russian flag under the North Pole'.

Other governmental papers have also painted a bleak picture. The United States Navy document, 'A Cooperative Strategy for 21st Century Seapower', argued that 'climate change is gradually opening up the waters of the Arctic, not only to new resource development, but also to new shipping routes that may reshape the global transport system. While these developments offer opportunities for growth, they are potential sources of competition and conflict for access and natural resources'.[4] And in March 2009, the British government's chief scientist, Professor John Beddington, warned that the world could face a 'perfect storm' of food, energy and water shortages within just 20 years. Speaking before a conference on sustainable development, he predicted 'a very gloomy picture' in the years ahead and argued that 'things will start to get really worrying' unless the underlying causes – massive population growth and climate change – were addressed immediately.[5]

Various events in the Arctic region seem to reinforce the impression that trouble is brewing. Within days of the Arctic expedition, President Putin announced his intention to resume the old Cold War practice of sending Russian planes to 'buzz' the defences of several neighbouring countries, flying as close as possible to their airspace without quite violating it. 'I have made a decision to resume regular flights of Russian strategic aviation', as he said in televised remarks, 'and our partners will view the resumption of flights of Russia's strategic aviation with understanding.'

Since then, British and Norwegian fighter jets have regularly scrambled to intercept Russian warplanes that fly close to their country's national borders, warning them not to stray any further. Strictly speaking, the Russian provocation is not a violation of international law but it does amount to what is unofficially known as a 'breach of etiquette', designed to make a point about Russia's national prestige and standing. These 'breaches of etiquette' had been a regular occurrence, almost a ritual, in the days of the Cold War, but had faded after the break-up of the Soviet Union in the early 1990s and had now made a comeback because Russia's coffers were filled with earnings from the export of oil. Since then its military forces have not only regularly tested the air defences of various NATO countries but also occasionally conducted low-level naval exercises in the very midst of Norway's oil and gas platforms in the North Sea and even carried out a mock bombing run against Norway's northern command centre at Bodo. Since the end of 2008 these missions have continued, even though Russia's economy has been badly affected by a dramatic drop in the price of oil, but they are still a regular occurrence: in 2008 NATO fighters scrambled to intercept 87 Russian bombers outside Norwegian territory, just one less than the previous year.[6]

Such 'breaches of etiquette' could conceivably be a sign of an aggressive mindset that would deliberately use military force to seize control of Arctic resources. Certainly some countries in the region consider the prospect of armed confrontation over the Arctic to be a real one. In 2008, the Norwegian media obtained a copy of a leaked report from the chief of the armed forces that considers just such a scenario, quoting General Sverre Diesen of the Norwegian military as saying that there was no immediate danger of war 'but there are grey zones'.[7] The previous year Diesen had spoken in terms more reminiscent of the Cold War when he said that 'under certain circumstances there is undoubtedly room for the possible use of military power' and added that 'the use of limited military operations in support of political demands, or the use of military power as part of a broader political crisis management, cannot be excluded in our neighbouring areas'.[8]

The Canadian prime minister, Stephen Harper, also admitted that such actions were a cause of alarm: 'I'm less concerned with the US, who, while not formally acknowledging our claim (over disputed parts of the Arctic), at least acknowledges that we make the claim and cooperates with us on the defence of North America. I think the greater worry is some of the other nations that we believe have been paddling around up there and not necessarily acknowledging their obligations to communicate with the government of Canada.'[9] The American response has hitherto been fairly muted but there are signs of change. In January 2009 the White House released a presidential directive on the Arctic region, and a few months before had announced plans to deploy an unmanned aerial vehicle, a drone or 'Predator', along its northern borders with a view to stationing 'several more' in the region by the end of 2010. At the same time the director of Homeland Security, Michael Chertoff, visited Alaska to assess the coast guard's operations there.

Some other developments have scarcely been more reassuring. In the summer of 2008, a Russian military chief, Lieutenant General Vladimir Shamanov, emphasized that his armed forces would have to be ready for combat operations in the Arctic – 'modern wars are often won and lost long before they start' – and would fight to defend the areas that Russia claimed formed part of its continental shelf.[10] At the same time, the Russian navy resumed its patrols of the seas around the Svalbard archipelago, an area of dispute between Moscow and Oslo. Although there had been no activity by Russia's military in this region since the collapse of the Soviet Union, its naval commanders stated their plans to increase military activity in these waters, and the heavy Northern Fleet vessel, *Severomorsk*, moved into the seas that surround Spitsbergen Island in the summer and was joined soon after by a missile cruiser, *Marshall Ustinov*.[11] 'Periodic missions of the Northern Fleet's battle vessels will be made to Arctic areas with the necessary regularity', as a spokesman for the Russian navy rather chillingly announced.

In December 2008, the Kremlin also published the draft text of a new national security document that seemed to confirm the worst fears of many people. In one passage on the future of the world's energy resources, the draft text points out that:

> *international policy will focus on the access to the energy sources of the world, including the Middle East, Barents Sea, the Arctic Region, Caspian Sea and Central Asia. The struggle for the hydrocarbon resources can be developed to the military confrontation as well, which can result with violation of balance on the Russia's borders with the allies and increasing of the nuclear countries.*[12]

Did the Kremlin mean that other countries might want to use military force to seize energy reserves and that Russia should be prepared for such an eventuality? Or were the Russians saying that they might be taking such an aggressive approach themselves? For some people such an eventuality seemed all the more likely when, three months later, Moscow announced plans to create army units in its Arctic territories that would 'guarantee military security in different military-political situations'. The formation of this new military force was incorporated in a new strategy document that declared the Arctic to be Russia's most important arena for 'international and military security' in its relations with other countries. The document also called for the creation of a new intelligence network to provide 'effective control of economic, military and (ecological) activity' in the region.[13] The 'freezing temperature' units would have special ammunition, weaponry and transport and be readily deployable across the vast region.

There are several different ways in which a 'resource war' in the region could conceivably break out. The most extreme, and far-fetched, is simply when one country invades territory that indisputably belongs to another under international law, usually searching for an excuse under the terms of the United Nations Charter to justify its act of aggression.[14] So if, in the future, any country enjoys overwhelming military superiority over its rival, whose natural resources it is perhaps desperate to seize, then it is plausible to argue that the Arctic could perhaps be the setting for this form of 'resource war'.

Fortunately, wars rarely break out in this way for the simple reason that very few would-be aggressors have enjoyed the military superiority to start them. It is much more usual for countries to work together and counterbalance the overwhelming power of another state. As one eminent commentator has written, it is necessary 'to acknowledge the extent to which war as a path to conflict resolution and great-power expansion has become largely obsolete'. Instead, warfare has in many cases 'truly become an option of last resort'.[15]

What is much more likely is that one country could use military force to seize disputed territory, or rather disputed territory whose precise legal status is unresolved. It is in this category that whole swathes of the Arctic region fall, in several quite distinct ways.

First, there are some areas where the claims of rival countries overlap, such as in the Beaufort and Barents Seas, or in a small section of territory, lying close to the North Pole, that Russia, Denmark and Canada could all claim as part of their respective continental shelves.[16]

Second, there are other regions that only one country can claim but which, if its legal efforts fail, would then make a tempting target for another state. For example, Canada is trying to prove that its continental shelf extends beyond its 200-mile economic zone, but if it fails to provide enough evidence then another state, such as Russia or the United States, could conceivably send warships and icebreakers to claim any section of these waters for itself.

Third, there are areas that are claimed only by one country, which could use military force when its legal and geological efforts are thwarted. If Russia should fail to demonstrate that its continental shelf extends as far north as the mission of Chilingarov and Sagalevich was designed to prove, then it could conceivably disregard international law, declare that the region forms part of its own territory and threaten to use force to back-up its claim.

Finally, a government could employ military force to assert its claims over an area that can otherwise only be 'no man's land', or what the 1982 Convention simply refers to as 'the Area' that lies 'beyond the limits of national jurisdiction'. There is one unclaimed stretch of Arctic seabed that lies beyond the theoretical maximum limits of the outer continental shelves of each of the 'Arctic Five'. It will therefore be administered as 'the common heritage of mankind' by an intergovernmental organization, the Jamaica-based International Seabed Authority, which the Convention specifically established to undertake this task.[17]

To take one last scenario, a 'resource war' could be fought more by accident than design if international powers start to step up their military presence in any region and exchange aggressive rhetoric. In this state of mistrust, small incidents on the ground can quickly spiral out of control, leading to a much wider confrontation. This could happen even if there are no territorial disputes in the Arctic, in the same way that so many other conflicts – most obviously the First World War – began in a similar state of mistrust or 'fear'.[18]

A United Nations panel is due to reach a categorical decision about who owns what in the Arctic by 2020. But until the panel delivers its verdict, there is a danger that some countries could act unilaterally. Perhaps fearful that the UN could rule against them, a government could take steps to claim a disputed region for itself. Technological progress is likely to make such steps more tempting, for by 2020 the technology to extract a far higher proportion of the Arctic's oil and natural gas natural frontiers is likely to have been developed. By the late 1980s the deepest offshore operations reached around 1200 feet, and now two decades later some exploration wells have been drilled almost eight times deeper.

An exaggerated risk

It is certainly true that in recent years disagreements about who owns some resource-rich waters have led to exchanges not just of heated words but also of violent blows. The legal status of the Spratly Islands in the South China Sea has long been hotly debated in the region and has created a state of high tension between China, Vietnam, Taiwan, the Philippines and other neighbouring countries. In 1988 this spilled over and nearly caused a regional war when Chinese gunboats sank Vietnamese transport ships that were supporting a military landing party near Johnson Reef. And in recent years, speculation that these waters could be a major source of petroleum has made the dispute even more bitter.

The underlying theme of this book is that the events of August 2007 are most unlikely to be the prelude to a future resource war fought over the Arctic. On the contrary, it is usually unnecessary and sometimes wholly counterproductive for any country to use military force to seize control over a foreign supply of natural resources. The Russian government would immediately alienate the sympathy of foreign investors, who are vital to the success of its economy in general and its energy sector in particular, and suffer a stock market slump if it undertook such drastic action. And even this assumes that the Arctic does have any natural resources that are really worth fighting over.

Most international powers have much more to gain from using the UN in order to stake their claim to the Arctic. To make their case as compelling as possible, they will be likely to rely on the presentation of highly sophisticated scientific evidence about very specialized issues, most notably the formation of the complex geological structures that lie beneath this disputed region. Such claims are likely to be backed up by the threat of military force, a threat that will usually be latent, at other times much more explicit, to lend them extra credibility. This, in turn, creates another serious danger, a danger of accidental war waged by a power that fears imminent attack by a rival, and then strikes its own pre-emptive blow.

If any particular controversy perfectly illustrates how irrational and exaggerated such speculation of a 'resource war' really is, then it is the dispute over Hans Island in the Nares Strait that lies between Greenland and Canada (Map 2). Because some geologists have speculated that these waters might have large deposits of oil and gas, the two governments have strongly disputed each other's territorial claim to the island. These disagreements have sometimes escalated into bitter squabbling and have led to acts of military posturing and showmanship. To the onlooker this dispute is not easy to understand because even if there are commercial quantities of oil and gas in the Nares Strait, the question of who actually rules Hans Island is likely to be irrelevant. Any sizeable deposits are much more likely to be found in the surrounding waters than on such a tiny island, and a border agreement that both governments signed in 1973 would determine their ownership.[19]

Nor, on close inspection, are some of Moscow's supposedly belligerent statements really quite as threatening as they might sometimes sound. The Kremlin's announcement, made in March 2009, of the formation of a new military force was even welcomed by some of those who studied the fine print. Norwegian State Secretary of Defence, Espen Barth Eide, told a British newspaper that he was 'not concerned' by the announcement but regarded it as a way of fostering cooperation in the region. 'I don't think an increased military presence needs to increase tensions if the interested parties are informed', he said. And there was, he continued, no reason to doubt Moscow's stated goal of trying to establish 'a zone of peace and co-operation' in the region.[20]

There is no reason why the prospect of finding large quantities of natural resources in the Arctic region should undermine the commitment made by the five coastal states in May 2008, when representatives gathered in Greenland to issue what has become known as the Ilulissat Declaration. Reaffirming their wish to pursue 'the orderly settlement of any possible overlapping claims', they also declared their commitment to the 1982 Convention, even though the United States is not a member:

[T]he law of the sea provides for important rights and obligations concerning the delineation of the outer limits of the continental shelf,

the protection of the marine environment, including ice-covered areas, freedom of navigation, marine scientific research, and other uses of the sea.[21]

Instead, many actions that might be deemed to be 'warmongering' amount to empty posturing and, in the words of the chief of the Russian navy, Vladimir Vysoktsky, are merely 'psychological'.[22]

The real danger
The retreat of the Arctic's ice instead poses another risk to peace and stability, one that is much more serious than the advent of any 're-source war'. As the waters of the Arctic Ocean steadily become more navigable, Russia and the United States may start to feel threatened by the growing presence of foreign governments in areas that they regard as strategically important, or even as their own backyard.

This could happen if a rival government establishes a commercial or, more drastically, a military presence in the region, or if commercial vessels or warships make their way through Arctic waters, simply exercising their right of 'innocent passage' through the territorial seas that lie adjacent to every coastal state. These ships could also provoke serious incidents if they venture through disputed waters.

For a country that is already mistrustful of another, such a presence might easily confirm its suspicions, reinforcing a picture of hostility and enmity that already seems plain to see. It is possible to imagine a strong reaction in Washington if, for example, Chinese companies should start to establish themselves in a country like Greenland, which is both strategically important as well as rich in resources. Or if Iranian warships 'innocently' made their way close to the Northwest Passage at a time of heightened tension over Tehran's nuclear ambitions. Accidents can also spark confrontations: it was fortunate that a serious collision between Russian and American submarines in Kolski Bay, in the waters outside Murmansk, happened at a time when Cold War relations had thawed considerably.[23]

There is an obvious counterargument: warships from Russia, the United States, China and every other country can currently sail in high seas close to each other's mainland, or make 'innocent passage' within a short distance of their shores. There are also places, such as Cuba and Poland, where Russian and American forces can establish themselves in a way that the other would find highly provocative, or even intolerable.[24] Why, then, are the Arctic's waters and territories more likely than anywhere else to become a future danger zone?

Most importantly, the regional presence of highly valued natural resources will give countries from all over the globe (not just the 'Arctic Five') a particular reason to establish themselves there. So if Chinese energy companies should explore for oil in Russia's Arctic waters, perhaps not far from the American border in the Bering Strait, there would be serious tensions between Washington and Beijing. China, as a later chapter points out, is in the process of undertaking a major overhaul and expansion of its naval forces, and the Arctic is one theatre where its ships might eventually come into close proximity with those of the Americans. Washington might also feel threatened if Chinese state-owned organizations invested in places such as Greenland, which the United States considers strategically important.[25] The Chinese could also conceivably eye the natural resources of Baffin Island in the Canadian Arctic, where some of the world's purest iron ore has been found and is already in the process of being exploited.[26]

The Arctic also has crucial strategic importance as some of the Arctic's islands and shores, notably Greenland and Svalbard, hold the key to the defence of Atlantic shipping routes, Russia's ports and industrial complexes, America's radar network as well as Alaska's oil installations. In the longer term, some of its seas may eventually become vital international trade routes that link east and west. This doesn't just mean that more ships will be making their way through their waters, but also that foreign governments will have better reason than before to establish a presence there.

The region is special for the simple reason that there are few other strategically important areas close to the two key members of the 'Arctic Eight'† – the United States and Russia – where an enemy force could conceivably establish a landed presence. Either country could hypothetically set up a military base on Greenland's east coast and in doing so make the other feel threatened. Decades hence, when the local climate may have become much less harsh, both could also beef up their forces close to the Barents Strait, facing each other from their respective territories in the same way they did in central Europe during the Cold War.

In other words, even if we suppose that the Arctic is completely devoid of natural resources, the region's increasing strategic importance could still exacerbate a state of mistrust between rival countries. Moscow could conceivably step up its military presence there, establishing what its Security Council chiefs have called 'a main

---

† The 'Arctic Eight' are Russia, the United States, Canada, Norway, Denmark, Iceland, Finland and Sweden.

strategic resource base' and by doing so make other countries equally fearful.[27] Or it is possible to imagine several foreign ships sailing, without Moscow's permission, towards the Vilkitsky Strait, a vital link between the Kara and Laptev Seas, and, at a moment of high international tension, the Russian authorities then taking preventive action to thwart an attack that they feel sure is imminent (Map 2).

The five Arctic coastal states are not accustomed to maritime traffic moving through those seas that are only now just starting to become accessible, or to the idea that a rival government might in some way establish itself in the region. Both Canada and Russia regard the Northwest Passage and the Northern Sea Route, which runs along the Russian coast, as their own respective 'historic waters'. They strongly dispute the alleged right of foreign ships to pass through them without permission and Russia, in particular, views their passage as an unwelcome intrusion into its territory. The United States might not have any comparable legal claim over the seas that lie north of Alaska but the mere prospect of foreign ships sailing through these waters is not something that American strategists are any more accustomed to than their Russian and Canadian counterparts.

Exactly when Russia, the United States or any of the other Arctic countries might start to feel threatened in this way, whether by the passage of ships or by any apparent occupation of Arctic land, is hard to say. What is certain is that although there are no precise figures on maritime traffic in the High North, experts know that it is already increasing considerably. According to one highly authoritative source, approximately 6,000 vessels ventured into the Arctic marine area in the course of 2004, around half of which were fishing vessels, while the rest were commercial ships and carriers.[28] In 2007, when seasonal ice was considerably lighter than the previous year, the Canadian coast guard also recorded a big jump in the number of ships moving into Arctic waters, while the Russians have started to make good use of the western end of their Northern Sea Route.[29] As the Secretary-General of NATO has pointed out, 'several Arctic Rim countries are strengthening their capabilities, and military activity in the High North region has been steadily increasing'.[30]

It is possible to imagine Russia or the United States taking action in the region that others might regard as belligerent, even if they are undertaken defensively. As a United States presidential directive on the Arctic, published in January 2009, argued, 'human activity in the Arctic region is increasing and is projected to increase further in coming years. This requires the United States to assert a more active and influential national presence to protect its Arctic interests and to project sea power throughout the region'.[31] The document also stressed that the United States has to 'project a sovereign . . . maritime presence in the Arctic in support of essential United States interests'. Washington certainly thinks that Russia is likely to pose a big threat to the region's stability and will pursue what the CIA calls 'a more proactive and influential foreign policy, reflecting Moscow's re-emergence as a major player on the world stage', while 'few countries are poised to have more impact on the world over the next fifteen to twenty years than China'.[32] The Arctic may prove to be one forum where these and other countries could assert themselves over the coming years.

Premonitions of the type of situation that could be realized in the years ahead came in the summer of 2008, when the economy of Iceland, which stands on the periphery of the Arctic, began to implode. In August, Reykjavik first asked Moscow for a loan and 3 months later reiterated its request, asking for $6 billion. Many observers felt sure that Russia would try to attach political strings to any such loan, seeking preferential rights over Iceland's fisheries, energy and mining sectors and perhaps even assuming control over an air base, once used by the Americans but abandoned in 2006, at Keflavik. 'If Russia becomes the country which saves the Icelandic economy, Russia could also end up securing an extended level of power in the North Atlantic', as one media editorial argued.[33] But any such move would have caused serious tension with the United States.

The next three chapters look at the setting – the people, the place and the vexing question of who the region actually belongs to – where some of the controversies and disputes are being played out.

2

The Arctic Thaw

In the spring of 1993, Inuits began to notice big changes in the formation of the winter sea ice near their homes in the Alaskan village of Shishmaref, a few miles off the coast of the Seward Peninsula. Until the spring thaw set in, the men had always made regular trips by snowmobile to hunt for seals, and until the mid-1980s they had always been able to drive a long way onto the ice to find their prey. But this year it was simply too dangerous to even walk out onto the frozen sea because the ice was thawing much earlier than ever before. The hunters therefore decided to start using boats instead. 'We just thought it's warming up a little bit', as one of the Inuit men told an American reporter. 'It was good at the start – warmer winters, you know – but now everything is going so fast.'[1]

At the same, time foreign visitors to the region also noticed similar changes, discovering a very different Arctic landscape from the one they had expected to find. In the late summer of 1997 a group of American geophysicists travelled to the Arctic to investigate reports that the ice was disappearing. One earlier mission, in 1975, had described an ice floe with an average thickness of nine feet and the geophysicists found, 22 years later, that it barely reached 6 feet in exactly the same place. One of the scientists on board recalled their reaction: 'we imagined calling the sponsors at the National Science Foundation and saying, "well, we can't find any ice".'[2]

The indigenous people of other Arctic regions were also starting to notice that something was radically transforming the traditional landscapes where their forebears had lived and worked for thousands of years. In the late 1990s, a number of houses and buildings in remote parts of Alaska had lost their upright shape and instead started to lean over at peculiar, and sometimes very dangerous, angles. Some of them were starting to slump downwards, while the windows and doors of other buildings were gradually sinking closer to the ground.

It wasn't long before scientists worked out what was happening. Much of the Arctic landscape is permafrost (ground that is frozen all year round). In recent years the permafrost's deep underground layers of ice have started to melt, and when the ice turns to water, anything built on the ice is liable to topple and fall.

This underground thawing is having other effects too, such as the increasing frequency of landslides in places where ice is frozen into bedrock but then begins to melt. Ellesmere Island in Canada has witnessed a very significant increase in both the number and severity of these landslides, known to geologists as 'detachment events' because the 'active layer', the layer between the underground permafrost and the surface soil that thaws in the summer months, becomes detached from the permafrost beneath and slides off. This has removed whole swathes of surface soil, sometimes covering areas hundreds of yards across but just a foot or so deep, from the land. Similar things have been happening in other parts of the world, not just the Arctic. During the heat wave that affected much of Western Europe in the summer of 2003, a huge segment of the Matterhorn broke off the mountain slope, blocking a key route used by Alpine climbers and leaving a group of them stranded.

Since the late 1990s, experts have made considerable efforts to record the rate at which this permafrost is melting. Experts at the Global Terrestrial Network for Permafrost have drilled boreholes in carefully chosen spots to make accurate records and found clear indications of a warming trend throughout the permafrost zone. In particular, findings at Norway's Svalbard archipelago, in the far north west of the Barents Sea, show that ground temperatures have risen four times faster than they did in the previous century. 'What took a century to be achieved in the twentieth century will be achieved in twenty-five years in the twenty-first century, if this trend continues', as one of the leading geologists involved in the project pointed out.[3]

The melting permafrost is having one other unmistakable impact on the Arctic tundra: the wilderness where the soil is too cold for trees to take root. In recent years, the tundra has started to retreat considerably because as the temperature rises and the permafrost melts, trees are springing up, and thick forests, known as taiga, are proliferating northwards. 'The effects of climate change in Alaska will be among the most visible in the world', says Professor Dominique Bachelet of Oregon State University. 'The tundra has no place else to go, and it will largely disappear from the Alaskan landscape, along with the related plant, animal and even human ecosystems that are based upon it'.[4]

Some of the most up-to-date research on the retreat of the tundra has been undertaken along the eastern slopes of Siberia's northern Ural Mountains. In particular, a number of leading international ecologists have shown how larches and, further south, conifers, firs and pines are now thriving in this region, even though no living tree has grown there for thousands of years.[5] Scientists report that it is only in the course of the past century that leading edges of conifer forests began creeping some 50–100 feet up the mountains, and in some places these forests have succeeded in completely overrunning tundra. Some scientists estimate that between one-half and two-thirds of the tundra could be completely covered by forest by the end of the twenty-first century.

Research into the state of the Arctic's waters has been going on for somewhat longer. Scientists first began to monitor sea ice in the Arctic Ocean in the late 1970s, when it was judged to be melting at a rate of around 6.5 per cent each decade, but amidst growing concern they stepped up their efforts in the late 1990s. Since then, research into the melting of Arctic ice has been extensive, detailed and thorough, leaving little doubt about the sheer scale and speed with which this transformation is happening.

Almost every year new research is published that seems more pessimistic and shocking than the last. In the autumn of 2002, a NASA satellite study caused a stir because it showed that permanent ice cover was vanishing at roughly three times the rate that scientists had previously thought. This survey was carried out using data that was compiled over more than two decades from 1978 to 2000, and in this time about half a million square miles of supposedly permanent ice had completely disappeared. Not only that, but the rate at which it was disappearing seemed to be accelerating fast. As a senior scientist at NASA's Goddard Space Flight Centre in Maryland, and the chief author of the study, has put it, 'this year we had the least amount of permanent ice cover ever observed'.[6]

Since then, scientific warnings have become even more dire. In 2005, surveys estimated that there was less ice in the Arctic Ocean than at any previous time, and a year later scientists at the United States National Snow and Ice Data Center argued that earlier predictions would prove wildly off the mark. Using an extensive amount of data supplied by American and Canadian satellites, they even claimed that the entire Arctic Ocean would be virtually ice-free by the year 2060 and that the rate at which the ice was melting had now reached 8.6 per cent – equivalent to 23.3 million square miles – every year. 'I'm not terribly optimistic about the future of the ice', said Mark

Serreze, a research professor at the University of Colorado at Boulder. 'Although it would come as no surprise to see some recovery of the sea ice in the next few years – such fluctuations are part of natural variability – the long-term trend seems increasingly clear'.[7] The sheer speed with which the frozen seas are melting is taking everyone by surprise, and numerous experts argue that the 'official' figure promulgated by the United Nation's climate panel in 2007 drastically understates the sheer gravity of the crisis. Speaking at a seminar for scientists and politicians that was held in the Norwegian town of Ny-Alesund, the world's most northerly permanent settlement, lying just 750 miles from the North Pole, and a centre of international scientific research into the region, Norway's environment minister, Helen Bjoernoy, did not mince her words. Not only are 'reductions of snow and ice happening at an alarming rate', she told her audience, but 'this acceleration may be faster than predicted' by a UN climate panel that had reported its findings earlier in the year. Other experts share her pessimism. Christopher Rapley, director of the British Antarctic Survey, takes the view that 'there may well be an ice-free Arctic by the middle of the century'.[8]

In the spring of 2009, the British explorer Pen Hadow also focused the attention of the world on the region. Hadow was leading the Catlin Arctic Survey, a four-man trek to the North Pole that set out in early March to get a better idea of the shrinking ice cap and obtain much more specific data than satellites could provide. Before long Hadow discovered that most of his ice samples were less than three feet thick, suggesting that the older, thicker ice had either floated away or, more likely, simply melted. He made his findings just as NASA was issuing more warnings that sea-ice cover over the Arctic had reached a new low point and that the region could experience an ice-free summer as early as 2013.[9]

Everyone agrees that the Arctic is melting fast, although there is marginally more disagreement about exactly why. A number of scientists take the view that the contemporary world is experiencing a natural environmental cycle, no different from the many other changes – sometimes dramatic and profound – that have previously affected the planet. It is well known that the world's climate has changed constantly over the past few millions of years and conditions in the Arctic have changed at least as much as elsewhere. Half a million years ago the southern tip of Greenland, which is now ice-capped, was covered with thriving boreal forest that was full of spruce, pine, alder, and yew. And 4,000–8,000 years ago, willows, birches and roses were all thriving on the northern tip of Norway's

Svalbard archipelago, an area that is now covered with ice. At the beginning of the twentieth century, some parts of the Russian Arctic were warmer than they are today, and one section of the Northern Sea Route, which runs along its coast from Murmansk as far as the Bering Sea, was completely ice-free. Some scientists have argued in academic journals that record levels of melting in recent summers need to be seen from this long-term perspective because they are the result not so much of man-made global warming, but more of a cyclical north-south shift in the Arctic's atmosphere.

But while climatic conditions over the past 10,000 years have been unusually stable, creating a temperature range that has been ideal for human life, most scientists agree that the changes are the effect of man-made carbon dioxide emissions. According to the scientists and other experts of the Intergovernmental Panel on Climate Change, which has published its findings in 2001 and 2007, there is a less than 10 per cent chance that the current warming trend is the result of natural variations in the climate.

The first proper research into the environmental impact of man-made carbon dioxide emissions was undertaken in the late 1970s, when President Carter commissioned a group of scientists to further investigate some initial findings. From its base in Massachusetts, the 'Charney Panel', as it became known, undertook some rigorous research and reached alarming conclusions. 'If carbon dioxide continues to increase', they argued, 'the study group finds no reason to doubt that climate changes will result and no reason to believe that these changes will be negligible.' And if carbon dioxide emissions doubled from the level they had reached in the pre-industrial age, they continued, then the global temperature would rise by between 2 and 2.5 degrees Fahrenheit, perhaps even within 'several decades'.

Thirty years on, the warnings of the Charney Panel seem prophetic. The rate at which carbon dioxide is pumped into the atmosphere has increased every year – it now stands at around seven billion tons – and the earth's temperature has increased more or less in line with the predictions originally made by the American scientists. Since 1990, almost every subsequent year has been hotter than the last, breaking new records and leaving scientists struggling to work out the implications for the world's environment. In early 2009, a leading expert, Professor Chris Field, even warned that both carbon dioxide emissions and the world's future temperatures had been dramatically underestimated and would be 'beyond anything' that had been predicted.

In the Arctic, as elsewhere, global warming is having an effect that is hugely complex and far-reaching. Inevitably, some people are benefiting, while many more are losing out. And like the Alaskan Inuit, who started to use boats to cut through the slushy ice, almost everyone – foreign powers as well as the region's indigenous peoples – has to adapt to the fast changing landscape.

Winners and losers of Arctic climate change

In the spring of 2005, a Siberian city hosted an event that would have been unthinkable a decade before: an auction of large quantities of mammoth tusks that local people had unearthed over the preceding few summers. Until they finally became extinct 4,000 years ago, huge numbers of these creatures had roamed parts of Europe, Asia and North America, but not much trace of them was to be found anywhere except in the Arctic, where the ice has preserved their remains. However, over the past few years the ice has started to thaw so rapidly that these relics from the Ice Age are becoming very much easier to find. Other relics from earlier ages, such as the bones of dinosaurs, have also been found here and elsewhere north of the Arctic Circle, most notably in Alaska.

Government representatives watched proudly as 50 tonnes of tusks – with a street value of about $25,000 – went on sale. 'There are those who say that to sell the riches of the republic abroad is a bad thing', argued Tatiana Gladkova, a provincial minister for entrepreneurship and tourism, 'but the problem is, if you don't gather the tusks and bones in time they start to decompose. So we've decided, better to make money than to let these riches go to waste'. Gladkova knew that for many nomadic tribesmen this booming market represented an opportunity to make money, and this was why, under a recent law, they had been allowed to collect what they found and then sell up to half a tonne to licensed traders. Most of the merchandise was sold to Japanese and Indian buyers, who are adept at using mammoth ivory as decorative jewellery. One particularly large tusk fetched $2,000.[10]

Situated more than 3,500 miles east of Moscow, and six time zones ahead, the Autonomous Republic of Yakutia (or Sakha as it is officially known) lies north of the Arctic Circle. Much of the ground surface in the Yakut Arctic is permanently frozen, but here the active layer covering the permafrost is starting to melt, leaving rich pickings for traders in the lucrative ivory trade. And many others are cashing in on a boom in tourism sparked by the more agreeable climate. Since the 1970s, the number of tourists visiting the region has increased by nearly five-fold, and every year around 1.5 million visitors are taken by cruise ship, bus and plane to places that were considered impenetrable wildernesses not long ago.

Of course, this influx sometimes poses serious risks and causes damage. This is not only because to reach the Arctic the visitors are creating the very carbon dioxide emissions that cause so much environmental damage; it is also because in some places, such as Ny-Alesund in Norway's Svalbard archipelago, they are leaving an eco-trail that has disrupted scientific efforts to gather data from the region, while elsewhere the accumulation of garbage has become a serious problem for local authorities. Around 80,000 tourists now arrive in Svalbard every year – an increase of one-third in just half a decade – and the constant trail of visitors is wearing down the vegetation on the surrounding islands. Local officials are also concerned that one of the many cruise ships could cause a serious oil spillage.[11]

Nonetheless some locals are doing well out of the tourist trade. In 2000, a United States official pointed out that over the preceding 12 months 'visitors spent almost $1 billion in Alaska, and tourism employed over 20,000 persons directly and over 30,000 indirectly; about three-quarters of these were Alaskans. Nearly one in ten jobs puts tourism up there with commercial fishing in terms of employment opportunities for Alaskans'. She added that 'tourism also shares another very important similarity to commercial fishing; there are opportunities and potential opportunities throughout Alaska from Anchorage to the smallest, remotest village or region'.[12]

But not many of those who live within the Arctic Circle are reaping the benefits of global warming. While the big Arctic thaw is bringing the best of times for some of the region's indigenous population, there are many more for whom it is bringing the worst. For example, most of the native peoples of Siberia (among them the Eveni, Evenki, Dolgane and Yukaghir peoples) have always relied on reindeer, fishing, hunting and horse-breeding to provide them with income, food, transport and clothing. But since the early 1990s many have found that their traditional ways of life are increasingly threatened.

It was at this time that their reindeer started to die in much greater numbers at particular times of the year. Although no one is sure of the reason, it seems that the warmer climate is bringing more rainfall, which in turn freezes more easily in the very places where the reindeer have always found the lichen and other mosses that they feed upon. Not only that, but the animals are increasingly preyed upon by wolves that are quick to exploit the changing landscape, finding perfect cover in the sprawling forests. The indigenous nomads and semi-nomads who live in the region, making up around a quarter of

Yakutia's million-strong population, are also confronted by numerous other challenges: the melting of sea ice is swelling rivers and flooding villages, and many of the lakes used by local people for fishing are being drained by a number of newly formed underground streams.

In short, many traditional ways of life in this particular quarter of the Arctic Circle are under threat. Many people have already migrated southwards in search of a new life, learning the Russian language and new skills, and many more are likely to leave their traditional homeland in the years ahead.

The same effect is as pronounced for the local Inuit people in other parts of the Arctic Circle, such as northern Canada and Alaska. In 2003, representatives of Alaska's 13,000-strong Inuit population launched a legal challenge to the Bush administration, claiming that its failure to ratify the Kyoto Treaty and cut America's carbon dioxide emissions amounted to a gross violation of their human rights. In Alaska and their other traditional habitats (around 30,000 in Greenland and at least 45,000 in Canada) the Inuits claimed to be 'bearing the brunt of climate change'. As their spokesperson put it, 'without our snow and ice our way of life goes. We have lived in harmony with our surroundings for millennia, but that is now being taken away from us. We are an endangered species'.[13] Instead, as another representative of Greenland's Inuit population has said, a vital link between man and nature is in the process of being ruptured: 'We fear that valuable knowledge will be lost among hunters with regard to how the environment behaves, a sense of the ice and snow formations, how animals behave and hunting practices if we continue to experience this warming in the Arctic. This is valuable information that users of nature know from first-hand experience.'[14]

Wherever it is felt, global warming is bound to have an impact as varied as it is complex, but everyone agrees that the Arctic is changing rapidly and that the effects of this change will be profound and far-reaching on those who live within the region and beyond.

The Arctic thaw and the outside world

These changes are posing challenges for the local nomads and herders whose traditional ways of life are coming under increasing pressure, but there are several other reasons why scientists are monitoring environmental changes in the region with so much concern. One is the 'albedo effect' caused by the reflectivity of solar light: when sunlight strikes snow and ice it is bounced back into the atmosphere instead of being absorbed into the earth's surface and then converted to heat.[15] So if a white landscape becomes boreal forest, then what was once a solar reflector becomes a heat collector, aggravating the warming of the planet rather than mitigating it. As an American expert at the National Snow and Ice Data Center in Colorado explains, 'areas which formerly had ice are now open water, which is dark. These dark areas absorb a lot of the sun's energy, much more than ice; and what happens then is that the oceans start to warm up, and it becomes very difficult for ice to form during the following autumn and winter'.[16] In other words, there is a classic vicious circle at work because global warming is melting Arctic ice to create open waters, which then absorb even more of the sun's rays, converting them to heat instead of reflecting them back into the atmosphere.

Scientists are also living in fear of another, very real, scenario. Since the end of the last glacial cycle, more than 120,000 years ago, the Arctic ice has incarcerated the remains of animals and plants, the decomposition of which has created huge quantities of methane that in summer can be seen bubbling to the surface. Over this period, the permafrost has acted as a lid that has kept the methane sealed in, but scientists now fear that the gas could easily be released into the atmosphere as the permafrost thaws. Methane is a greenhouse gas about 20 times more powerful than carbon dioxide, and if it escapes on the scale that some scientists think possible then its impact on the world's climate would be devastating. In the summer of 2008, researchers were alarmed to find that some of these deposits were already reaching the surface. Orjan Gustafsson, of Stockholm University, described how in the course of one research trip:

> *an extensive area of intense methane release was found. At earlier sites we had found elevated levels of dissolved methane. Yesterday, for the first time, we documented a field where the release was so intense that the methane did not have time to dissolve into the seawater but was rising as methane bubbles to the sea surface. These 'methane chimneys' were documented on echo sounder and with seismic [instruments].*[17]

The great thaw might also spring other surprises on the outside world. Some scientists fear that the preserved carcasses might contain deadly viruses that, after lying dormant for thousands of years, could suddenly return to devastate humanity. In the course of their Arctic travels, experts have certainly been mystified by the primitive life forms (fortunately quite harmless) that they have so far discovered: one British scientist, based at the Scottish Association for Marine Science in Oban, unearthed what he called 'a deep-sea mystery': a simple life form, just a half inch long, that he has been quite unable to classify, from a rock sediment in a fjord at Rijpfjorden, in the Svalbard archipelago.[18]

But the main cause of concern about the Arctic thaw is its effect on global sea levels. Floating ice, of the sort that surrounds the North Pole, poses no danger because it is already displacing water; like ice cubes in a glass of water, the sea level will remain unchanged when the ice melts. But the melting of the massive ice sheets that cover Greenland would have a catastrophic effect; some of the world's leading experts have repeatedly warned of the 'imminent peril' this eventuality poses and pointed to the 'devastating' rise of sea levels, perhaps as much as several metres every century. The UN's Intergovernmental Panel on Climate Change has also predicted that these levels will eventually rise anywhere between 4 inches to 3 feet.

This is not the sole, or even the main, reason why the Arctic has started to arouse the interest of the watching world. Of much more immediate and pressing concern for most governments are new opportunities to exploit the region's vast, untapped natural resources. Over the past decade geological surveys have shown that the Arctic has huge underground reservoirs of oil and natural gas. Now that the ice is melting, and the technology and expertise to undertake deep-water drilling has been developed, these resources are for the first time open to exploitation, and they promise to bestow huge benefits on whichever country can claim them as their own.

3

The Great Explorers

Contemporary interest in the Arctic is growing fast, but this is not the first time that the region has caught the eye of the outside world. Ever since the end of the fifteenth century, sailors and governments alike have been intrigued by the possibility of discovering a navigable waterway that would connect the Atlantic and Pacific Oceans and open up the vast markets of the Orient, which had been made so alluring by the story of the legendary Marco Polo. Any such route would have offered a far quicker and safer journey than the epic voyages around the Cape of Good Hope that, until the opening of the Suez Canal in 1869, ships had always been forced to undertake.

The Northwest Passage

Many early efforts to discover the Northwest Passage were made by English sailors, or other Europeans who were granted the patronage of the English Crown. An example was Giovanni Caboto, an Italian who had searched unsuccessfully in Spain and elsewhere to find sponsorship for ambitious overseas voyages before coming to England as a last resort. Changing his name to John Cabot, he persuaded King Henry VII and some Bristol merchants to finance a journey to explore the fabled Northwest Passage and eventually set off in May 1497. He was gone 3 months, landing on an unclaimed stretch of territory that he called New Found Land, and on his return was awarded the grand sum of ten pounds by a grateful English king.

Nearly a century later, a succession of English 'sea dogs', notably Martin Frobisher, Humphrey Gilbert and John Davis, all made their own separate efforts to map these unexplored regions. The risks of exploring any undiscovered territory were considerable, but to undertake such an enterprise in the Arctic's extreme climatic conditions required immense personal courage as well as superb seamanship. Frobisher wrote powerfully of 'horribile snows' and how 'the yce comming on us so fast, we were in great danger, looking every houre for death'. The dangers became painfully obvious in the case of the explorer Sir Hugh Willoughby, who had left England in May 1553 but became disorientated by savage storms and fierce winds off the Norwegian coast. Deciding to ride out the winter months in the relative sanctuary of an offshore river, Willoughby and his 63 men met a gruesome end in the bitter winter frosts, and their corpses, together with Sir Hugh's will, were discovered by Russian fishermen the following summer.

There were numerous other dangers: ferocious and fast-moving, the polar bear terrified these early Arctic explorers. As they crossed the ice or foraged for food on nearby land, the explorers were often vulnerable to attack, and one sailor recorded how a 'great leane white bear' grabbed an unfortunate Englishman and 'bit his head in sunder . . . which she tare in peeces'.[1] Some ships collided with whales and sank and there was the constant risk that disease, fights and even mutiny could break out among the crew, all of whom soon suffered from what one explorer, William Parry, called 'the most dreary isolation and the total absence of animated existence' during their long months at sea.[2] Although some of the indigenous people they encountered along the way were friendly, others were deeply hostile. Five members of Frobisher's crew rowed ashore near Alaska and were either kidnapped or killed by Inuits, while on one desperate occasion Frobisher himself had to run for his life, taking an arrow in his buttock from an Inuit marksman and fleeing from the scene, in the words of one chronicler, 'rather speedily'.

Such dangers posed considerable risks not only for the seamen but also for their commercial sponsors. Many of these explorers had the backing of businessmen who recognized just how important their discoveries would be in the world of commerce, or who were convinced that the region could boast quantities of gold and other minerals. Henry Hudson, who made his way to Iceland and then around the southern tip of Greenland in 1610, had funding from several trading houses, notably the Dutch East India Company, which had been formed to develop trade and ties with newly discovered parts of the world. Investors who hoped to find an ice-free passage to the Indian subcontinent were disappointed by his findings, but Hudson did return with accounts of the whales off the Norwegian coast, and within months a major English whaling industry had sprung up, in close competition with Dutch rivals.

It was in the early eighteenth century, however, that the outside world, the British in particular, made great strides in exploring the Canadian Arctic. This was partly because the Royal Navy had been left with a surplus of ships at the end of the Napoleonic wars in Europe and many officers who were eager to find peacetime employment, and who were often buoyed with patriotic pride. It was also because the British government knew that any Arctic sea route would potentially offer a shorter route to the jewel in her imperial crown: India.

British interest in the region had been stirred during the war years by the travels of David Buchan, a Scottish naval officer who had patrolled the coasts of Newfoundland in search of the French fleet. In 1818, three years after Napoleon's defeat, he volunteered to undertake a much more ambitious project. This time he would head for uncharted waters and lead an expedition to the North Pole alongside another intrepid British naval commander, maverick and explorer, one whom he specifically asked to take his side. The name of the young lieutenant, a 32-year-old veteran of numerous naval clashes, such as the battles of Trafalgar and Copenhagen, was eventually to become almost synonymous with Arctic exploration: John Franklin.

The first of three major expeditions that Franklin was to make there proved to be difficult, costly and nearly disastrous. He was financed by major entrepreneurs who were interested in exploiting the local fur trade, as well as accessing the passage. Franklin moored off the coast of Alaska, where he personally led an overland party of 20 men along the Coppermine River, which today stretches through Canada's Northwest Territories. This terrain would have been challenging even to the most experienced land explorer, which Franklin certainly was not, and within days the party faced starvation and had been reduced to eating old shoes and other scraps of leather. Eight of his men died in this expedition, and the others were lucky to escape with their lives.

Five years later, in 1825, Franklin was much better prepared as he undertook another journey to the region. This time he took his ships to explore the Beaufort Sea, moving along the Alaskan shore for some 500 miles and drawing up detailed maps before heading back. His most renowned voyage, and the journey that associated his name so closely with a very British brand of heroism, adventurism and tragedy, began exactly 20 years later. Now 59 years old, many of his friends and family urged Franklin to retire quietly from Arctic exploration but were dismayed to find that he was determined to go.

By this time, senior figures in the Admiralty were very keen to reach the last, unmapped areas of the Canadian Arctic, covering about 70,000 square miles, and they regarded Franklin, the veteran of two earlier missions there, as the best man for the job. On 19 May he and his second-in-command, Captain James Fitzjames, led 130 men on board the HMS *Erebus* and HMS *Terror* and headed for the waters of the northern Atlantic. They never returned, and although other sailors caught occasional glimpses of them along the Canadian coast, no trace of either of the two ships or their crew was ever found.

Over the next years, many intrepid individuals searched for clues to the fate of Franklin and his men, almost all without success. However, they did explore the remaining unmapped regions of the Canadian Arctic. The Englishman, Robert McClure, set sail from London in December 1849 to search for Franklin, but though he found no clues, and nearly died of starvation in the process, he and his crew did manage to cross the Northwest Passage by ship and sledge. By the standards of the day this was an astonishing feat, and McClure and his men, feted as British national heroes, were generously rewarded.

Soon afterwards, in May 1853, an American doctor and sailor, Elisha Kane, sailed from New York to search for the British expedition that had disappeared eight years before. In the course of his journey he succeeded in going further north than anyone had previously travelled, charting the coasts of Greenland and Ellesmere Island, discovering the ice-free Kennedy Channel and making his way into those places that are today known as Smith Sound and the Kane Basin. He was no natural sailor and suffered from chronic seasickness almost as soon as a ship set sail. Yet he was also supremely determined and throughout his journey always showed exemplary courage. His diary entry for 20 August 1853 recorded the dangers he and his crew faced:

> We were dragged out by the wild sea, and were at its mercy . . . at seven in the morning we close upon the piling masses of ice . . . down we went with the gale again, helplessly scraping along a lee of ice seldom less than thirty feet thick . . . one upturned mass rose above our gunwale, smashed our bulwarks and deposited a half ton of ice in a lump upon our decks. Our staunch little brig bore herself through all this wild adventure as if she had a charmed life.[3]

His voyage ended in near disaster when, in May 1855, he was forced to abandon his 140-ton brig, the *Advance*, and with his crew undertook a heroic north-easterly trek to reach the sanctuary of Upernavik, on Greenland's west coast. They returned to New York, amidst jubilant scenes, a few months later.

For all the ingenuity and determination of so many explorers, it was not until the beginning of the twentieth century that anyone managed to finally navigate their way across the entire length of the Northwest Passage. In 1903, a clever and resourceful 29-year-old Norwegian, Roald Amundsen, left the coast of Greenland with a handful of others on board a hunting vessel, the *Gjoa*. Initially he moved steadily through the islands of Canada's Arctic coast, but was eventually forced by bad weather to stop, and for two long winters lived among the Inuit people of King William Island. It was not until 1906 that he finally navigated the Northwest Passage, arriving at the mouth of the Mackenzie River and then completing his epic journey by sailing around the Alaskan Peninsula and on to San Francisco in October.

The Northeast Passage

Besides making such great efforts to map the Northwest Passage, a succession of European explorers and their sponsors were also looking eastwards, fascinated by the possibility of finding another route that would lead them to the riches of the Orient. From the end of the sixteenth century, numerous expeditions had set out to explore these unknown seas, and sailors brought back extraordinary stories of the vast riches, dangerous natives and fabulous animals that they claimed to have seen with their own eyes. One crew returned to England claiming to have seen unicorns and brandished a skull with one horn in a bid to prove it. However, most expeditions found their progress blocked by thick pack ice.

One of the earliest ventures to explore the Northeast Passage was made in 1580, when the Muscovy Trading Company commissioned two highly experienced sailors, Arthur Pet and Charles Jackman, to lead an expedition in the region.[4] Although they discovered the Kara Sea and the offshore archipelago of Novaya Zemlya, the expedition was ravaged by bad weather and Jackman's ship eventually disappeared without trace. Fourteen years later a Dutch navigator, William Barents, made three journeys of his own, discovering the Svalbard archipelago in the process, but like his predecessors, he too was beaten back by atrocious weather. Barents died in June 1596 during the arduous return journey, and only 12 of the 17 men who left Holland made it back after encountering atrocious weather and conditions. In 1607 and 1608 Henry Hudson also made two trips of his own but soon found his routes blocked by ice, and the disappointing outcome of his journey was one reason why, over the coming century, very few Europeans showed much interest in exploring the passage.

At this time nearly all of the explorers who headed for the region were Russians, or else had the backing of the Czar. In 1648 a Russian expedition set out in seven vessels to explore the Siberian coast, and although several were wrecked in the process, the remaining few went round the eastern tip of the Chukotka Peninsula, through the Bering Strait and around the north-eastern tip of Asia, where a band of 25 survivors, led by a Cossack called Simeon Dezhnev, built an outpost and lived for several years. Decades later, stories of Dezhnev's achievements intrigued Czar Peter, who commissioned a Danish sailor, Vitus Bering, to explore these unknown seas of the north. In August 1728 Bering and his crew made their way through a narrow strait, later named after him, and wintered on the Kamchatka Peninsula before returning to St Petersburg in March 1730.

Although Bering had succeeded in exploring and mapping much of the region, it was not until 1878 that anyone succeeded in sailing the entire length of the Northeast Passage, when the Swedish explorer Erik Nordenskjord completed this epic journey and became a national hero, and a very rich man, as a result.

The North Pole
The discovery of an ice-free passage, one that could link east and west, clearly offered huge commercial and strategic benefits to every maritime nation. Explorers therefore had little trouble finding sponsorship from governments, business organizations or wealthy individuals for any journey that they wanted to make to the region. By contrast, locating the North Pole – the Earth's precise axis of rotation – had intrigued both scientists and adventurers for centuries, but in the world of commerce it seemed to be a rather empty gesture: even if it could be pinpointed, the Pole was really just like any other stretch of land, water or ice. For many adventurers it represented a great prize, but almost no one could raise the funds to make a journey and seize it.

For this reason, few people made any specific effort to find the Pole unless it also helped them to map the Northwest Passage, even if the personal bravery of those who made the effort was just as remarkable. By the end of the nineteenth century only a handful of journeys there had been made, most of which had ended in disaster. The least costly of these was undertaken by a British naval officer, William Edward Parry, who had set sail in 1827 with the specific intention of being the first to locate the exact spot and raise his national flag. Setting out from the northern shores of Spitsbergen, he and his men set a new record, reaching a higher latitude than any previous explorer, but in the end he had to admit defeat before returning safely to base.

Decades passed before anyone tried to surpass this feat, and the stories of those who did were typically tragic. A party led by an

American, Isaac Israel Hayes, set out in 1860 to reach the Pole but was eventually forced to turn back by unexpectedly severe blizzards and by the death of a man who had fallen through the ice and frozen to death.

Eleven years later another American explorer, Charles Francis Hall, led a disastrous mission to the earth's northern-most point, enjoying generous congressional patronage to do so. Initially everything went well for the USS *Polaris* and its crew of 35 men, who safely reached the coast of Greenland and established a base camp. But it was not long before tragedy struck. Hall became violently ill and died in agony. His second-in-command took over, but, although a very able and experienced seaman, he was unable to prevent the *Polaris* from being surrounded and nearly crushed by huge packs of ice. In the ensuing chaos, about half of the crew jumped ship for the relative safety of the ice floe while the others stayed determinedly on board, drifting with the vessel for several more days before it finally ran aground. Some of the sailors were fortunate enough to be led to safety by Inuits and then rescued by passing whaling ships, lucky to escape with their lives.

Other voyages of the age fared even worse. In 1881 the American explorer George DeLong set sail from San Francisco on board the USS *Jeannette* in a bid to find a direct route to the North Pole through the Bering Strait. But like the *Polaris* a decade before, this ship also became helplessly stuck in pack ice. 'We started for the Pole', as DeLong wrote in his log, '[but] we are beset in the pack in 71 plus (latitude); we drift northwest; our ship is injured . . . we drift back southeast.' He added later, with a terrible sense of grief and pain, that 'we have failed, inasmuch as we did not reach the Pole'. DeLong ordered his men to abandon ship and try to head for Siberia in three small boats. But most of the mariners perished in the days ahead, becoming disorientated and lost in their arduous surroundings, and the bodies of DeLong and his last companions were later discovered near Mat Vay in Siberia.

Another subsequent mission to find the North Pole, made in 1897 by three Swedes who tried crossing the area by hydrogen balloon, also ended tragically when the fog weighed the balloon down, forcing them to land and leaving them stranded in a remote area of the Svalbard archipelago. Their frozen bodies, and the logbook they had kept meticulously until their diary entries suddenly broke off, were not discovered until 1930. Others came within a whisker of death. In 1893 the Norwegian Fridtjof Nansen led a very ambitious bid to reach the Pole on the ship *Fram*, but he and his crew were forced to spend nine months hibernating, like native Inuit, in a simple hut covered with walrus skins. They only made their way back home because of a near-miraculous encounter with a British expedition that had known nothing of their whereabouts.

Although a number of people claimed to have been the first to reach the Pole – notably the Americans Frederick Cook and Robert Peary in 1909 – it was not until 1926 that anyone made a confirmed, undisputed sighting of what was still considered, in the world of exploration, to be a great prize. Once again it was the intrepid Norwegian, Amundsen, who seized the attention of the watching world. Although he was by this time in his early fifties, Amundsen was still immensely ambitious to reach the Pole and his appetite had been whetted by his success in the Antarctic in 1911, when he had narrowly beaten the legendary British explorer, Captain Scott, in the race to the South Pole.

In early 1926, Amundsen's generous American patron, Lincoln Ellsworth, put up the money to develop a new airship that was specially designed for both the huge distances and the atrocious weather conditions in the Arctic, and before long the *Norge* was ready to fly. Piloted by an Italian, Umberto Nobile, the airship had taken off on 11 May from Spitsbergen, and after several days flying the crew waited anxiously for the navigator to confirm that they had reached the exact spot. After the airship landed on the ice below, one member of the jubilant crew described the event in his logbook: 'The beautiful, padded Norwegian silk flag whistled down; a cross-bar fixed to a long aluminium pole, like a standard, which gave it excellent steering. It landed perfectly, bored into the ice and in the light breeze the Norwegian colours unfolded.'[5]

One race for the Arctic was over, but more than eight decades later another has begun.

Part 2
The Issues

4

Who Owns the Arctic?

For one Western tourist who was taking a cruise around the Svalbard archipelago in the summer 2005, the advent of global warming presented an opportunity that was simply too good to miss. He had heard that a number of tiny islands, many no bigger than a tennis court or baseball pitch, had suddenly and unexpectedly appeared in parts of the Arctic Ocean. Covered by massive glaciers for thousands of years, it is only now, as the ice shelf continues to retreat, that they have begun to surface. Unmarked on any map, many of these islets are in the north Barents Sea, near Svalbard, while others have also been seen off the shores of Greenland, Iceland and elsewhere.[1]

The traveller regarded these newly discovered lumps of rock as a huge temptation. As the ship pulled closer, he became so excited that, with a real spirit of adventure, he waded ashore, scribbled his name on a can of baked beans, stuck it into the soil and then loudly proclaimed that the island was his own.[2] In the true spirit of the astronauts who landed on the moon, or of Captain Cook in the New World, this undiscovered piece of territory seemed, for a few brief moments at least, to belong to him.

This story says something about what lies at the heart of all the various controversies and disputes in the contemporary Arctic. This is not the presence of petroleum or any other highly prized natural resource. Nor is it the region's superb strategic location. After all, numerous other parts of the world are bestowed with either, or sometimes both, of these assets, but in recent decades have never been quarrelled over by foreign powers. Both Russia and the United States have vast oil deposits and no one disputes whom those resources belong to, even if the status of foreign companies as they extract oil or any other substance from the ground is often a highly contentious issue.[3]

The difference is one of legality. When any natural resources are located within established, undisputed national borders, they are unlikely to create or aggravate a serious international dispute because everyone agrees to whom they belong. The problem comes when the ownership of the region where these assets are located is open to serious question.

In the past few years, this question has been asked about many parts of the world. Sometimes different answers can lead to serious domestic disputes, just as the identity of contemporary Britain is currently being challenged by a brand of Scottish nationalism that has undoubtedly drawn strength from the exploitation of North Sea oil, and just as parts of West Africa continue to be torn apart by bloody and protracted 'resource civil wars' waged by militias with rival claims to reserves of petroleum.[4]

At other times, such resources may belong to a state, which, although formally recognized by the United Nations, is regarded by some countries as 'illegitimate' in some other way. In this situation, these resources can make international tensions much worse. Many of the borders in the Middle East were drawn up hastily and at times almost randomly after the First World War and their validity has been questioned by some Arab leaders. 'Lack of legitimacy was a basic feature of the new state system', says one leading historian of the Middle East.[5] So Iraq has long claimed Kuwait as its own territory and this was the premise upon which Saddam Hussein ordered an invasion of the principality in August 1990, even though disputes over its oil were the immediate cause.[6]

Finally, there are places that seem to belong to no one, and which foreign powers therefore feel free to claim as their own. This is exactly what happened during the 'Scramble for Africa' that began in the 1880s, when rival European governments raced to colonize whole swathes of a newly discovered continent that seemed to promise minerals and other natural resources on a vast scale. In the contemporary world, most governments are more likely to petition the International Court of Justice (ICJ) for formal recognition over an unclaimed stretch of land or water.

The various different Arctic controversies and disputes fall into each of these three categories. The question of who rules Greenland, for example, is essentially a domestic dispute because for more than 200 years this vast landmass has been a sovereign part of Denmark. Elsewhere, some countries have sometimes failed to reach a lasting agreement about exactly where their borders should be drawn.

Large parts of the Arctic fall into the final category because, like pre-colonial Africa, they have always been a no man's land or sea. Until recently almost no government had attempted to stake its claim to the wilder, more remote regions that lie further north, either because there seemed no point in doing so or because they had no historical, cultural or geographical basis for making such a claim. Only over the past decade has this started to change because the ice has started to melt and huge energy resources have been discovered and become increasingly accessible. Of course the 'Arctic Five' can claim to have sovereignty over their surrounding waters, but beyond that lie frozen seas and wastelands that seem to belong to no one. It is only if Russia and other states can demonstrate that their continental shelves run further out to sea – as the underwater journey of Sagalevich and Chilingarov was intended to demonstrate – that they can potentially extend their 200-mile zone.[7]

The Arctic's legal challenges

There are a number of reasons why the legal challenges of determining the ownership of the Arctic's disputed regions are formidable. Sometimes it is simply because the scope and meaning of international law is itself unclear, for although a great deal of law has been codified into various treaties, the ICJ in The Hague still looks to vague, and occasionally contradictory, sources to pass judgement. International treaties are only binding on their signatory parties, and crucially the world's great superpower, the United States, has (at the time of writing) still not ratified the 1982 United Nations Convention on the Law of the Sea.

However, the disputes in the Arctic are likely to be particularly controversial for a number of reasons. One is that some parts of the region were once claimed by a number of explorers from several different countries. The Svalbard islands were probably first discovered by Vikings but were then occupied by both Norwegian and Russian explorers as early as the sixteenth century; their natural resources were unearthed much later. Another reason is that the Arctic has a uniquely complex geography: geographers and lawyers alike are not entirely sure if whole areas of the region, covered as it is for much or all of the year by thick ice, constitute 'land' or 'sea'.[8] Sheet ice on the land is no different from any other piece of territory, but the status of other types of ice, such as fast ice, which is formed by seawater and clings to the coastline on a seasonal basis, and the vast floes of pack ice that move on the ocean for much of the year, are much harder to define. A Soviet naval officer, serving in the Northern Sea Route Authority, gave a description of this complex picture:

> *The ice cover of the Central Arctic is not a continuous massif of old ice. It consists of ice fields and fragments of different thickness and age, with*

open leads between all the mobile floes, no matter what their thickness, degree of hummocking, geographical position or season of the year.[9]

Some international lawyers have wondered if the 1959 Antarctica Treaty can help shed light on this, or any other issue. But this agreement is unhelpful because it leaves open the question of whether ice can ever be the subject of a territorial claim, and because none of the countries that did make any such territorial claims under the Treaty ever referred to ice shelves. In any case it is uncertain how helpful any legal comparisons between the Arctic and Antarctic really are. The Antarctic is a continent, surrounded by a vast maritime belt, that rests on one thousand feet of land covered by a solid ice cap about three thousand feet thick. By contrast, the Arctic is an ocean that is surrounded by a vast and nearly continuous continental belt, and the North Pole rests on extremely deep water that is covered by thick, moving ice.

All sorts of other legal questions remain unanswered. Does the entire Arctic fall into a special category of 'ice-covered areas' that the 1982 Convention seems to create?[10] And how can any ice-laden waters ever be described as 'high seas', over which ships always have certain freedoms, in the same way as any other?[11] Without a precise definition it is impossible even to determine what the rules are, let alone how they should be applied.

These are some of the general questions that underwrite the variety of border disputes in the Arctic, while more particular issues arise in the context of the southern regions on the one hand and the uninhabitable High North on the other.

Disputes within the southern periphery

Over the centuries, much of the Arctic's southern periphery has attracted a steady flow of migrants and has been gradually absorbed by neighbouring governments. This means that the question of who rules has long been settled in many cases.

The most obvious single examples are those sovereign countries that are located, wholly or in part, north of the Arctic Circle. The three Scandinavian countries, Norway, Finland and Sweden, all lie mainly to the south of the Circle, but are either integral to, or have well-established claims over, areas that lie north of the latitudinous line or are located exactly on it. For centuries, around half of Norwegian territory has been located north of the Circle, and its territorial claims even over more remote Arctic territories have long been undisputed: in 1920, the world's leading powers agreed to recognize

Oslo's sovereignty over the Svalbard archipelago, which lies about halfway between the Norwegian mainland and the North Pole.[12] Tiny Grimsey Island, which is located exactly on the boundary of the Arctic Circle, has long been governed from Reykjavik.

Russia first started to stake its own claim as far as the Arctic Ocean in the early seventeenth century, when its armies had started to push northwards, lured by the prospect of controlling the lucrative local fur trade. The resistance they encountered from most of the indigenous tribes was limited, and by the middle of the century Cossack troops had moved as far as the river Lena, just a short distance south of the Arctic Circle. Over the coming decades, Siberia's Arctic coast would be mapped by a number of Russian explorers, notably Dmitri Ovtsyn, Fiodor Minin and Khariton Laptev, before a steady stream of Russian migrants began to colonize the region in ever greater numbers.

By contrast, the involvement of some other countries north of the Circle is a relatively recent affair. The far north of Alaska has been formally incorporated into the United States only since 3 January 1959, when the province was recognized as the 49th state, although it was nearly a whole century before, on 30 March 1867, that the Senate had voted to purchase the region from the Russian government for a lump sum of $7.2 million.[13]

But there are also other parts of the southern Arctic where the question of who rules has, by contrast, long been disputed.

'Internal waters'

In the Arctic Ocean, and elsewhere in the world, the status of some stretches of water is difficult to define partly because of the complex formation of the islands in their midst. The Northwest Passage, for example, stretches between the Davis Strait and Baffin Bay in the east and the Bering Strait in the west (Map 2). But the cluster of numerous islands, rocks, barriers and reefs in this area makes its true nature very hard to determine in both geographic and legal terms. At what point, geographers and lawyers both ask, does a cluster of islands, lying adjacent to the coast, become an extension of the mainland, thereby making its waters 'internal' and essentially no different from a river or canal?

In the case of Canada and Russia, this question is difficult enough to answer. But the controversies have been more heated because the 1982 Convention on the rights of any country to move through internal, or any other, waters is not fit for purpose.

Canada's 'internal waters'

Canada's own Arctic regions have long been an integral part of its sovereign territory. These huge expanses of land, which cover millions of square miles, were first brought under the control of the central government in the course of the nineteenth century. In 1870, a private commercial organization, the Hudson's Bay Company, transferred ownership of its territories in the far north to the newly formed dominion of Canada. A decade later Great Britain formally ceded its claim to the myriad of Arctic islands where a succession of English seafarers, notably Martin Frobisher and William Baffin, had planted the national flag. Today the Canadian Arctic is made up of three separate provinces: Nunavut, which alone covers 750,000 square miles (nearly one-fifth of Canada's land mass), Yukon and Northwest Territories. The national anthem even includes a reference to 'the True North, strong and free'. As a government minister claimed emphatically in September 1985, 'the Arctic is not only a part of Canada, it is part of Canadian greatness'.[14]

But although no one disputes Canada's ownership of its Arctic lands and the thousands of offshore islands, the status of the surrounding waters is very much harder to determine. The issues are twofold: can the Canadians draw their borders around the outer fringes of these islands, claiming that the waters within are 'internal'? And, if so, can any other country claim that they have a right to move through those internal waters?

The Canadians themselves are adamant about the status of these waters. In 1969, Prime Minister Pierre Trudeau stated that 'the area to the north of Canada, including the islands and the waters between the islands and the areas beyond, are looked upon as our own and there is no doubt . . . that this is national terrain'.[15] Sometimes these claims have led to diplomatic incidents, a few of which have been minor, quickly forgotten and even humorous: in 1977, when a Soviet ice station, SP22, drifted a couple of hundred miles off course in the Northwest Passage, a Canadian plane flew overhead and dropped a message that read 'Welcome to Canada'. But there have also been moments of serious tension between Canada and the United States over the issue of where 'internal waters' lie.[16]

Some of the rules of international law that cover these points are clear: under the Convention on the Law of the Sea, which Canada ratified in 2003, every coastal country can claim two different stretches of water as part of its sovereign territory.[17] The first are the 'internal waters', such as rivers and canals that lie on its 'landward side'.[18] The other is the belt of adjacent water, known as the 'territorial sea', that is located 'up to a limit not exceeding twelve nautical miles' from its coast (Map 1).[19] Although, under the same agreement, international shipping has a 'right of innocent passage' through the territorial sea, the coastal state has a right to close these waters 'if such suspension is essential for the protection of its security'.[20] Beyond this 12-mile area and the coastal state's 'contiguous zone' and 'exclusive economic zone' that lie even further out to sea, are the 'high seas' that are 'open to all states'.[21]

What is not so clear is whether the Convention gives Canada the right to draw its borders around its fragmented northern coasts. This can sometimes be done by 'a state constituted wholly by one or more archipelagos', although 'other islands' may also have the same right.[22] However, long before the 1982 treaty came into effect, the ICJ had decreed that a state with a fragmented coastline can sometimes draw its baselines around the outer points of any offshore islands, even though they 'must not depart to any appreciable extent from the general direction of the coast'.[23]

Foreign ships still have a right to use 'internal waters' if a strait that is 'used for international navigation' runs through them. In this situation 'all ships and aircraft enjoy the right of transit passage' through these internal waters.[24] A ship that makes 'transit passage' through a strait enjoys much more freedom of navigation than it would have if making an 'innocent passage'.[25]

These are the issues that lie at the heart of one long-running dispute between Canada and other foreign governments, notably the United States. Canada claims that the Northwest Passage is comprised of its 'historic internal waters' and thus falls under its jurisdiction and control.[26] Its lawyers point to the 1951 'Anglo-Norwegian Fisheries case', a Norwegian claim but which some experts say has similarities to Canada's geographic claim. Ottawa's title to the fragmented coastline, or 'coastal archipelagos', is particularly strong, they argue, because centuries of traditional practice by the indigenous Inuit people make their waters 'historic'.[27]

By contrast, the United States has disputed Canada's claims, denying that it has any 'internal waters' in the Northwest Passage and pointing out that, in any event, there is an 'international strait' there.[28] This is an opaque legal area. According to the 1982 Convention, a 'strait', under maritime law, is a body of water 'used for international navigation'. This phrase clearly implies 'usage' over a period of time, even though before the treaty came into force the ICJ had occasionally argued that this is of no necessary relevance.[29] The trouble for the Americans is that their claim is far from convincing – only 11 foreign transits were made through the whole length of these waters between 1904 and 1984 – and because they have not been previously used as an international navigation or shipping route on any significant scale, many observers say that they fail to qualify as a strait.

The Canadians have also pointed out that the Passage, at its narrowest points, is less than 24 miles across and any shipping therefore moves through its overlapping territorial seas, which under the 1982 Convention fall within a 12-mile radius of both coasts.[30] But this claim would still not prevent the United States or any other country from arguing the existence of a 'strait', which can run through internal waters, territorial sea or an exclusive economic zone. This was one reason why, in 1993, Ottawa tried to buttress its claim by passing a piece of domestic legislation, the Nunavut Land Claims Agreement, that stated 'Canada's sovereignty over the waters of the Arctic archipelago is supported by Inuit use and occupancy'.[31]

Such arguments have failed to convince Washington, and the dispute between the two countries seems set to continue. In January 2009, just days before leaving office, President George W. Bush issued a directive bluntly proclaiming that 'freedom of the seas is a top national priority'. It continued by stating that:

> *The Northwest Passage is a strait used for international navigation, and the Northern Sea Route includes straits used for international navigation. Preserving the rights and duties relating to navigation and overflight in the Arctic region supports our ability to exercise these rights throughout the world, including through strategic straits.*[32]

Russia's 'internal waters'

Moscow has also long argued that the Northern Sea Route that crosses its Arctic shores is a Russian, rather than an international, sea lane (Map 2). In a document that was published in 1990, the route was described as 'the essential national transportation line of the USSR that is situated within its inland seas, territorial sea (territorial waters), or exclusive economic zone adjacent to the USSR Northern Coast'.[33] But while Moscow's claim goes back at least to the 1940s, the most important single declaration of recent years was issued only in 1984, when a Soviet proclamation drew a clear baseline around parts of the northern coasts and islands and decreed that any waters that fell within that border were 'internal'.[34] To win a right to sail through these waters, foreign governments would have to demonstrate that there was already an international strait running through them.

There could be a serious dispute in the years ahead if, for example, American vessels try to cross the Northern Sea Route but find their journey blocked by Russian warships. This is what happened in the 1960s, when the United States government sent a number of icebreakers and marine research vessels into these waters, which it claimed were either 'high seas' or 'territorial seas' through which they had a right of innocent passage. Between 1962 and 1964 several such voyages went unchallenged by the Soviet authorities, but in 1965 the journey of the United States coast guard cutter *Northwind* through the Vilkitsky Strait provoked strong diplomatic protests by Moscow. Washington abandoned this attempt and 2 years later cancelled other missions along the same route by USCGC *Edisto* and *Eastwind*.

At the time Moscow had decreed that the Vilkitsky and other straits, if not the seas around them, were its 'territorial sea' and that it needed prior notice to arrange icebreaker escort.[35] An alternative line of argument, based on the decree of 1984, was that the strait fell within its baselines and its waters were therefore 'internal'.[36]

Border disputes

Some parts of the Arctic are contested not just because their landscape is unusually complex and the law uncertain, but because rival claimants appear to have equally strong claims. This can happen when an island lies exactly halfway between two countries with competing claims, and when there is no clear way of deciding the outcome. In such an inhospitable region, there is rarely a local population that can have a decisive say in the matter by simply casting its vote.

In this situation, most lawyers turn to the 1982 Convention. This lays down that 'where the coasts of two states are opposite or adjacent to each other' then the 'median line' that lies 'equidistant' to the two shores determines the border in the same way that the North Sea, for example, has been divided between Britain, Norway, Denmark and several other European countries (Map 3).[37] But this very general rule gives no more than an indication about how to decide a dispute. A government can still point to a 'historic title or other special circumstances' that give it a right to ownership, or claim that its continental shelf runs past the median line.

These types of disputes can be resolved amicably, usually through international arbitration, in the same way that, in 1931, Norway formally recognized Canadian sovereignty over the Sverdrup Islands in the Arctic. But at other times contestants will present their case before the ICJ or, rarely, resort to force of arms.

Beaufort Sea

One of the ongoing controversies in the southern Arctic is whether this 'median line' should determine the demarcation of the Beaufort Sea, which lies off the shores of both Alaska and Canada's Yukon Territory (Map 2).

For Washington, the fairest way of adjudicating the boundary is to apply the widely used 'equidistance principle', which is incorporated by the 1982 Convention and more closely reflects the direction of the respective coastlines. Since the coastline slants from east to west, so too should the maritime border lie at the same perpendicular angle, about 30 degrees to the east. But Canada insists that the equidistance principle does not apply because it runs contrary to the 'special circumstances' (well-established historical practices) that the 1982 Convention mentions. An 1825 treaty between Russia and Great Britain defined the eastern border of Alaska as 'the meridian line of the 141st degree, in its prolongation as far as the Frozen Ocean'. In other words, as far as the thick pack ice that lies miles off shore. The Americans counter-argue that the border should follow the 141st meridian, but only on land: the seas should be divided in a different way and that 'the Frozen Ocean' always referred to the coastline, not the pack ice that lies much further out to sea.

On the map the disputed area of sea looks like an insignificant wedge, but in practice this area of 7,000 square nautical miles could prove hugely important in a region that geologists feel sure is rich in natural resources.[38]

Hans Island

There are several other disputed areas of the Arctic whose ownership, some rival claimants say, cannot be determined simply by easy reference to the 'equidistance' of the 1982 Convention. What happens, some countries ask, if the continental shelf of only one country extends beyond the equidistant line?

An example is the dispute that surrounds Hans Island in the Arctic Ocean (Map 2). Tiny and uninhabited, measuring barely a mile across, it is in some ways surprising that its status should ever have been a matter of international dispute. But situated in the Nares Strait, and lying exactly halfway between Greenland (which is ruled by Denmark) and Canada's Ellesmere Island, it has long been a source of disagreement between the two governments, which both continue to claim it as their own sovereign territory. The Danes say that the island belongs to them because 'relevant evidence in connection with defining the area of Greenland, such as geological and geomorphological evidence, clearly supports this point of view'.[39]

Although the island was discovered in the late nineteenth century, the origins of this dispute go back to 1933, when the Permanent Court of International Justice formally declared that Greenland was sovereign Danish territory.[40] Denmark soon claimed that Hans Island was geologically just an extension of Greenland and has subsequently undertaken numerous scientific surveys of the Nares Strait to prove its point. But these claims have been strongly disputed by the Canadian government, which since the early 1970s has argued that the island falls under its own jurisdiction. Although in 1973 Canada and Denmark reached an agreement to draw a border between Greenland and Ellesmere Island, the status of Hans Island was left undetermined. The competing claims to the island have never been finally settled in international law and have become much more contentious since the early 1980s, when the area's oil-bearing potential had started to become clear.[41]

Barents Sea

The setting for some particularly long-lasting and bitter border disputes in the Arctic region is the Barents Sea, which has been the focus of some sharp disagreements between the Russian and Norwegian governments for some years (Map 5).

There are three disputed parts of the Barents. One is the Svalbard archipelago, a cluster of islands that lie 300 miles off Norway's north coast, while further south, along the Russian and Norwegian shores, is another disputed section of the Barents Sea known as the 'Grey Zone'. This is an area covering 19,475 square nautical miles where the border has long been disputed.[42]

A third disagreement is over the status of the 'Loophole', a large triangular region situated north of the Kola Peninsula, west of Novaya Zemlya, south-west of the Svalbard archipelago and roughly equidistant from all three. It covers 60,000 square miles.

The dispute over Svalbard revolves around an international agreement that was signed in 1920. The Spitsbergen (Svalbard) Treaty recognized Norwegian sovereignty over the islands, but also contained an unusual clause that grants other countries equal rights to any natural resources found on the land. The crucial part of the treaty is Article 3, which states that 'ships and nationals' of the signatory states 'shall be admitted under the same conditions of equality to the exercise and practice of all maritime, industrial, mining or commercial enterprises both on land and in the territorial waters, and no monopoly shall be established on any account or for any enterprise whatever'.[43]

The big question is what constitutes these 'territorial waters'. Does Russia or Iceland, for example, have an equal right to fish in all of the surrounding seas, whether it is a 200-mile economic zone or the full 350-miles over any outer continental shelf, or only within the 12-mile 'territorial sea'? The lawyers who drew up the treaty would certainly have had a very different idea from their contemporaries of what constitutes 'territorial waters'.[44] Could the Norwegians establish an exclusive economic zone, or a restricted fishing area, surrounding the islands beyond that 12-mile limit, which would belong only to them?

Such questions surfaced in 1970, when Norway argued that the treaty gave other countries an equal right to fish only in the high seas and not within their own maritime zone that they claimed surrounded the islands. The Norwegian government announced the establishment of an exclusive economic zone, but in 1977 made a more modest claim, declaring that there was a fisheries protection zone – one that allowed other signatory countries to fish there provided they complied with Norwegian regulations – within the surrounding 200 miles. Every one of the signatories to the 1920 agreement accepted Norway's claim with one exception: Russia, whose fishing industry had always found these waters a highly fruitful source of stock.

Russia has always recognized that without the 1920 agreement and under the 1982 Convention alone, it would have no right to the fish stocks or any other natural resources in Svalbard's surrounding waters. Instead, the Russians know that the ICJ would simply draw a 'median line' between Svalbard and Franz Josef Land, which has been Russian territory since 1926, unless they could prove that it has the 'historic title or other special circumstances' that the Convention requires. Given the ambiguity that surrounds the 1920 agreement this is very far from certain, and the Russians have only quietly protested at the Norwegian claim because since 1977 they, like everyone else, have still been allowed to fish there on the same terms as everyone else. But such uncertainties have not prevented the Norwegians from strictly enforcing their claims, even opening fire in 1994 at an Icelandic trawler that was fishing there illegally.[45]

Nonetheless, the meaning of the 1920 treaty is becoming more important than ever because the waters of the Barents Sea are now thought to be particularly rich not just in fish, but also in oil and gas. Today the Norwegian government still claims that the 1920 agreement has only ever applied to resources that are discovered on land and therefore does not include offshore deposits of oil or natural gas, which it argues will be inside its territorial waters. But other countries, including Britain, take a different view. In 1986, the Foreign Office in London claimed that 'in our view Svalbard has its own continental shelf, to which the Treaty of Paris (Svalbard Treaty) applies. The extent of this shelf has not been determined'.[46] London also sparked a minor diplomatic row in the summer of 2006 when it failed to invite Norway to a meeting with the United States, Russia and other member states of the European Union to discuss the future of the islands. The UK and other countries wanted their own oil companies to have equal access to Svalbard's waters in the event that the Norwegian government opened up these areas to tender.[47]

Hundreds of miles to the south is the Grey Zone, which is the setting for another simmering border dispute. This revolves around the same issue as the Beaufort Sea controversy: the question of how to determine the maritime boundary of waters between states with adjacent coasts. The Norwegians claim that drawing a 'median line', equidistant to the nearest part of each state's mainland, gives the fairest outcome. But the Russians have long argued that the median line is inappropriate because there are 'special circumstances'. This claim is based largely on a Soviet order of 1926, decreeing that the border should follow a more westerly line that runs all the way from the Russian-Norwegian border straight up to the North Pole, while bypassing the Svalbard archipelago. Tensions between Russia and Norway over the disputed Grey Zone surfaced in the early 1970s, but were abated in 1978 when they both agreed to share fishing rights there, even though the ownership of the disputed region was not finally settled.[48]

The third and final dispute in the Barents Sea concerns an area known simply as the 'Loophole'. This large triangular region is the subject of disagreement because it falls beyond the 200-mile limit that both Russia and Norway can claim as their exclusive economic zone. Strictly speaking, its waters are therefore 'high seas' and will remain so defined unless a coastal state can demonstrate that its outer continental shelf reaches beyond the 200-mile limit.

Fishing vessels have a right to go to the 'high seas' of the Loophole but have to cross Russian or Norwegian waters to get there. Some trawlers are tempted to take fishing stocks en route, or to exploit this particular area so heavily that a much wider area is affected. The same problem – of 'high seas enclaves' that are surrounded by national waters – bedevils several other areas. The Donut Hole, for example, is an enclave in the central Bering Sea that is surrounded by Russian and American waters. For many years international fishing vessels journeyed through these waters to reach the Hole and fish in this small enclave. When the stock of Bering Sea pollock diminished sharply in the early 1990s, both Washington and Moscow sought to crack down on unregulated fishing and in 1994 brokered the Donut Hole Agreement, which imposed strict quotas on foreign vessels.

The issue between Russia and Norway over the Loophole, however, is based on the question of whose continental shelf extends over it. In November 2006, 10 years after it had ratified the 1982 Convention, the Norwegian government formally submitted a claim to the UN, arguing that its continental shelf extended into three areas. One of these was the Loophole, while the other two were the Western Nansen Basin in the Arctic Ocean and a region, known alternatively as 'the Herring Loophole' or 'Banana Hole', which lies in the Norwegian Sea.[49]

As the underwater mission of Sagalevich and Chilingarov made so clear, the Russians are making their own comparable claim about the size of their continental shelf. Drawing a more westerly line through the Grey Zone than the Norwegians, they extend it northwards beyond their 200-mile economic zone and follow it through the Loophole, beyond Franz Josef Land up as far as the North Pole. This is the same course as the borders that were drawn by the Soviet authorities in 1926.

Nationalism

In legal terms, other Arctic disputes are narrowly domestic matters, even though they also have wider repercussions. An example is Greenland, which was first colonized by Danish settlers in 1721 and has been ruled from Copenhagen since 1933, when the Permanent Court dismissed Norway's claim to ownership. But in the post-war years there has been a growing demand among Greenlanders for independence, an issue that is ultimately for them and for the Danish government to determine, rather than the outside world.

These national aspirations came to the political surface in the late 1970s, when the 57,000-strong population voted in favour of home rule and were subsequently granted more freedoms from Denmark while at the same time remaining part of its sovereign territory. But even these concessions failed to satisfy many people, notably the leading advocate of Greenland's total independence, Jonathan Motzfeldt of the social democratic Siumut Party, who urged his followers to press for more freedom. There was a further rift in 1985, when Greenland voted to withdraw from the European Union even though Denmark remained a member, and in 2003 it was granted a limited say in matters of foreign policy and international security. This is discussed further in Chapter 12.

Overlapping continental shelves

In several parts of the Barents and Norwegian Seas, various coastal countries are making overlapping claims over the size and limits of their continental shelves. Assuming that each state can prove its case, it is far from clear how the judges of the ICJ will resolve this dispute. The same is equally true of areas of the far north into which the 'Arctic Five' could claim, or already have claimed, that their continental shelves extend. There are some areas close to the North Pole where the claims made by Russia, Canada and Denmark might potentially all overlap.

There is no real legal guidance on this point since the 1982 Convention only vaguely states that these disputes should be decided 'by agreement on the basis of international law . . . in order to achieve an equitable solution'.[50] And although the ICJ has passed judgement on three overlapping continental shelf disputes since its inception in 1946, each case was decided well before the Convention was drawn up and agreed upon.[51]

Claimant countries might be able to buttress their case by arguing that they have some form of 'historic title' to the disputed region. The ICJ was sceptical of this kind of argument in one of the three cases it adjudicated, but nonetheless acknowledged that history should be a factor in resolving overlapping continental shelf claims and that geology alone was not likely to offer a well-defined boundary. In that case Tunisia had an 80-year historical practice of fishing in the contested area and this gave it some 'historic title' to the contested region.[52]

Disputes in the High North
Slicing the Arctic pie

Another contentious issue is exactly how disputed seas should be carved up. This is already causing disagreement between the United States and Canada in the Beaufort Sea, and between Russia and Norway in the Grey Zone of the Barents. It is also creating tension among the 'Arctic Five' as they decide how to divide up the rest of the Arctic Ocean that lies further north.

Since the late 1940s, international lawyers have looked to the 'median line method' to divide disputed waters. The 1958 Geneva Convention on the Continental Shelf, for example, argued that the borders should be drawn according to the length of a country's coast; in other words, that every point of a median line is equidistant to the nearest point on the coast. This approach, which is easy and convenient to apply, was the starting point for the ICJ on each of the occasions when it has considered the vexing issue of how to deal with overlapping continental shelves.

But a coastal state might also have legal grounds to claim territory around a pole on a 'sector' basis (Map 4). This approach allows them to claim a pie-shaped area that is formed by drawing lines that run from its coasts to the pole. In other words, a disputed area is cut like a cake. This is not a recent legal invention but instead has long-standing historic roots. When Canadian explorers first staked their claim to parts of the Arctic in the late nineteenth century, they claimed that their country owned everything between the 60th and 141st meridians of longitude all the way to the North Pole. Canada's most famous early proponents of this approach were Senator Pascal Poirier, in the early twentieth century, and Captain J. E. Bernier, who took 'formal possession' of the whole Arctic archipelago on 1 July 1909 by placing a plaque on Melville Island that still reads:

> *This Memorial is erected today to commemorate the taking pos-session for the DOMINION OF CANADA of the whole ARCTIC ARCHIPELAGO lying to the north of America from long. 60°W to 141°W up to latitude 90°N.*[53]

Other countries have also favoured this approach. In 1926, the Soviet authorities had decreed that their national border ran northwards from the city of Murmansk to the North Pole and then headed straight back down into the middle of the Bering Sea.[54] They declared that this triangular segment of the Arctic belonged to Russia and represented its natural sphere of influence. The Central Executive Committee then issued a formal decree that incorporated these claims.

Moscow based its claim to the Arctic on the sector principle when it first submitted its case to the UN Commission on the Limits of the Continental Shelf in 2001, even though it actually has little to win or lose from either approach. By contrast, the United States and Norway have a great deal to gain from the sector method, while the median line principle strongly favours Canada and Denmark, almost doubling what they would expect to win under the alternative approach. This is ironic because, in order to stake its claim over the islands of the Northwest Passage, Canada had once found the sector principle more convenient.

These different approaches to the demarcation of borders illustrate how challenging some of the disputes in the Arctic might turn out to be. Fortunately most of these future disputes are likely to be resolved peacefully. Most of the Arctic countries are peace-loving and have neither the will nor the means to wage war against each other. There are two places where Denmark and Norway have long disagreed about where their maritime borders should be drawn. One is north of the Svalbard archipelago, in the waters of Western Nansen Basin that lies close to Greenland. The other is the so-called 'Banana Hole' that lies in the midst of the Norway Basin, the Lofoten Basin and the Greenland Sea, and where the two countries, and Iceland, have made overlapping claims about where their outer continental shelves lie (Map 5). Both countries, as well as Iceland, have amicable relations. In 2006, Denmark and Norway agreed not to obstruct each other's subsequent efforts to prove to the UN that their continental shelves extend into these disputed areas.[55]

But it remains possible that another country, most obviously Russia or the United States, might calculate that it has more to gain by using military force to seize disputed regions. A region rich in energy resources, or which has a superb strategic setting, could conceivably make a very tempting target.

5

Black Gold

In the summer of 1990, a leading Canadian geologist was flying by helicopter to a research station near the Borup Fjord on Ellesmere Island. Glancing down at the terrain hundreds of feet below, he noticed that part of a huge ice formation had a distinctive yellow tarnish, and after landing nearby, he drove to the area to take a closer look.

At the offices of the Geological Survey of Canada, colleagues looked at the samples he had taken and confirmed what he already suspected: that the tinge was caused by hydrogen sulphide, induced by sulphur-oxidizing bacteria thriving within the glacier. Among members of the scientific community, this revelation caused a flurry of excitement. Experts at NASA, who had spent years investigating the terrain of other planets in the solar system, were taken aback by the possible significance of the discovery: if there is life in the depths of an Arctic glacier, they asked, could there not equally be some forms of life on the frozen environments of outer space? For the geologist, the news meant something else entirely: the presence of sulphur is often an unmistakable sign of underground petroleum. Ellesmere Island, in other words, suddenly seemed to promise oil.

In the summer of 2008, a leading scientific research organization, the United States Geological Survey (USGS), published a report, formally known as the 'Circum-Arctic Resource Appraisal', which had taken 4 years to complete and whose conclusions had been eagerly awaited, not only in the scientific world but also by many groups. The matter had once been academic, but since the late 1990s, it has started to become important for one simple reason: the ice is retreating and opening the way for underwater exploration, and exploitation of resources. Although this has always promised to be an immensely complicated task, the contemporary oil industry has considerable technological expertise at its disposal. 'For a variety of reasons, the possibility of oil and gas exploration in the Arctic has become much less hypothetical than it once was', emphasized Donald Gautier, a chief USGS geologist, when the report was published.[1]

The agency's findings seemed to make a compelling case that the Arctic is set to become a new frontline for oil and natural gas exploration. Using the latest scientific methods and instruments, the geologists argued that the region has as much as 90 billion barrels of undiscovered oil reserves, and 1,670 trillion cubic feet of natural gas. This is equivalent to around 13 per cent of the world's total undiscovered oil and about 30 per cent of its undiscovered natural gas, while the researchers also reckon that the region holds a huge quantity of natural gas liquids, amounting to perhaps as much as 44 billion barrels in total.[2] The 'extensive Arctic continental shelves', the researchers argued, 'may constitute the geographically largest unexplored prospective area for petroleum remaining on earth'.[3]

In particular, the scientists emphasized one very important aspect of these findings. These reserves were not the total quantity of underground oil, known in the industry as 'oil in place'. Instead, they were an estimate of how much of this 'oil in place' is actually 'recoverable'; in other words, how much of it can be lifted out of the ground using methods and technology that are already being used elsewhere in the world.

This is a crucial difference, and the scientists were well aware of how much weight international governments might be tempted to give their findings. 'Before we can make decisions about our future use of oil and gas and related decisions about protecting endangered species, native communities and the health of our planet, we need to know what's out there', said the director of the Survey, Mark Myers. 'With this assessment, we're providing the same information to everyone in the world so that the global community can make those difficult decisions.'[4]

The revelation that the Arctic can boast natural resources on such a vast scale has fostered speculation that the region will be the setting for future 'resource wars'. The confrontational rhetoric of some political leaders, as well as provocative actions such as the flag-waving underwater expeditions made by Russian submarines in August 2007, have only helped to fuel fears that the Arctic could be a future battleground for oil and natural gas. But such talk is misleading. There are many reasons why this worst-case scenario is – in theory at least – most unlikely to ever come about. A much more complicated picture is likely to emerge.

Oil and natural gas are very different commodities, surrounded by quite different issues, but this chapter will focus purely on oil.

Oil and governments

Although it is an exaggeration to say that an Arctic 'resource war' over oil is probable, the interest of foreign governments in the region is perfectly understandable. There are two quite different benefits that oil gives any government that can claim title over it: security of supply and export revenues.

Security of supply

Some countries are still haunted by memories of the desperate situation in which the United States and its strategic allies in the Western world found themselves in the wake of the Arab oil embargo that followed the Yom Kippur War in October 1973. Having lost the war, the Arabs sought to compel the United States government to change its position on the Arab-Israeli dispute by starving it of oil exports. This effort at 'political blackmail' (to use Henry Kissinger's term) not only exacted a heavy economic price but also succeeded in engineering what a historian of the crisis has called 'one of the gravest splits in the Western alliance since its foundation in the days after World War II, and certainly the worst since Suez in 1956'.[5]

Today, however, it would be quite impossible for any oil producer to starve a consumer in the same way. In the intervening years, energy markets have been transformed and oil is now bought and sold in a truly open, global market that prohibits producers from dictating where their oil goes. After the crude oil is loaded onto tankers, international traders make electronic bids for the cargo as it makes its way to prospective markets. To starve a particular consumer of supplies, a producer, or any other country, would have to impose a military blockade stopping all oil cargoes from pulling into harbour.

Of course, any oil exporter can still deliberately disrupt its exports, cutting back on its production levels or refusing international shipping permission to use its ports. This is what Iraq did briefly in April 2002, when it protested at an Israeli incursion in the West Bank by imposing a month-long embargo. It is also what others have threatened to do, even though such a move would, in all likelihood, be economically suicidal. Ayatollah Ali Khamenei, Iran's Supreme Leader, has been known to issue vague threats that 'if [the Western countries] do not receive oil, their factories will come to a halt. This will shake the world'.[6] In this situation, consumers would still be able to buy crude oil from other suppliers, but probably at a higher price for the simple reason that any disruption, in any part of the world, is apt to cause an imbalance between supply and demand.

Instead of a producer deliberately cutting back on its output, it is today much more likely that war, terrorist actions, accidents and severe weather conditions will block supplies and send the barrel price soaring. The most vulnerable single area is the Strait of Hormuz in the Persian Gulf, through which tankers move around one-fifth of the world's oil, although the Niger Delta, Iraq and Venezuela are also susceptible. Following Hurricanes Katrina and Rita in 2005, the United States experienced a supply disruption of around 8 per cent, causing a price spike that was mitigated only because President Bush released a certain number of barrels from emergency reserves.[7]

It is in the event of such disruption that a consumer might arguably be able to benefit from 'security of supply'. If there is a tight oil market, it can increase production from its own oilfields, helping to redress an imbalance between supply and demand, instead of vainly imploring foreign producers to do so on its behalf. It was in this spirit of impotence that, in the summer of 2008, when the global price of crude oil began to climb to record highs and eventually reached a barrel price of $147, the British Prime Minister, Gordon Brown, met with Middle Eastern leaders and other representatives of the Organization of the Petroleum Exporting Countries (OPEC) and urged them in person to step up production while pointing to the 'scandal that forty per cent of the oil is controlled by OPEC'.[8]

Rightly or wrongly, many people felt that the sharp price increases in the summer of 2008 were an alarming premonition of the future. However complicated the causes of the oil price bubble may have been it is easy to understand why anyone should take such a view. Almost every day there are reports in the media that the age of 'easy oil' is over and that new reserves will become increasingly hard to find, despite growing demand, in the years ahead. The arguments of the advocates of 'peak oil', who claim that global output has reached its peak, seem compelling to many people.[9]

'Peak oil' is a hugely contentious issue, but what is not in doubt is that almost everyone is more uncertain than ever before about where future sources of supply are going to come from. The International Energy Agency (IEA), which acts as a watchdog for the governments of the developed world, predicts that the world will need as much as 100 million barrels of oil every day by the year 2015 (daily consumption in 2007 stood at around the 86 million mark). At the same time, supply is widely anticipated to peak and then gradually decline, although of course no one is quite sure when. In December 2008 Fatih Birol, the IEA's chief economist, told a newspaper that conventional crude output could reach a plateau by 2020, a far more pessimistic prediction than the IEA had ever previously made.[10] But what really matters is the underlying sense of gloom, in both the industry and in government circles, about the future. Even leading figures in the world of oil who are very far from being 'peak oilers' feel far from sure about what the future holds. James Mulva, chief executive of ConocoPhillips, and Christophe de Margerie, his counterpart at the French energy giant, Total, have said that in their view, daily world production is most unlikely to ever surpass the 89 million-barrel figure.

Unless new replacement fuels are discovered to redress this increasingly uneasy relationship between supply and demand, the result will be dramatically higher fuel bills. This would exact not only a painful economic price, but would also carry big political risks: in the summer of 2008, for example, higher fuel bills triggered large-scale rioting in many parts of the world, including France, Nepal and Indonesia.

Some experts argue that one way of meeting the threat of such price spikes is to acquire ownership of the world's remaining oil reserves: if the global price of oil shoots up, then a government can arrange for a nationalized upstream company to pump oil at a faster rate, or for a distribution and marketing company to divert crude from refineries abroad to those at home. In practice this presents all sorts of problems: in the Western world, governments have no direct means of making private oil companies toe the line unless they nationalize them. But this may seem a minor objection to a government that is deeply concerned about achieving 'security of supply'.

Export revenues

Anyone who has spent much time in oil-producing countries usually has a similar story to tell. In each of these states, usually not far from where the impoverished masses live and work, is a privileged elite whose lifestyle seems luxurious even by the standards of the Western world's most affluent. In the streets of north Tehran or Khartoum, land cruisers are driven by the fortunate few who wear expensive suits and dark glasses while in the Nigerian capital, Lagos, some people had 'champagne, watches, cars or – if they were too poor – just motorcycles' at the height of the oil boom of the mid-1970s.[11]

Such scenes are a reminder that besides 'security of supply', oil offers something else to a government that can lay claim to the underground reserves – export revenues. In the case of both private and nationalized companies, these revenues are drawn from taxes that are either imposed on company profits or on the actual movement of goods as they leave the country of origin and head for their destination markets. How much a government takes can vary enormously: in recent years, Saudi Aramco has paid around 93 per cent of its profits in royalties and dividends to the state, keeping the rest for itself so that, in the words of one Aramco official, 'it does not have to ask permission from the government to get the money back'.[12] The Russian government also takes a very high percentage, and in 2004 introduced a punitive tax that allowed it to appropriate around 80 per cent of oil revenues. Western governments, by contrast, are unlikely to take as much from the privatized energy companies, such as BP, Royal Dutch Shell and Total. It was precisely for this reason that in the summer of 2008 the British government argued in favour of a windfall tax that would take much more money from UK-registered oil majors at a time when their profits were being hugely inflated by the soaring price of crude.

This is why oil-producing states across the world reaped such large profits from the dramatic rise in the price of crude that lasted from the end of 2003, when a barrel fetched around $25, until the late summer of 2008, when the price peaked at $147. Russia, for example, had faced a serious economic crisis in the late 1990s when its $200 billion economy nearly defaulted, but by the spring of 2008 its gross domestic product reached $1.4 trillion (35 trillion roubles), driven almost entirely by the sale of oil and natural gas. In the Middle East, many governments were also similarly awash with petrodollars. These sums of money remain vital to every aspect of the economies of almost every chief oil exporter, whether it is to pay their civil servants, to finance a state-induced spending boom or to subsidize the price of gasoline at home, thereby offsetting any price increases in the wider global market.

How much oil, then, does the Arctic have to offer, and could it be the setting for a future 'resource war' waged by oil-thirsty countries desperate to acquire its assets for these two reasons?

The Arctic's existing oil supplies

Alaska is one Arctic region where oil has been flowing for some considerable time. Although Inuits had noticed oil seepages for thousands of years, the first proper oil exploration operations got underway here only in the early years of the twentieth century and the first producing wells had begun to operate at full capacity in 1911. It was not until much later, however, that the region really caught the eye of the big oil companies. In July 1957, a Californian exploration company struck an underground reservoir that flowed at a daily rate of 900 barrels, and this immediately prompted others to step up their search for Alaskan oil. The single most important discovery was at Prudhoe Bay on the Arctic coast, which was unearthed in 1967. It began operation a decade later and by the mid-1980s had become North America's largest oil field, producing around 2 million barrels every day and meeting around one-fifth of American domestic demand.

For some years, Alaskan oil has offered the United States limited 'security of supply' because a huge 23 million acre area of the province's North Slope forms part of America's National Petroleum Reserve. This area was originally set aside in 1923 by President Harding, who saw it as a source of emergency supply in the event of any serious disruption to imports, and in 1976 the United States Department of the Interior began to administer the site, which is currently estimated to contain around 10.6 billion barrels of oil, and renamed it as the National Petroleum Reserve – Alaska.

Both the central government and the state of Alaska have also drawn very considerable tax revenues from the local oil industry. In 2005, taxes and royalties from oil production accounted for 87 per cent of the revenues that flowed into the state's general financial fund, subsidizing the provision of basic services ranging from schools to roads and enabling all Alaskans to avoid paying state income tax. The US central government also earns huge sums from the sale of exploration rights: in 2008 oil companies spent $2.6 million acquiring leases on government-controlled offshore tracts.

There are also some parts of northern Siberia, lying just north of the Arctic Circle, where the oil industry is relatively well established. The most important of these is the Timan-Pechora Basin, located on the territory of the Nenets Autonomous Okrug and the Komi Republic in northern Russia, which is a mature hydrocarbon province. This area has a long history of oil and gas exploration and production. The first field was discovered in 1930 and, after another 80 years of exploration, more than 230 fields have been unearthed and more than 5,400 wells drilled. By early 2009, more than 16 billion barrels of oil and 40 trillion cubic feet of gas had been extracted from this part of the Russian Federation.

Future sources of oil

In September 2008, the European Union (EU) energy commissioner, Andris Piebalgs, argued that the Western energy firms would need to look to the Arctic region in order to acquire energy security. 'You even need to go into hostile environments' such as the Arctic, he claimed. 'You can't say "this is a sanctuary" because it will not work . . . otherwise where will we get energy from?' Provided 'all environmental precautions' were taken, Piebalgs continued, he was supportive of the position taken by the giant Norwegian oil and gas firm Statoil, which has already invested huge sums in searching the Arctic coastline for new reserves. Statoil's director, Helge Lund, has argued that 'any realistic energy strategy in the future will have to rely on oil and gas' and that a 'massive exploration effort' is required in the Arctic.[13] These views were echoed soon after in the EU's first official document on the Arctic region, which argued that its 'resources could contribute to enhancing the EU's security of supply concerning energy and raw materials in general'.[14]

Most experts feel sure that the region still has vast, untapped sources of oil that could conceivably dwarf its existing output. The 2008 survey by the USGS concluded that one-third of the Arctic's undiscovered oil, about 30 billion barrels, lies off the coast of Alaska. 'It is the most obvious place to look for oil in the North Arctic right now', as the chief geologist in the survey has pointed out. 'It is virtually certain that petroleum will be found there.'[15] Western Siberia is also considered to be very promising. The USGS estimates that there are 3.6 billion barrels of undiscovered oil throughout the West Siberian Basin province as well as considerably more in other parts of northern Russia that lie north of the Arctic Circle.[16]

The American experts also considered the coast of Greenland to be the other chief oil-bearing Arctic region. Although some efforts to explore this area were made in the late 1970s, oil was first discovered here only in 1992, seeping out of rocks not far from a stretch of coast in the Disko-Nuussuaq region of West Greenland. The area was properly surveyed in 2007, when a huge offshore tract off the eastern coast, covering nearly 200,000 square miles, was the subject of another USGS survey. Judging that several areas were 'potentially good source rocks' and 'potentially promising' for liquid petroleum, the scientists reckoned that there are approximately 17.5 billion barrels of oil off Greenland's coasts.[17]

Not surprisingly the prospect of reaping a future oil bonanza has caused enormous excitement among Greenlanders, as well as consternation in Copenhagen, which has ruled this continental landmass since 1720.[18] 'This is an epoch-making time, and how we handle it will be of colossal significance', as Aleqa Hammond, Greenland's minister of Foreign Affairs and Finance, put it in 2008. 'Greenland will be a player in the global arena in many more ways than we can even begin to imagine.' And it has certainly created real interest in the world of commercial oil. In October 2007, Greenland's government awarded exploration licences to Chevron, ExxonMobil and Husky Energy, all of which wasted no time in collecting seismic data to determine the best drilling sites.

Although the most oil-rich areas of the Arctic are widely considered to be in Russia and Greenland, there are others that are also thought to be full of promise. In particular, very positive signs of oil have been discovered in an area, known as Derki, which lies on Iceland's Jan Mayen Ridge. In the summer of 2008, an Icelandic oceanographic research ship, the *Arni Fridgeirsson*, returned from the region after mapping around 15,000 square miles of ocean with the latest scanning technology, and found strong indications of oil in an underwater terrain that appeared to strongly resemble the North Sea. At the same time the Icelandic government has been working hard to attract investment in this region from some of the world's biggest oil companies, and in early 2009 had started to finalize the terms for its first offshore licences. Several British groups and Statoil were among those that were said to be interesting in bidding for about 100 exploration licences.

Icelandic officials admit that bringing this oil to the surface would not be an easy feat because the depth of the water ranges from 2,500 to about 6,000 feet, but argue that it is a much more feasible operation than before. A manager at Iceland's Energy Authority has pointed out that in the 1990s, plans to explore the region had been scrapped because the area was considered too challenging, but a decade on, deep water projects in the Gulf of Mexico and in Brazilian waters showed that 'the technology now exists'.[19]

An Arctic resource war?

Revelations that the Arctic is home to untapped quantities of petroleum have prompted speculation that the region could be the setting for a future resource war waged for control of its oil. As fears mount that the world is starting to run dry (the theory goes), governments will be more tempted than ever to rely on military force to seize areas deemed to be rich in petroleum. Fortunately, however, this gloomy scenario is likely to paint too pessimistic a picture.

The location of the resources

The most important reason why the Arctic is unlikely to be the setting for a new 'oil resource war' is that most of the region's reserves are thought to lie not in disputed territory but within established borders. The 2008 USGS survey located most of the region's oil deposits in Alaska, Greenland, Siberia, the East Barents Sea and the Amerasian

Basin, areas where the question of territorial sovereignty either does not arise at all or only exists between close allies.[20] Although the survey did find evidence of oil in the disputed waters around Svalbard, there are many other petroleum-rich areas over which the 'Arctic Five' do not have to compete.

In the areas that are disputed, the rival claimants are generally governments with amicable relations that are too strong to be undermined by disagreements over one particular issue. One such disputed region is the Beaufort Sea, where the line of demarcation between Canada and the United States has been a subject of considerable controversy for some years.[21] This is an area that geologists feel sure has enormous promise, since it is an extension of the proven reserves in the nearby Mackenzie River and North Slope. Although the first major efforts to find black gold here were made in the late 1960s and the first platform of the Amauligak Project started to pump out oil in 1986, it is only recently, as the ice has receded, that extensive operations have really got underway. Canada's National Energy Board has now discovered a considerable amount of recoverable oil – somewhere between 585 million and 1.44 billion barrels – in this area.

In 2003, when the United States government auctioned oil and gas leases in the disputed region, Ottawa filed a diplomatic protest, raising the spectre of long-term legal wrangling that scared off international energy companies. The prospect of a military clash between the two NATO members is of course unthinkable as the ties between Canada and the United States are simply too strong to be severed by a single issue. The same is true of the dispute between Denmark and Canada over the ownership of Hans Island, whose surrounding waters geologists have long regarded as an area of great potential. It is highly unlikely that anything more serious than heated words would ever be exchanged between these two governments.[22]

Much more plausible is speculation of a possible clash between Russia and Norway over disputed parts of the Barents Sea. To date, there have been few significant discoveries in the area, despite considerable efforts to find new reserves there. The sheer size of these wells, such as the massive Russian gas complex at Shtokman first unearthed in 1988 and Norway's vast Goliath oil field discovered in 2000, compensates for their paucity of number. Such discoveries dramatically raise the stakes in the dispute over the three large areas of the Barents Sea that the two countries have long contested: the 'Grey Zone', the 'Loophole' and the waters surrounding the Svalbard archipelago, where the Russians claim they have fishing and mining rights.[23]

Many experts feel sure that some, and perhaps all, of these disputed areas have considerable oil-bearing potential. In 2007 the Russian research vessel, *Professor Kyrentsov*, undertook several studies of the underwater geology around Svalbard and its findings prompted experts in Moscow to deliver an upbeat assessment. These findings reiterated the estimates made by the Norwegian Petroleum Directorate, which commissioned some exploratory drilling in September 2005 and found the northern regions of the Svalbard waters to be full of potential. In a press release issued in May that year, the oil minister, Thorhild Widvey, commented that 'I believe the north will develop into one of Europe's most important petroleum-producing regions. Here Norway has great opportunities'. The Grey Zone is also thought to be particularly promising, and Professor Jan Inge Faleide of Oslo University, for example, has described it as a 'hot' region where there are 'large geological structures in the area that may contain oil and gas'.[24]

This has sometimes come close to causing trouble. In 2002 Oslo gave permission for a Russian company, Marine Arctic Geological Expedition, to undertake seismic surveys of the Svalbard continental shelf, but did so only on the strict condition that they were done for 'scientific research' rather than 'petroleum exploration'. But the Russians effectively ignored this and instead used a seismic vessel to look for oil, prompting Norway to take a harsher line and more vigorously enforce its ban on petroleum exploration.

Because the Norwegian authorities have continued to deny Russia permission to conduct any more surveys around Svalbard, EU defence chiefs have warned that 'a serious conflict could emerge between Russia and Norway' over 'the large deposits of gas and oil that are currently locked under a continental shelf' in the waters that surround the archipelago.[25] For a number of reasons such disagreements are much more likely to create tensions and controversy rather than confrontation. This is partly because the two countries have a strong interest in cooperating, rather than working against each other, and cannot afford to forfeit the other's trust or lose its goodwill. As Chapter 9 points out, Russia is reliant on Western expertise to develop its offshore oil and gas fields just as Norwegian energy companies, which are world leaders in this technically highly demanding area, regard Russia's fields as a huge commercial opportunity.[26] It is significant in this regard that some Russian officials confess to sabre-rattling: Mikhail Margelov, head of the international affairs committee of Russia's Federation Council, has admitted that 'the real reason for the arguments' between Moscow and Oslo 'is the oil rather than fish', but added that 'Russia has no intention to monopolize the hydrocarbon market', and is ready to cooperate with Norway in the development of offshore fields.[27]

This is one reason why, in 2005, representatives of the two countries signed a broad agreement to work together to search for Arctic oil and gas, prompting commentators to make upbeat statements about what the deal signalled. Vladimir Ryashin, a Moscow-based representative for a Norwegian oil organization, felt that Russia's position was 'a reflection of an attitude that their general intention is positive, and an invitation to be very active. It's a hint that Russia is ready for compromises, and they expect the Norwegians to take the same position'.[28]

Russian fishermen have long been highly dependent on the Svalbard waters, and some estimates reckon that as much as one quarter of the national catch comes from here. But Russia has no clear legal right to fish outside Svalbard and has not wanted to risk sacrificing its current freedoms by challenging Norway's rights before the judges of the ICJ. As one researcher has written:

> In a broader perspective, there is little to suggest that the Russian authorities have an interest in provoking a judicial chaos in the fisheries protection zone. This would lead to increased pressure from third states with no tradition of fishing.[29]

The Russians do not wish to provoke a legal fight over such an important issue that they might well lose. Nor for that matter can Russia, Norway or any other country just assume that there are any oil reserves in the Arctic that are worth fighting for; even estimates that use the latest, most up-to-date methods can be highly misleading.

Statistical reliability

Something that plagues the entire oil industry is the sheer unreliability of statistics. What this means is that no government can be quite sure that the Arctic has reserves that could justify entering a fight. Instead it is equally likely that a small and misleading number of big discoveries, such as Goliath and Shtokman, have created a false impression about what the rest of the region offers and hugely inflated many people's expectations.

Oil and gas companies base their estimates on the results of various types of exploration activities, including regional geological studies, seismic surveys, drilling, sampling, pressure testing and reservoir modelling. These findings are combined with feasibility studies and a commercial evaluation based on economic considerations. No matter how sophisticated the methods, such estimates are always going to be imprecise. Oil is seldom located in underground lakes or reservoirs, but is often absorbed into porous underground rocks in a way that makes it almost impossible to measure accurately. Many of these deposits run so deep that even in the early stages of exploitation it is still impossible to guess about their size and location. This is why the story of oil exploration is one of massive misjudgements.

Until the 1920s almost every expert thought that the Middle East had no oil and urged Western governments to search Central America or the Far East to find new supplies.[30] More recently, some of the 'predictions' about the growth of future oil demand have become almost notorious for their unreliability. These figures are often revised by huge degrees and are nearly always treated with scepticism by many in the trade. 'Oil market data is generally a black art like using a set of chicken bones', in the words of one analyst. 'If Columbus had thought he'd hit India when in fact he was in the Caribbean, that's about the level of oil market data. It is like paint thrown across a canvas. You get the broad outline of the situation but even then . . . the paint moves of its own accord.'[31]

Trying to make even a rough estimate of oil reserves is difficult, but there is good reason to suppose that any assessment of the Arctic region will be particularly challenging. This is not because the region's geology is unusually complex or because much of the Arctic Ocean is unusually deep. It is simply because the Arctic's thick pack ice seriously obstructs the scientific equipment that is used to estimate how much petroleum lies buried deep below the surface.

The USGS report in 2008 admitted its limited scope, pointing out that:

> *Because of the sparse seismic and drilling data in much of the Arctic, the usual tools and techniques used in USGS resource assessments, such as discovery process modeling, prospect delineation, and deposit simulation, were not generally applicable. Therefore, the Circum-Arctic Research Assessment relied on a probabilistic methodology of geological analysis and analog modeling.*[32]

The authors of the 2008 report did not define what they meant by 'geographic analysis and analog modeling' but since the report was published some of the researchers have emphasized just how speculative their conclusions were. Donald Gautier, a leading geologist in the appraisal assessment team, has cautioned that with little drilling or seismic surveying in many of the Arctic basins the new resource estimates are highly tentative. 'I would emphasize that this is a very uncertain area and these are probabilistic estimates with a great deal of uncertainty associated with them', as Gautier told one newspaper.[33] Just as many question marks hung over an earlier report published the previous year on oil prospects in Greenland. This had noted that any effort to survey its north-east regions was bound to be imprecise because it 'shares important characteristics with many Arctic basins, including sparse data, significant resource potential (and) great geological uncertainty'.[34]

Critics of the 2008 report argue that the USGS has a track record that perfectly illustrates just how unreliable such 'estimates' can be. In particular, its 'World Petroleum Assessment', published in 2000, produced figures that were wildly at variance with those the organization had made a few years later. In 2000, it estimated the offshore reserves in eastern Greenland at around 46 billion barrels, but 8 years later was forced to massively downgrade this figure.

The findings of other respected engineering firms and consultancies have been more cautious than those of the USGS. In 2006, a British organization, Wood Mackenzie, and Fugro Robertson, a leading petroleum engineering company, published their own assessment of the Arctic region as a source of long-term energy supply. Although it has a lot of natural gas, the authors of *The Future of the Arctic* argued, the region may not have nearly as much oil-bearing potential as some people hope. Instead their findings were 'disappointing from a world oil resource base perspective' because they showed that key basins of North America and Greenland had only about one-quarter of the oil volumes other assessments claimed. And given that only the North Slope in Alaska and the Pechora Sea in Russia seemed to be particularly promising, the researchers argued that 'this assessment basically calls into question the long-considered view that the Arctic represents one of the last great oil and gas frontiers and a strategic energy supply cache for the US'. Instead the United States would need to 'look elsewhere to meet rising demand', and recognize that OPEC member states 'such as Venezuela', and Russia, are more promising.[35]

It is significant that many of the assessments of the Barents Sea have been proved wrong. In the 1980s it was regarded by some people as promising oil territory until a number of exploration wells yielded disappointing results. In May 1985 a United States Congress Report entitled 'Oil and Gas Technologies for the Arctic and Deepwater' was revised just before publication, and the region's potential oil resources were downgraded by a massive 73 per cent and gas by even more. Geologists thought they knew the reason: 'The Barents Sea rose and fell during the last ice ages. Sediments several kilometres thick were scraped off. Gas deposits underneath expanded and the oil was forced out of the reservoirs', as a leading expert, Professor Jan Inge Faleide, has pointed out. 'The drilling should have been done 10 million years ago.'[36]

The root of the issue, Dr Rob Mandley of Fugro Robertson emphasizes, is the sheer paucity of reliable information on the Arctic's reserves. 'For example, there are hardly any offshore Russian oil fields east of the Kara Sea, which means a huge area is almost completely untouched by modern, up-to-date methods of exploration and surveillance.'[37]

How does this affect a government as it weighs up the case for using military force to seize territory where oilfields are said to exist? If any estimate is as uncertain as the survey carried out in 2008 by the USGS, a government might draw two possible conclusions. It may take the view that the likelihood of finding fewer resources than predicted is heavily outweighed by the inevitably high cost of war (as Chapter 9 shows, even a brief conflict, such as Russia's clash with Georgia in the summer of 2008, can still have a very heavy political and economic impact).[38] On the other hand, the uncertainty of scientific opinion is no guarantee against a 'resource war' in the Arctic because a government might conceivably underestimate the costs of war but argue that the underground oil reserves may be far larger than the experts say.

However, there is a more important reason why governments are unlikely to risk war fighting over the Arctic's oil reserves, no matter how extensive they prove to be. This concerns not the location or size of these deposits but their recoverability: vast quantities of untapped oil are of little significance if they are simply too difficult or expensive to get out of the ground.

Recoverability

Although it is used extensively in the world of oil, the issue of recoverability is often an uncertain one. Everyone agrees that oil is recoverable if the technology has already been developed to exploit it, but this begs other questions. Above all, potential investors need to judge if the output of a new oilfield will yield revenues that justify the sheer cost of extracting the oil with know-how that is often extremely expensive to develop and operate. For energy companies, the price of making the wrong decision is likely to be huge – by the end of 2008

Shell had poured more than $2 billion into the exploration of the Alaskan coast but had nothing to show for it, and the future of its involvement there currently seems uncertain.

Although USGS geologists have claimed that the Arctic's oil is 'recoverable' in both technical and commercial terms, this assertion needs to be clarified. One staff member, Brenda Pierce, later commented that the assessment did not take into account the technical difficulties of operating in extreme conditions. 'We assumed these resources are recoverable in sea ice and despite water depth', as Pierce later commented.[39] The report itself points this out:

> The study included only those resources believed to be recoverable using existing technology, but with the important assumptions for offshore areas that the resources would be recoverable even in the presence of permanent sea ice and oceanic water depth. No economic considerations are included in these initial estimates; results are presented without reference to costs of exploration and development, which will be important in many of the assessed areas.[40]

There are some areas of the Arctic Ocean, it is true, where the waters are relatively shallow and any oil would be comparatively accessible. The offshore waters adjacent to East Greenland, surveyed by the USGS in 2007, generally reach less than 1,500 feet, while the average depth of the Barents Sea is just 750 feet. But other regions – like those in which Chilingarov and Sagalevich moved in August 2007 – are far more daunting and often reach depths of around 14,000 feet that would be too deep for the world's leading energy companies to work in. Some exploratory drilling projects in the Gulf of Mexico and off the coast of Brazil have been undertaken in depths of 12,000 feet, but production has not gone below 6,000 feet. The average depth of the Amerasian Basin, for example, is 12,960 feet.

Even if oil is found within this range or the technology to work in deeper waters is developed, another challenge comes from the presence of sea ice, which would seriously hamper any effort to extract it. 'Drilling on the ocean shelf is currently restricted to ice-free periods in the summer', as Dr Mandley of Fugro Robertson explains, 'and it is only if there is a significant reduction in ice cover that drilling would become much less costly and production much more economic.'[41] The trouble is that no one is sure when this will happen: it could be 25, 50 or even 100 years or more before the ice has retreated enough to make drilling commercially viable.

There are some oil-rich Arctic regions that are relatively ice-free.

In the West Barents, south-west Greenland and the Labrador Sea, for example, there is often no pack ice and only limited seasonal ice. But elsewhere ice presents a formidable obstacle. The 2006 report argued that while the Kronpins Christian basin, off the coast of northeast Greenland, is one of the very few areas that has undiscovered resources exceeding 10 billion barrels of oil (the other areas being the South Kara/Yamal region of Western Siberia and the East Barents), it is nonetheless covered by extremely thick ice that constantly pushes against the shore. Icebergs also pose a serious risk in some places, notably Baffin Bay.[42]

Adding significantly to the costs of drilling in such a difficult environment would be the imposition of massive insurance premiums. As a later chapter points out, extracting oil in an ice-laden environment could easily lead to disaster; there is a real risk that a drifting block of ice could collide with an oil rig or pipeline, inflicting serious damage on the infrastructure and causing a spillage on a massive scale.[43]

Some experts have calculated that the cost of extracting Arctic oil is rarely likely to be lower than $46 per barrel, which would prove prohibitively expensive. Any country that seeks 'security of supply' could do much better than encouraging its energy companies to undertake huge commercial risks in the Arctic. There are many parts of the Middle East, Africa, Siberia and South America that are still relatively unexplored and other places that can continue to produce oil well into the twenty-first century with much lower overheads than the Arctic.

By contrast the exploitation of much of the Arctic's oil would require the building of new infrastructure – such as pipelines and storage terminals – that would be hugely expensive. True, there are some deposits that lie close to existing working fields and which could therefore be tapped using existing infrastructure. Some of these unexploited fields are in close proximity to the Trans Alaska Pipeline System that connects the North Slope to its mainland markets, or to the natural gas complex near Hammerfest that links the West Barents. And the massive Prirazlomnoye field could also help exploit the undiscovered deposits of the Pechora Sea. Known in the oil business as 'niche' opportunities, these fields make relatively low-risk but potentially high reward investments that would prove to be commercially very tempting. But there are also areas of high promise, such as northern Greenland and the Laptev Sea, that are not only very remote from markets but also wholly devoid of existing infrastructure.

The situation could change if regional ice continues to melt at a dramatic rate, making exploration and development much easier and cutting the cost of producing a barrel of oil closer to $20. This still looks unlikely for many years, and in the meantime the contrast is clear with the Middle East where a barrel can cost as little as $5 to produce.

The Beaufort Sea provides one example of just how expensive many drilling projects in the Arctic could turn out to be. In 2005, the Oklahoma-based Devon Energy Corporation was searching for natural gas, but chanced upon a pool of oil containing around 240 million barrels. Although the price of oil was at this time soaring, leaving energy companies with far more disposable income than before, its directors decided not to make any effort to exploit their discovery. 'We have confirmed the presence of both oil and gas', as one spokesman put it, 'but at the end of the day it's beyond economic reach. We would need some critical mass going. It takes a lot of time and energy to get these things to market . . . at this juncture, the company has better places to invest its money.'[44]

Even if the Arctic does contain the large reserves that the USGS has claimed and these deposits are commercially recoverable, then they need to be seen from the proper perspective. At an EU summit on energy security, held in September 2008, one expert pointed out that an additional 90 billion barrels of oil is 'only' equivalent to 3 years of global production and would do nothing to address the widely anticipated 'supply crunch' in 2015–20. 'Those who think we are going to find a solution to our oil problem in the Arctic are clearly wrong', concluded Willy De Backer. He added that 'it's not the first time that the "new energy bonanza" story has come up' since, only a decade or so before, 'everyone thought the Caspian was going to provide the miracle solution'.[45]

The scope for dispute

A depressing conclusion could perhaps be drawn from all this. It is plausible to argue that some countries will be tempted to use military force to seize potential oil-bearing regions on the premise that, at some future point, the technology and expertise will be developed to exploit them. After all, until the mid-1960s no one would have been taken seriously if they had suggested that the North Sea harboured vast reserves of oil, or that they would be recoverable in such deep waters – just as some European governments later felt seriously aggrieved because they had divided the North Sea before much of its oil had been found. (Norway's massive Ekofisk field is in an area that Denmark or Britain could potentially have claimed for themselves.) So too could some countries calculate that it is worth their while using military force to seize Arctic ground that might eventually prove rich in natural resources.

It is certainly true that this gives every government a strong interest in staking its claim to Arctic territory peacefully, just as Russia and Canada are making considerable efforts to map their outer continental shelves and to present their findings to the United Nations. This is a long way from the deployment of military force. The costs of war are punitively high in every sense. For the moment both the presence of oil in the Arctic's disputed regions, as well as its commercial recoverability, are as seriously in doubt as the theory of 'peak oil', which has attracted considerable criticism from eminent commentators. By the time oil production does eventually peak, and the Arctic's black gold does become recoverable, it is quite possible that alternative replacement fuels will have been pioneered.

There is certainly scope not just for heated disagreements but also for episodes of brinkmanship that could perhaps spill over into confrontations that no party really wants. Some incidents might also come close to open conflict before the various contestants pull back. At Pristine airfield in Kosovo in June 1999, Russian and British soldiers came perilously close to exchanging fire, while in 1993 a single incident on the border between North and South Korea nearly caused a full-scale war that would have embroiled the entire peninsula and brought the forces of the United States and perhaps China into battle. The prospect of such exchanges justifies the establishment of new diplomatic channels comparable to the East-West telephone 'hotline' during the Cold War.

There are other ways in which oil might cause international tension and disagreement. In some parts of the world where large, underground reservoirs of oil straddle international borders, it is not uncommon for one country to accuse a neighbour of stealing its reserves of oil. It was exactly such disagreements that triggered Iraq's invasion of Kuwait in August 1990, when Saddam Hussein accused his southern neighbour of stealing the resources of the Rumeila field. The same accusations were still being made even a decade later. 'The theft of Iraqi oil by Kuwait is not new', as Saad Qassem Hammudi, a senior member of the Baath Party in the days of Saddam Hussein, alleged in September 2000, 'it is a fact established in Iraqi documents and reports since 1990.'[46]

When any country is buoyant with oil revenues, political tensions are likely to surface. Disagreements about how any large sums of money should be spent are of course inevitable but can have far-reaching implications if they exacerbate the cause of political

separatism. Sometimes this can take the form of a strident nationalism, just as in 1951 long-running disputes about oil revenues ruptured
relations between Iran and the United Kingdom. At other times,
the provincial and regional governments of those places where oil
is found can claim a greater share of the revenues at the expense
of a central administration. Regional disputes about how Iraq's
petrodollars should be spent, for example, have dogged the Baghdad
government since the deposition of Saddam Hussein in 2003. As a
later chapter explores in more detail, it is in just the same spirit that
the prospect of an oil bonanza is now aggravating tension between
Greenland and Denmark.

Although Arctic oil is unlikely to cause a future conflict, the region
is also thought to be rich in other natural resources that could perhaps
be a cause of rifts and rivalry.

6

The Arctic's Other Resources

Until the end of the 1990s, the remote Norwegian coastal town of Hammerfest, which lies 400 miles north of the Arctic Circle, was in a state of true decline (Map 5). Almost entirely dependent on reindeer farming and the fishing industry, it had been relatively prosperous in the 1960s, when fish stocks in the Barents Sea were particularly plentiful, but had then gradually started to suffer hard times. Its small population, of around just 9,000 inhabitants, began to dwindle as an increasing number of young people made their way southwards to find opportunities that simply did not exist at home. Visitors remarked on ubiquitous signs of decay and neglect, as schools and hospitals slowly crumbled, water pipes burst and levels of mortality outstripped the birth rate. Regularly rain-soaked, blessed with only a few limited hours of daylight for at least half of the year, and with winter temperatures regularly dipping well below freezing, Hammerfest was a distinctively unenviable place to be.

Just a decade on, the same town is bustling, thriving, and in some ways quite unrecognizable. Far from being a decrepit backwater, its central streets are peppered with new retail shops that stock all the latest and most expensive Western brands. Housing has been in such short supply that property prices have rocketed and the local construction industry has boomed. So many jobs have been created that there is a serious local shortage of labour, both skilled and unskilled. And although very few outsiders were once seen here, today it is a relatively cosmopolitan place where people from many parts of the world come to live and work. The background noise is often incessant, particularly from the passenger jets that regularly ferry visitors in and out.

What lies behind this transformation is a discovery of natural resources on an epic scale. The size and significance of this discovery was captured perfectly on the night of 21 August 2008, when locals watched with amazement and a certain degree of trepidation as a giant jet of orange flame roared into the sky from a nearby offshore island. For the first time, gas was being flared off from Melkoeya, heralding the opening of a huge, underwater complex, known as Snoehvit or 'Snow White', where huge quantities of natural gas have been discovered and are now being exploited. This particular field has already proved highly productive and yet, by the standards of a reservoir's lifespan, it is only in its relative infancy. Nine underwater wells in three fields have become operational since it was first opened, and this is expected to eventually increase to 20 wells over the next few years.

Everything about this site pays testimony not just to the scale of new Arctic opportunities but also to the phenomenal technical sophistication with which this potential is being exploited. To begin with, the natural gas comes shooting out of the depths of the ocean floor at a very high temperature of about 200 degrees Fahrenheit, and at an intense pressure, before being moved for more than 60 miles through a series of underwater pipelines that run along the ocean floor and terminate on Melkoeya.

Until about 2005, this was a largely barren island with almost nothing except rocks and shrubs, but when natural gas was discovered nearby, construction work began on a massive scale and within months almost the entire island had been virtually rebuilt. Two thousand labourers worked round the clock under vast floodlights, digging tunnels leading to the mainland, dynamiting and then clearing 6 million cubic feet of rock, pouring more than 30,000 lorry loads of concrete onto the site and laying down several million feet of cable.

On its arrival at Melkoeya, the natural gas has already been cooled considerably by its passage through freezing waters. But at this point it is chilled even more by what is, in effect, a giant, 150-feet-high refrigerator – known to workers on the island as the 'cold box' – that now forms an unmistakable part of the skyline. Once inside, the natural gas is then subjected to a formidably complex scientific process. Carefully filtered, it is cooled right down to a temperature of –259 degrees Fahrenheit, when it turns into a liquid that is barely a fraction of its gaseous volume. So if 600 cubic feet of natural gas is piped to the island, this can be liquefied and then condensed into just 1 cubic foot before being shipped as LNG (liquefied natural gas) in specially constructed tankers to markets the world over.

Nearly all experts feel sure that, like Snow White, the wider Arctic region is also full of promise as a source of natural gas, and perhaps has much more gas to boast of than oil. Could this mean that the presence of natural gas reserves, or any other highly valued resource such as minerals or fishing stocks, could be the trigger for a regional war? Although the issues that surround oil and gas are different, the essential conclusion is the same, and it is most unlikely to be the cause of any future confrontation. Once again, a much more complicated picture will emerge.

Natural gas and the future
Unless alternatives are pioneered, natural gas is set to become an increasingly important fuel in tomorrow's world. It is cleaner and more environmentally friendly than both coal and oil, emitting less sulphur, carbon and nitrogen and leaving behind almost no ash particles if it is burned. At the same time it can potentially be used just as extensively both in the home and workplace: more than half of American houses already use natural gas as their main heating fuel and it is employed in all sorts of industrial processes to create all manner of different products.

The raw statistics speak for themselves. In 2006 the world's consumption of natural gas already stood at around 105.5 trillion cubic feet, of which roughly one-fifth was taken up by the United States. But the annual United States government document *International Energy Outlook* predicts that by the year 2030 global consumption could jump by more than half. This is partly because many people will turn away from oil if its price rises as much as many experts predict. But it is also because governments are likely to encourage the use of a substance that is less environmentally damaging than oil or coal. So natural gas will be increasingly used to generate electricity, the IEA report points out, because of 'its relative fuel efficiency and low carbon dioxide intensity' since it is the cleanest-burning fossil fuel for toxic air pollutants and it emits about half the greenhouse gases of coal.[1]

Producing countries will be able to continue reaping considerable profits from this growing demand for natural gas. Russia gets most of its foreign exchange earnings from the sale of both oil and gas, and in 2007 its massive energy conglomerate, Gazprom, earned a colossal 873 billion roubles from the export of natural gas.[2] Another key producer is Norway, whose economy has in recent decades been sustained by the output from the North Sea.[3]

The Arctic's natural gas
Most experts feel sure that the Arctic region will play a vital part in meeting future demand. The survey published by the USGS in the summer of 2008 estimated that the region harbours 1,669 trillion

cubic feet of natural gas as well as 44 billion barrels of natural gas liquids, which would amount to around one-third of the world's undiscovered gas. They also argued that more than 70 per cent of the undiscovered natural gas is located in just three of the provinces it surveyed: the West Siberian Basin, the East Barents Basin and Arctic Alaska. The vast majority of these reserves are also said to be located offshore.[4]

Other researchers have reached similar conclusions. Shortly after the USGS report was issued, two leading British organizations published their own assessments of the Arctic's natural gas resources. Using detailed scientific analysis of individual basins and industry data on exploration wells and existing discoveries, Wood Mackenzie and Fugro Robertson emphasized that while the Arctic's oil-bearing potential has probably been exaggerated the region does have very large gas reserves, which constitute nearly all the assets that have either already been discovered in the region or else are waiting to be discovered.[5]

The Arctic's current output certainly gives one indication of how much potential the region might have. Some of Russia's most important fields are at Yamal-Nenets, part of which juts out into the Kara Sea above the Arctic Ocean. Since the early 1980s, 11 gas fields, as well as 15 oil and gas condensate sites, have been discovered here and the aggregate reserves of the largest fields, namely Bovanenkovo, Kharasavey and Novoportovskoye, are thought to account for more than 200 trillion cubic feet of gas, 100.2 million tons of condensate, as well as 227 million tons of oil.

But the single most important natural gas field in the Russian Arctic was discovered in the centre of the Barents Sea, further west, where Soviet geologists unearthed an offshore field in the late 1980s. Further investigation revealed the sheer size of the discovery, which exemplifies the Arctic's full potential. Covering a huge area, the new field, named Shtokman, is estimated to have reserves of 110 trillion cubic feet of gas as well as a further 31 million tons of condensate (Map 5).

However, by the standards of the day, Shtokman presented insurmountable engineering challenges. Lying 340 miles off the coast, and situated in waters 1,000 feet deep, the Russians have always completely lacked the expertise to develop its resources. Even if a field like this had been located on land, its exploitation would still have been difficult enough because its deposits lie in four main layers, each of which have to be brought to the surface in different stages.

Some geologists feel sure that both Shtokman and Snow White are just the tip of an energy iceberg in the Barents Sea and are an unmistakable sign that much more is waiting to be unearthed. Their upbeat assessment has been subsequently confirmed by a series of important, though less dramatic, finds. In November 2008, for example, Statoil announced the discovery of another reserve, located 50 miles north-east of Snow White, that reportedly contains between 70 and 500 billion cubic feet of recoverable natural gas. 'It is, of course, promising that we once more have proven gas in the Barents Sea', pointed out Geir Richardsen, head of exploration activities in the far north for Statoil. 'We need time to make an evaluation and analysis to understand the volume and size of the find.'[6]

Alaska is also reckoned to have some very large, recoverable natural gas reserves. These include the Wyoming Basin and the National Petroleum Reserve, while the North Slope of Alaska has about 119.15 trillion cubic feet of conventional recoverable gas resources. The North Slope is also an area deemed to be full of huge quantities of hydrates, which are formed when gas and water are locked in an icy solid that forms in very low temperatures. In a report published in November 2008, USGS scientists reported that around 85.4 trillion cubic feet of natural gas is recoverable from Alaska's gas hydrates, which would be enough to heat more than 100 million average-sized homes for more than a decade. 'This is a huge source of untapped energy', as Interior Department Secretary Dirk Kempthorne commented. 'The assessment points to a truly significant potential for natural gas hydrates to contribute to the energy mix of the United States and the world.'[7]

Canadian reserves may well prove to be as extensive. The Mackenzie Delta, located in the Northwest Territories, holds an estimated 5–6 trillion cubic feet of recoverable underground natural gas reserves and four companies (Imperial Oil, ConocoPhillips, Shell Canada and ExxonMobil) are currently in the process of exploiting the region's three major fields.

A resource war for Arctic gas?

Although the Arctic is undoubtedly rich in natural gas as well as oil, it is highly unlikely that any future resource war will be waged for control of these assets. This is partly for some of the same reasons that weigh against a regional war for oil: many of the areas where large reserves of natural gas have been detected lie within established borders, not disputed zones. Of course, there are clear exceptions, most notably the Barents and Beaufort seas. In the summer of 2008, there were reports that a giant new gas field had been discovered in the 'Grey Zone', adjacent to the Russian and Norwegian mainland.[8]

But, as the previous chapter has pointed out, armed clashes in these disputed areas are most unlikely, even if rival camps may heatedly exchange some sharp words.

Commercial viability

There are some reasons why conflict over natural gas is even less likely than over oil. One key difference between the commodities is that gas is generally more difficult and expensive to extract and move to market. 'A remote oilfield in the Arctic or anywhere could be exploited by tankers, and crude oil could be placed in local storage tanks if thick winter ice makes access to the area seasonal', as Andrew Latham, a director of Wood Mackenzie consultancy, points out. By contrast, 'remote gas always requires huge infrastructure, whether it is piped or moved by LNG tankers'.[9] Latham has also added that 'export and technology constraints are expected to delay production of a large portion of the commercial gas (in the Arctic) until 2050', echoing the views of experts at the EU headquarters who emphasize that 'exploitation of the Arctic's reserves will be slow, since it presents great challenges and entails high costs due to harsh conditions and multiple environmental risks'.[10]

This means that an energy company needs to be absolutely sure that its huge capital outlay can be offset by the promise of even bigger reserves than any oil investor would look for. But for the moment at least, no one is absolutely sure that there are gas reserves on this vast scale in any disputed part of the Arctic. For any government to risk conflict over resources that have such a questionable commercial value would either be unthinkable or else require mass deception or massive misunderstanding.

Future sources of supply

There is another difference between the two commodities that makes a resource war over natural gas, wherever it is deemed to lie, even less likely than over oil. This concerns how much natural gas is left in the world, or more specifically, how much governments *fear* a future shortage of natural gas. While fears about the future of oil are rife (if far from universally shared) most experts agree that the world still has plenty of natural gas. So while there has been much talk of 'peak oil', references to 'peak natural gas' or to 'the end of gas' are completely unheard of. Instead the *International Energy Outlook* predicts that supply will match demand in the year 2030, and points out that:

*Historically, world natural gas reserves have generally trended upward.
As of 1 January 2008, proved world natural gas reserves, as reported
by Oil & Gas Journal were estimated at 6,186 trillion cubic feet –
virtually unchanged from the estimate for 2007 of 6,168 trillion cubic
feet. Reserves have remained relatively flat since 2004, despite growing
demand for natural gas, implying that, thus far, producers have been
able to continue replenishing reserves successfully with new resources
over time.*[11]

Part of the reason for this difference is that oil has been extensively
hunted, used and exploited for centuries, whereas the relationship
between the human world and natural gas, although increasingly
passionate, is a much more recent affair that is borne of far more
advanced technology and expertise.

There is another reason why both producers and consumers have
reason to share this relative optimism about the future of natural gas
supply. This is the growing ease with which the commodity can be
moved from its source to its destination market.

The emergence of LNG

Gas is far more expensive to move than oil because it has a much lower
energy content: one square yard of oil contains around 170 times
more energy than an equivalent measure of gas. As a result there are
far fewer commercially viable ways of moving gas, which at one time
was only moved along specially constructed pipelines often stretching
for thousands of miles. These are difficult, expensive and time con-
suming to build, and if this supply was cut off, whether by accident
or design, then a consumer might have no other source it could turn
to other than emergency stockpiles. During the 1990s, the technology
and expertise to freeze, liquefy, store and then transport natural gas
by giant tanker became much more widely used. This was not because
of any scientific breakthrough (the technology has been around for
decades) but because the costs of building the infrastructure, although
still enormous, started to become more competitive when compared
with the construction of pipelines. As a result banks regarded such
projects as less risky and were therefore more willing to lend money
to investors. Today, as the operation at Hammerfest illustrates, it can
sometimes be less financially demanding to ship the substance in the
same way as crude oil, loading it onto tankers that move over vast
distances instead of relying solely on pipelines.

This development is already having enormous implications. On
the one hand, producers can feel more confident about future sources

of supply. Gas fields that would have been too difficult to connect with pipelines can now be developed because tankers can move their output instead. Snow White is a classic example because the construction of a pipeline from the site to the wider continental pipeline grid, which feeds the European consumer market, would have been prohibitively expensive: the vast cost of building a pipeline that is more than around 2,000 miles in length is generally considered to be much harder to justify in raw economic terms. If the distance is greater than 2,000 miles or so, then it is probably more cost effective to use LNG.

The development of LNG is also reassuring for consumers. Instead of being forced to rely on a very limited number of suppliers, consumers have now started to diversify their sources. The UK, for example, was once heavily dependent on piped gas from the North Sea, but has now started to import shipments of liquefied gas from places as far afield as Qatar and Algeria. These shipments already meet about one-tenth of its national demand. By the year 2020 British officials hope that tankers from every corner of the world, including Egypt, Nigeria, Oman and Trinidad, will make up more than one-third of its gas supplies. American imports of natural gas are expected to mirror the same trend, increasing rapidly from 631 billion cubic feet in 2005 to more than 2 trillion cubic feet in 2015 as new liquefaction facilities come on line both at home and abroad. At the beginning of 2008, the United States had five LNG import facilities in operation that can handle more than 5.8 billion cubic feet every day. Four additional facilities are also being built in the Gulf of Mexico and two in the offshore waters of New England, which, when completed, will more than double the nation's import capacity.

The implications for both the consumers and producers of natural gas are considerable. If consumers are able to rely more heavily than before on shipments of liquefied natural gas, then they no longer have the same need to acquire 'diversity of supply', just as no producers can expect to monopolize supply. In other words, there is little strategic point in either consumers or producers seizing control of natural gas reserves in any part of the world, including the Arctic.

Of course this is certainly not to say that those reserves have nothing to offer. Arctic gas would give the EU, for example, an extra source of supply that would reduce its dependency on Russia. In 2007, Gazprom supplied 4.4 trillion cubic feet of gas to the EU – around half of its intake – and such heavy dependency makes consumers extremely vulnerable to accidental or deliberate disruption. This danger became apparent in January 2006 and again in January

2009, when pricing disputes between Russia and Ukraine prompted Gazprom to briefly turn off its supply of gas. This had unfortunate consequences for some European states, notably Bulgaria, Poland and Hungary, since their own supplies were fed through the same pipeline network that moved across Ukraine and for a time many people braced themselves to face the bitter winter cold amidst bitter recriminations that the EU had been taken 'hostage'.[12]

Fearful of a repeat scenario, European countries have increasingly tried to look away from Russia and find ways of diversifying their supplies. The proposed Nabucco pipeline project would route natural gas from Caspian states to the EU, bypassing Russia's extensive pipeline network in the process. For the same reason, the EU Commission has shown a clear interest in the Arctic's energy resources. So in November 2008 an EU document argued that the Arctic is a 'unique region of strategic importance which is located in [the] immediate vicinity' of Europe and claimed that its 'resources could contribute to enhancing the EU's security of supply concerning energy and raw materials in general'.[13] European representatives have also pointed out that:

> *The Arctic region is believed to be one of the most important remaining petroleum provinces. Development of the Arctic energy resources can therefore be a major contribution to the world's energy supply in the long term. As part of the Arctic energy potential, the Barents Sea represents an opportunity to develop a new European petroleum province.*[14]

But this would not be a justification for the use of military force to stop these resources from being captured by another country, perhaps hostile, or to seize them back. The growing importance of liquefied natural gas offers consumers like the EU or the United States 'diversity of supply', just as its emergence is undermining any stranglehold and strategic leverage that producers like Russia may have previously enjoyed over their consumers. This completely undermines any argument for using force to seize natural assets in the Arctic or anywhere else, if not for showing a strong interest in them.

So it was significant that in September 2008 EU Energy Commissioner, Andris Piebalgs, argued that while Western energy firms should look to the Arctic region as a possible source of supply – 'having options is always a good thing' – he emphasized that Russia's importance should not be exaggerated.[15] Instead, he pointed out, 'the EU already has very diversified suppliers . . . Norway, Algeria, Caspian, Trans-Saharan . . . We are in a good situation'. He further cautioned against 'singling out one supplier' or 'diminishing one supplier, saying that it is more dangerous than the other'.

Monopolistic pricing

'Diversity of supply' has clear economic, as well as strategic, implications. In an ideal marketplace, consumers want several sources to choose from because they can more easily negotiate a fair price, whereas producers clearly gain if they are in a monopoly situation. Could this give Russia, as a key gas exporter, a good reason to use military force to seize the Arctic's gas reserves?

The Kremlin has certainly benefited enormously from buying gas from Central Asia at one price, and then reselling it to Europe at a much higher one. Until the emergence of liquefied gas, the price of the commodity was determined not by market conditions that are constantly fluctuating, but almost entirely by long-term contracts between suppliers and consumers. As they struggle to claw back the huge cost of building long-distance pipelines, Russia and other exporters have always sought to lock their consumers into lasting relationships, usually of a 25-year duration or more, and closely link the price of gas with that of oil.

Not surprisingly, for a time Moscow did everything it could to prevent the emergence of a spot market that would undercut the prices that suited them: most of its pipeline agreements have destination clauses that prohibit the resale of the transported gas. But once again, the emergence of liquefied gas is having drastic implications, and in the spring of 2007 the world's leading LNG exporter, Qatar, broke new ground by establishing an energy exchange at Doha, its capital, where shipments could be openly bought and sold by traders. The terms of pipeline supply contracts have usually been shrouded in secrecy, but the new spot market has brought much-needed price transparency instead.

Of course, the emergence of this spot market is not preventing Russia from doing its utmost to maintain a grip over its European customers: Gazprom's strong commitment to the 'South Stream' pipeline that links southern Europe to its energy corridors illustrates this determined drive. But even when a natural gas spot market does emerge, there are ways in which Russia or any other producer could influence the price of the commodity much more effectively than by using military force to seize the assets of just one particular resource-rich area: at the end of 2008, reports emerged that Moscow was making tentative moves to establish a gas cartel, which, like OPEC, could work together to hold sway over the price.[16]

Besides oil and natural gas, the Arctic is also home to some other natural resources, which international powers are keen to access. All of these are important enough to cause disagreements and tensions, or to aggravate existing ones, but are much less likely than energy resources to be a cause of heavy, serious conflict.

Rocks and precious metals

Disagreements about who owns the numerous other natural resources in the Arctic region could certainly fuel international mistrust and controversy and perhaps even cause brief, though serious, incidents in which ammunition as well as harsh words are exchanged. But they are not important enough in their own right to cause a 'resource war'.

Over the past few years governments and private investors have begun to regard the Arctic as a very promising source of mineral wealth and started to search for deposits of gold, diamonds, platinum, nickel kimberlite and other precious stones. To some extent this interest reflects the dramatic surge of recent years in the market price of minerals, driven mainly by a massive growth in demand from China.[17] Despite the market crash of late 2008, the value of these commodities has been driven high enough to make some very expensive and risky mining operations commercially viable for the first time.

The impact of climate change is also playing its part. Above all, the melting of the overland permafrost and the polar ice cap means that some mining sites are only now becoming accessible. So until the late 1990s glaciers covered around 80 per cent of northern and north-eastern Greenland, but the gradual retreat of the ice is enabling mining companies to explore areas that were previously inaccessible and to work there for longer spells than was hitherto possible. 'Global warming has extended the working and exploring development season by a few weeks, as higher temperatures mean the frozen ice is leaving a couple of weeks earlier', as one mining expert told an American newspaper. 'With the rapid melting of the snow early in June, surface exploration is proceeding a month earlier than would have been possible one or two decades ago.'[18]

An example of just such an operation is an old zinc and lead excavation site on Greenland's west coast, about 250 miles north of the Arctic Circle, known as the Black Angel mine. Once famous for the high quality of its zinc ore, it was shut in the early 1990s because commodity prices were depressed at a time of worldwide recession and because operating so far north was hugely expensive. But in the intervening years the local climate and conditions have changed considerably. Above all, geologists made a breakthrough in 2005, when they came across a huge deposit of sulphide, stretching more than half a mile, which had been uncovered as a glacier retreated. A British company, Angus & Ross, then started to mine the site and by early 2009, in the space of just 3 years, its operations there had become highly fruitful.

The great ice thaw is not only making it easier to get minerals out of the ground but also to move them to the market place. Big international companies are likely to step up their efforts to find precious stones in northern Canada, for example, partly because the economic case for building vital infrastructure to remote locations looks stronger than ever. In particular, the reduction of sea ice in the Northwest Passage might eventually mean that the annual shipping season – the summer months when cargoes can move relatively unimpeded – will become shorter than ever, and this would in turn make it more viable than before to justify the huge capital outlay of building a deep-water port on Canada's northern coast. This port, as well as numerous other sites, could then be linked to excavation sites by the construction of all-weather gravel roads that would have been too difficult and too expensive to build before local ice began to melt. In recent years, the changing picture in the Canadian Arctic has lured the South African-owned mining company De Beers, whose directors regard the region as 'a very exciting area of prospectivity for many different types of precious metals'.[19]

So far, all of these valuable minerals have been discovered well within existing borders and are therefore most unlikely to be the cause of any confrontation between rival powers. In any event, governments have other ways – more effective and less costly than the use of military force – in which they can access rare commodities. So in its paper 'The Raw Materials Initiative' the EU has argued that future shortages of some precious metals can be partly met by ensuring fair trade. This might mean stopping any country from placing restrictions on how and where it sells its exports; preventing any practices that unfairly distort the market price or put other countries at a disadvantage; lowering import tariffs on some raw materials; and encouraging free trade agreements, including accession agreements to the World Trade Organization, while fully enforcing existing ones. The document also points out that future shortages can be met by sustainable management of demand and resource efficiency.[20]

These considerations, which weigh so strongly against the possibility of a war fought over precious metals, are also true of another underground resource found in the region.

Coal

There are a few Arctic locations where disputes over coal have already surfaced and caused a lot of ill feeling between rival claimants before they were settled. Chief among them is the Svalbard archipelago, where the question of who has a right to mine the land, as well as who owns its surrounding waters, was hotly disputed until the advent of an international agreement in 1920.[21]

This issue had its origins in the nineteenth century, when hunting crews searching for seals and whales came ashore and started to dig out underground coal, initially just to keep themselves warm, but later to stoke the boilers of their newly pioneered steamships. But it was not until 1899 that anyone made a serious attempt to exploit Svalbard's coal on a commercial scale, when a Norwegian, Soeren Zachariassen, mined the northern shores of Isfjorden. In 1901, an American industrialist, John Munro Longyear, visited the region and made an immediate decision to invest there. Others tried to follow his example. A British company set up a mining operation at the same time, although on a much smaller scale, while a succession of Russians also started prospecting, including the great explorer, Vladimir Rusanov, who investigated the coal seams at Grumant, along the shores of Isfjorden, in 1912. When Norwegian investors bought out Longyear's Svalbard operation in 1916, the rivalry between Norway and Russia for the island's resources really began in earnest, each vying to keep one step ahead of the other. The Soviet Union opened an extensive mine at Barentsburg in the 1930s and another at the very remote location of Pyramiden on Billefjorden, which came into production in the 1940s, while a number of separate Soviet and Norwegian communities also flourished in different mining locations.

In one respect at least, those who worked on these collieries may have been somewhat surprised by the strength of commercial and political rivalry that surrounded them. For even by the dire standards of the day, conditions were almost intolerably tough. The main coal seams were often located high on the valley sides, forcing miners to trek up a steep track along slopes that were frequently covered with snow and ice. This would have been difficult enough even in daylight, but in the long winter months the journey usually had to be undertaken in almost complete darkness. Once they got to work, things were not much better since the coal seams were generally less than a few feet high, forcing them to work in cramped conditions, and the temperature in the mines was constantly below freezing. Even today the area retains its reputation as a particularly harsh environment: in 1996 a Russian plane carrying 141 people, including miners' families from the Ukraine, crashed in a blizzard, and the following year 23 miners died in a mine fire at Barentsburg.

Deep seabed mining

In the coming decades it is also possible that international companies will want to undertake deep seabed mining in some parts of the Arctic Ocean. But this is a very difficult and demanding enterprise even in the best of circumstances. In order to extract minerals from the seabed, a ship has to keep a very steady position (in deep waters this has to be done without an anchor) while a recovery vehicle is lowered to the ocean floor by a specially constructed pipe. But the piping can sometimes snap or become seriously distorted by the strength of the ocean waves, while the recovery vehicle can become lost or stuck on the seabed. Not surprisingly, it has been compared with standing on top of a skyscraper while using a vacuum cleaner attached to a long hose to scoop up marbles from the streets far below. The high risk of encountering floating ice in these waters means that it is likely to be many years before any such mining operations are undertaken in much of the Arctic Ocean.

Fishing disputes

Anyone old enough to remember the 'Cod War', which began in the 1950s and was resolved only in the mid-1970s, will realize just how bitter a dispute over fishing rights can become. Over three decades, Britain and Iceland intermittently exchanged angry words and several hard blows over the complex legal issue of where the lines of demarcation in the North Atlantic should be drawn. Both sides regularly deployed warships to escort their fishing vessels and deter the other side from harassing the crews, and on several occasions disputes nearly escalated into full-scale confrontation. On 11 December 1975, British tugs rammed Icelandic gunboats that had challenged their right to move through disputed waters, prompting one of the vessels to open fire with live rounds. Ships from both sides were damaged and retreated for emergency repairs amidst a flurry of accusations and counteraccusations. Six months later, relations between the two countries deteriorated once again when a British warship, HMS *Falmouth*, steamed at high speed into an Icelandic ship and almost capsized it.

It is just such a situation that could easily flare up in the Arctic's two main fishing zones over the coming years. One such area is the Barents Sea, where the competing legal claims made by Russia and Norway have already been closely looked at. The other is the Bering

Sea, which is famous for its harvest of salmon, crab, pollock, halibut
and groundfish. Every year United States commercial fisheries take
approximately $1 billion worth of seafood from these waters, com-
prising about half of America's national catch, while Russia's Bering
Sea fisheries are worth approximately $600 million, amounting to
about one-third of its own. In both cases, climate change could well
either cause future disputes or else aggravate existing ones.

The impact of climate change

The impact of climate change on the fishing stock in these, and other
areas, is very difficult to predict. Scientists admit that 'it is not clear
how climate change will affect . . . the most important zooplankton
species that acts as food for fish in Arctic waters', the *calanus finmar-
chicus*, which they consider to be a 'crucial question'.[22] And as the
Arctic Climate Impact Assessment emphasizes, the adaptability of
these, and every other life form, is simply impossible to guess, leading
to 'a high level of uncertainty'.[23]

The most likely scenario is that fish stocks, particularly supplies
of cod, are likely to start colonizing more northerly waters as they
become warmer. Cod stocks thrived during a relatively warm period
that lasted between the 1920s and 1950s, but were then badly hit by
a drop in water temperatures during the 1970s and 1980s. And even
if cod stocks do stagnate or diminish, in the Barents and Bering Seas
or elsewhere, their numbers could well be offset by an increase not
just in farm fishing (between 2004 and 2007 there was a threefold
increase in the production of farmed cod) but in other warm-water
breeds that feed off different ocean foods. 'In a warmer ocean, with
less ice in the Arctic, we can expect that a number of species will
extend their habitats further north', continue the scientists. The blue
whiting, for example, could move further northwards and might
well become established in the Greenland Sea. It is also possible
that herring could return to the Icelandic coast, where it had been
well established until the mid-1960s, when a sudden drop in local
temperatures killed off local plankton and decimated fish stocks.

The movement of fish stocks

At first sight it might seem to be a laudable development that many
breeds of fish will be able to move northwards and thrive in areas that
they were previously unable to even approach. But tensions might
arise if stocks migrate from the waters that belong to one country
into those of another.

One place where this could happen is the Bering Strait. In 2002 the Arctic Research Commission, a special panel appointed by the US president, reported its findings and concluded that some species of fish were already moving north through the Bering Strait and were likely to continue doing so. 'Climate change is likely to bring extensive fishing activity to the Arctic, particularly in the Barents Sea and Beaufort-Chukchi region, where commercial operations have been minimal in the past', argued the report. 'In addition, Bering Sea fishing opportunities will increase as sea ice cover begins later and ends sooner in the year.'[24]

Today, as the sea ice retreats, snow crabs, which are highly prized by fishermen and their customers, appear to be moving away from their traditional locations off Alaska and heading towards Russia, where the waters may be providing them with a better venue to find their sea foods. American crab boats already have to steam further than ever to bring a good haul, and some fishery experts have predicted that these creatures could eventually move out of American waters altogether.

Most fishermen are likely to accept these changes with stoicism, and perhaps find new commercial openings. 'If the crabs move over into the Russian zone', as the president of the Pacific Seafood Processors Association in Seattle has said, 'there's not much to be done about that except hope they come back some day.'[25] But some fishermen will be tempted to stray into Russian waters and risk seizure and the imposition of penalties. Others will move into areas of high seas that are unregulated by fishing quotas and exploit them to the full, leading to a serious depletion of stock as well as to angry confrontations with governments, rival fishermen and environmentalists.

An EU document, published in November 2008, pointed out:

Climate change might bring increased productivity in some fish stocks and changes in spatial distributions of others. New areas may become attractive for fishing with increased access due to reduced sea ice coverage. For some of the Arctic high seas waters there is not yet an international conservation and management regime in place. This might lead to unregulated fisheries.[26]

The EU proposed setting up safeguards as soon as possible to prevent this scenario from being realized. It is essential, ran the report, to put in place:

a regulatory framework for the part of the Arctic high seas not yet covered by an international conservation and management regime before new fishing opportunities arise. This will prevent fisheries developing in a regulatory vacuum, and will ensure fair and transparent management of fisheries in accordance with the Code of Conduct for Responsible Fishing ... until a conservation and management regime is in place for the areas not yet covered by such a regime, no new fisheries should commence.[27]

EU leaders have also expressed their concern that fish will migrate into waters where there are no fishing quotas at all, leading to their exploitation and depletion as well as clashes between rival fishermen. 'Climatic changes may also lead to changes in the migration patterns of important fish stocks', as Norwegian Foreign Minister, Jonas Gahr Stoere, pointed out in January 2009. 'Commercial fisheries may expand into the Arctic Ocean. Wherever commercial fisheries take place, an effective management regime is imperative in order to prevent depletion of stocks.' Norway and the EU Commission have both vowed to tackle this challenge by 'developing and implementing the integrated management plan for the Barents Sea and [believe] that this plan could serve as a model for the management of other maritime areas – including the Arctic Ocean'.[28]

The decline of global stocks

There is another reason why the Arctic could be the setting for confrontations over fishing rights. This is the relative availability of cod, one of the world's most highly prized fish, in the Barents Sea as a result of its exploitation elsewhere in the world. Mainly as a result of overfishing in other waters, the global catch of cod has slumped around 70 per cent since the early 1970s and in some key places, such as the North Sea, it has fallen even more. Most experts think that overfishing is still rife in many areas, despite clear warnings about the disastrous effect this is having, and if they are right then stocks are likely to carry on shrinking considerably.[29]

If this steady rate of global decline continues, it is likely to be to the Barents, currently home to the world's largest stock, that some fishermen and their respective governments may well turn in the years ahead. Likewise if climate change eradicates fish supplies, then the Barents may well turn out to be one of the cod's last remaining refuges. 'The only cod stocks that still support large fisheries', as the World Wildlife Fund (WWF) wrote in a 2004 report, 'are the ones outside Iceland with an annual catch around 200,000 tons and the world's largest cod stock in the Barents Sea, with an estimated catch in 2004 of almost 500,000 tons.' But even here supplies are under serious threat from fishermen who blatantly disregard international quotas. As the WWF report continues, there are 'serious concerns about high fishing pressures and illegal fishing. In November 2003, the joint Norwegian-Russian Fisheries Commission set the fishing quotas for 2004 to 486,000 tons, ignoring the scientific advice of a total catch of less than 389,000 tons.'[30]

This leads to an alarming possibility. If global stocks of cod, or any other fish, continue to diminish, then it seems quite possible that there could be an increasing number of clashes in the Barents Sea between Norwegian and Russian coast guards on the one hand and international trawlers – or, more specifically, poachers – on the other. After all, more trawlers than ever before might be tempted to start illegal fishing, exceeding quotas in the high seas, such as the Loophole, or else straying into national waters that lie within 200 miles of the coast. This would pose a clear threat to the livelihoods of Norwegian and Russian fishermen: after all, around half of Norway's annual catch and 12 per cent of Russia's fishing harvest comes from the Barents Sea, and any sudden depletion of its stocks would have a serious economic impact. If this does happen and supplies of cod run short, then this might conceivably create tension between Russia and Norway, as their own fishermen illegally stray into each other's waters. It is easy to imagine international tension brewing up over such an issue.

Incidents in the Barents Sea

There have already been quite a few minor incidents between Russia and Norway over fishing rights. One of the best known was a dramatic chase that took place near the Svalbard archipelago in October 2005, when two Norwegian fishing inspectors intercepted and then boarded a Russian trawler, the *Elektron*, that they suspected had been fishing illegally. The authorities ordered the captain, Valery Yarantsev, to head for the Norwegian port of Tromsoe for questioning, but to their horror they watched the *Elektron* speed off towards Russian waters, taking them along as captives. For the next five days the Norwegian coast guard pursued the trawler, eventually intercepting it and ordering the release of the two hostages. The Russian authorities later fined the captain $3,900 for poaching, although he was acquitted of detaining the fishing inspectors.

Again, in November 2007, the Norwegian coast guard detained a Russian trawler, the *Tyndra*, on suspicion of illegally fishing in its waters and forced the captain to surrender 170 tons of herring. It is easy to think that similar incidents in the future could easily escalate and spiral out of control as they nearly did in the early 1990s, when the Norwegian coast guard opened fire on Icelandic vessels.[31]

The clashes took place at a time when an increasing number of Icelandic fishermen were heading to the Barents Sea, regarding its waters as a plentiful and lucrative area of the high seas. This was mainly because the temperature and salinity of local waters changed significantly around 1990, providing cod with almost ideal conditions in which to thrive. In 1993 the third-party catch in the Loophole was estimated to be a 'moderate' 12,000 tonnes – although at this time the Norwegian coast guard had no powers to intercept and search foreign trawlers – but the following year it grew dramatically to 60,000 tonnes. This was almost entirely because Icelandic fishermen had turned away from their own waters, where cod stocks had suddenly become harder to find, and looked further afield. Emergency talks were held in Stockholm between the various foreign and fisheries ministers of Iceland and Norway, but they soon broke down, and the four ministers left hurriedly without even holding a scheduled news briefing.

It was not long before some people started to sound menacing. At a meeting with a minister from the Faroe Islands, the Russian Fisheries Minister, Vladimir Korelski, 'signalled an intention' to deploy a warship in the Loophole. And representatives of the fishermen's union and of the Norwegian Fishing Vessels Owner Association also sounded threatening when they predicted that, unless an agreement could be negotiated between the governments, 'Norwegian fishermen may have to take things into their own hands (including) the cutting of nets'. The Norwegian Fisherman's Union also called for a boycott of any Norwegian firms that supplied Icelandic trawlers and even threatened to use their vessels to blockade harbours.

The state of simmering tension reached a climax in the summer of 1994, when on at least two occasions shots were actually fired in the Svalbard fisheries zone. On 14 June, the Norwegian coast guard boarded four Icelandic trawlers and cut their fishing nets, firing a warning shot at a fifth. The next day, Bjoern Tore Godal, the Norwegian Foreign Minister, warned that his country was prepared to take whatever steps it deemed necessary to prevent the Icelandic vessels from fishing in its protection zone around the Svalbard archipelago, and things got even worse five days later, when the captain of the Icelandic trawler, *Drangey*, claimed that the Norwegian coast guard had attempted to ram his vessel. Later that day, the captains of seven Icelandic trawlers in the Svalbard zone announced that they would leave the area altogether, but they left open the possibility that they would move into the waters of the Loophole, further south, instead of returning home to Iceland.

The most serious single incident took place in August 1994, when shots were exchanged. It appeared that the Icelandic trawler, *Hagangur II*, used small arms to open fire at a Norwegian coast guard vessel, the *Senja*, that was attempting to stop it from fishing inside a restricted zone around the Svalbard archipelago. The Norwegians gave chase, firing non-explosive shells at *Hagangur II* before boarding and then escorting it to Tromsoe. Talks resumed at the start of the 1995 fishing season, but broke down in April over the size of the quota. The matter was initially settled in December 1996, when all three parties signed the UN Fish Stocks Agreement, and a regional accord between the three main contestants and the EU was finally signed in December 1999. Under the deal, Iceland won a small share of the cod stock in the Loophole in return for surrendering any fishing rights for cod in the fisheries protection zone around Svalbard.

There have been some other incidents around Svalbard. In the spring of 2001, when the Norwegian coast guard seized the Russian trawler, *Chernigov*, Norway's ambassador in Moscow was presented with a sharp formal protest, and Russian patrol vessels were later deployed to 'protect' Russian trawlers from the Norwegian coast guard. The following year the Russian Northern Fleet made the quite dramatic move of sending its large anti-submarine warfare destroyer, *Severomorsk*, to the Svalbard waters, and in 2004 fears of escalation prompted the Norwegian foreign ministry to abort the planned seizure of the Russian trawler, *Okeanor*.

Another 'Cod War'?

In the years ahead, it is possible that growing global demand for cod – particularly in the Far East, where fish is fast becoming highly fashionable – will put increasing pressure on the strict quotas that currently regulate the harvesting of the Barents Sea.[32] Trawler captains will be more tempted than ever to violate borders, risking detection, arrest and prosecution in the process, in order to earn high premiums from a market where cod will be a highly prized commodity. It is also possible that some governments, if not quite turning a blind eye, will be increasingly indifferent to such violations because they will want to avoid angry disputes with the fishing lobby and alleviate any political pressures that could result from that. Groups representing fishermen have repeatedly lobbied the Russian government to establish a secure presence around Svalbard, for example.[33]

While tension could rise and serious incidents (like those that took place in 1975 or 1994) might quite conceivably break out, this is far from being a recipe for a 'resource war'. The most obvious reason – that fish is clearly not as important a commodity as oil or gas, and will become even less important in the years ahead as the general public becomes increasingly accustomed to food shortages – hardly needs to be mentioned. But it is also because the fishing lobby, in almost every country, is simply not strong enough to cause serious political trouble and is likely to become much less important in the future.

The Norwegian government has always lobbied hard on behalf of its fishing industry for the simple reason that it has traditionally sustained the local economy of its remote northern provinces. But as the example of Hammerfest illustrates perfectly, climate change has also opened up some of these areas to oil and gas exploration, as well as to other industries, and in doing so provided new job opportunities that have considerably relieved some of this domestic political pressure. Russian fishermen could also find new openings in places like Novaya Zemlya. Hitherto always an area of high security that is accessible only to the armed forces, in time this might become a centre for commerce and business, not least to develop the offshore Shtokman gasfield.[34]

7

Sea Lanes and Strategy

In the summer of 1997, an American businessman by the name of Pat Broe astonished almost everyone by making an investment that seemed pointless at the very least, and one that would probably distract him from other, much more fruitful, opportunities.

His purchase, for the nominal price of just seven dollars, was the port facilities at Churchill, a tiny, windswept outpost on the southwest coast of Hudson Bay, below the Arctic Circle, that almost no one wanted to buy and almost everyone was anxious to avoid. It was home to only around 1,000 people who depended upon hunting, fishing and an influx of tourists who arrive every winter to watch and photograph polar bears. True, it had had its moment of glory during the Second World War, when the Canadian government had made good use of its facilities to ship to Russia thousands of tons of grain that were desperately needed to sustain the war effort. But once the conflict was over, the port had gradually fallen into disuse, having been made virtually redundant by the far more efficient, privately run operations in Thunder Bay and Vancouver. In the post-war years it had become largely forgotten, particularly since it had no roads linking it to the rest of Canada, and was highly dependent on the daily flights made by a number of small passenger aircraft to and from a tiny airstrip a few miles out of town.

For Broe, however, Churchill's saving grace was its railway, which had always been its main link to the outside world. In the mid-1990s, Broe was looking to expand his Denver-based railroad company, OmniTrax, and had already paid vast sums to acquire denationalized lines elsewhere in Canada. He now purchased the port at Churchill from the Canadian government just in case someone else might buy and then use it as a 'toll booth' that might eventually burden his own railroad.[1]

However, over the next decade or so, it gradually became apparent that Churchill had much more to offer than just old railway track. On the contrary, Broe's decision to invest in the place looked more like a stroke of supreme foresight and entrepreneurial brilliance. This was because, by late summer of 2007, sea ice in Hudson Bay had started to melt more quickly than ever before. Larger areas were navigable for longer summer periods and some experts even began to estimate that the port might eventually be open for 10 months every year instead of the usual 4-month period between July and November. Soon there was wild speculation that it could eventually become a vital part of a trans-Atlantic trade route for international shipping, linking Canada and the United States with Russia and drastically reducing the length of the existing journey. Because of its key coastal location, Churchill would become a commercial hub that lies along the way.

Broe is working hard to bring Churchill up to commercial scratch. Over the past few years OmniTrax has spent around $50 million modernizing the port to accommodate big ships carrying key exports like grain and farm machinery across the Atlantic to northern Russia, and to offload imported Russian products, such as fertilizer and steel, while in October 2007 Prime Minister Stephen Harper also announced the award of a $68 million grant to upgrade the ageing port and railway. Such large investments might eventually reap handsome dividends and one American newspaper even estimated that Mr Broe's nominal initial investment could one day net him about $100 million a year.

In late August 2006, as Pat Broe and his associates were busily rebuilding Churchill's facilities, some native Inupiat residents living near the city of Barrow, a long way to the north-west on the Alaskan coast and the highest point of the North American mainland, were looking along the shores with astonishment. They were stunned to see a large cruise ship, the *Bremen*, looming in the distance and then pulling into harbour, bringing several hundred German tourists to visit. They had left Europe and headed first of all to Greenland before making their way right through the Northwest Passage, where ice was increasingly on the retreat and in which more ships than ever before had by this time started to move. The lifestyle of some of these indigenous peoples is already starting to change in a number of very noticeable ways – some are even known to have been buying and using air conditioning units in their Arctic homes – but to see a passenger ship pulling into their harbour, even in the relatively ice-free weeks of late summer, was quite unheard of.

Like the Inupiats, almost everyone is amazed by the sheer speed with which the Arctic's ice in the Northwest Passage, and in the wider Arctic region, is melting. But in the case of sea lanes, no less than of oil and gas, speculation and fantasy need to be carefully distinguished from fact.

Arctic opportunities

What is true is that the Arctic region is changing in a way that is already bringing considerable new commercial opportunities. To quote a 'key finding' of the *Arctic Climate Impact Assessment*, 'reduced sea ice is very likely to increase marine transport and access to resources'. For example, the number of ships moving through Arctic waters is already increasing significantly. Cruise ships around Greenland and Svalbard are already fairly commonplace, while Russian ships are now using the western end of the Northern Sea Route throughout the year in order to move ore from the mine industrial complex at Noril'sk to the Kola Peninsula.[2] By February 2009, Russia's largest shipping company, Sovkomflot, had bought into service three new ice class shuttle tankers that were specially designed and built to move oil from the terminal at Varandey to Murmansk. Each of these three vessels was capable of moving in temperatures of around –20 degrees, breaking ice up to 6 feet deep without any icebreaker escort. It planned to bring more of these tankers into service to move oil from other Arctic fields, such as Prirazlomnoye, just south of Novaya Zemla.

Above all, the story of Pat Broe illustrates the commercial opportunities of a changing environment. When a Russian ship pulled quietly into Churchill's harbour, during a cold night in October 2007, its visit was viewed as something of a milestone because it was the first time that the port had ever accepted goods shipped directly from Russia. A vessel leaving Murmansk for Canada ordinarily navigates the Atlantic, moves through the St Lawrence Seaway, makes its way into the Great Lakes and then stops in Ontario's Thunder Bay. This is a protracted journey that takes a whole 17 days. But it would take the same ship just 8 days to reach the port of Churchill, still crossing the Atlantic to get there, while its goods could then be quickly moved to their destination markets by rail and road. This link between Churchill and Murmansk has been called the 'Arctic Bridge', since both ports lie north of the Circle.

Not surprisingly, on that October day delegates from the Russian embassy, the Murmansk Shipping Company and various government representatives greeted the captain and crew of the Kapitan Sviridov with very warm handshakes. 'Today represents the first successful shipment on the Arctic Bridge', proclaimed Mike Ogborn, the head of OmniTrax. 'It is a great step forward in showing the world that the port of Churchill is a two-way port.' Sergei Khuduiakov, an official at the embassy of the Russian Federation, concurred. 'The goal is very simple', as he put it, 'global warming gives us an opportunity to establish better marine shipping routes between Canada and Russia, and this project, the Arctic Bridge, has very good prospects.' Both countries, he concluded, are 'very interested in the development of our northern regions. Cooperation is very important for us'.[3]

Besides Pat Broe's new enterprise, there are other commercial shipping activities in the Canadian Arctic. Nickel concentrates are regularly shipped to Quebec from Deception Bay, and iron ore from the Mary River mine on Baffin Island. Could this be a sign that the region will become a new trade route linking the Atlantic with the Pacific?

Arctic possibilities

Although the great Arctic thaw is already bringing new opportunities, it is likely to be many years before trans-Arctic crossings become frequent or commonplace. Many media reports of a new maritime commercial 'highway' running through the Northwest Passage and along the Northern Sea Route have been greatly exaggerated (there were no commercial transits through the Passage at all during 2007 and 2008) and for the next decade at least, and in all likelihood for very much longer, there is little prospect of an 'Arctic Bridge' that runs through the Passage or along the Northern Sea Route and over which international shipping can cross.

Most experts do agree that, with every passing year, talk of a route that runs through the Northwest Passage, linking east and west, becomes somewhat less hollow than before (Map 2). A report prepared for the US Navy in 2001 predicted that 'within five to ten years, the Northwest Passage will be open to non-ice-strengthened vessels for at least one month each summer', while another report, issued jointly by the Institute of the North, the US Arctic Research Commission, and the International Arctic Science Committee, estimates that the Canadian Arctic will experience entire summer seasons of nearly ice-free conditions as early as 2050.[4]

These are statements that need to be carefully clarified. After all, much of the Arctic has long been accessible, as the Soviet nuclear-powered icebreaker, *Arktika*, proved in 1977, when it became the first surface vessel to reach the North Pole. The key question is how easily this can be done; in other words, how quickly such a journey can be undertaken, how many icebreakers, if any, are needed to accompany traditional cargo-carrying commercial ships and how much insurance premiums would cost to make such a journey. And if, as these scientists say, the Northwest Passage really is 'nearly ice-free' by the year 2050, then its usage would become commercially viable as insurance premiums fall and icebreaker escort becomes unnecessary. In the coming years shipping crews are likely to become gradually more confident about their ability to navigate safely through the Northwest Passage.

The ice is also very slowly receding along the northern coasts of the Russian Federation, and hopes have been raised, not least in the Kremlin, that this is set to become a key commercial shipping lane (Map 2). Stretching nearly 3,500 miles from the Norwegian coast all the way to the Bering Sea, the Northern Sea Route has usually been navigable from late June to mid-November, although nuclear-powered icebreakers can make their way along it all year round. Widely used in the days of the Soviet Union, it played a vital role in the Kremlin's plans to rebuild the Soviet economy both before and after the Second World War, and became even more important later on. In 1968, around 300 Soviet ships had carried 1 million tons of cargo along the route and by the late 1980s, as its popularity peaked, this tonnage had increased more than sevenfold. But the Northern Sea Route started to fall out of favour after the Soviet Union disintegrated, and in 2006 only 1.5 million tons of cargo was transported along it, including metals from the Noril'sk industrial complex, oil and gas exports from the new Varandey terminal on the Pechora coast, and food imports to settlements along the northern shores. But by the spring of 2009, no non-Russian commercial vessels had journeyed along the route since 1991, although there have been occasional transits made by research ships and military vessels.

Some scientists feel sure that over the coming decades this route, like the Northwest Passage, will also become marginally easier to navigate even in winter, although they have no idea by how much. 'Winter navigation along the western end of the Northern Sea Route, from the Barents Sea to the mouths of the Ob and Yenisey Rivers, will possibly encounter less first-year sea ice', as the authors of the *Arctic Climate Impact Assessment* write, 'while full transit of the Northern Sea Route through Vilkitsky Strait to the Bering Sea is very likely to remain challenging and require icebreaker escort'.[5] Whenever the Northern Sea Route does finally become more navigable, international shipping would be able to move along it, using its 'right of innocent passage' under the 1982 Convention, although the Soviet authorities have claimed that several of the adjacent Arctic seas are 'closed seas' or 'internal waters' through which no such right automatically exists.[6]

It is impossible to predict when, or if, any such maritime highway will ever become a reality, and the likelihood of it materializing in the foreseeable future has sometimes been considerably exaggerated in the media. This became clear in a major report, the *Arctic Marine Shipping Assessment*, released by the Arctic Council in April 2009. Although 'it is highly plausible that the Arctic Ocean could become completely ice-free for a short summer period much earlier than 2040', ran the report, computer predictions suggest that there will be 'only a modest decrease in winter Arctic sea ice coverage' and that 'there will always be an ice-covered Arctic Ocean in winter'. So while these changes act as 'a facilitator of marine access' and 'it is highly plausible there will be greater marine access and longer seasons of navigation', there will 'not necessarily [be] less difficult ice conditions for marine operations'.[7]

For shipping companies to make use of these Arctic transit passages would be commercially risky because they are likely to remain ice-bound outside the summer months. Maritime traffic is always under immense pressure to keep to tight schedules that the presence of ice would easily disrupt. So even though the Northwest Passage and Northern Sea Routes may offer shorter distances, journey times might well be longer. Nor could investors easily justify spending large sums of money on icebreakers or ice-strengthened ships if year-round transit of these Arctic routes proves impossible or impractical. This is because these types of ships have very limited commercial use outside Arctic waters and therefore might be redundant outside the summer months.

So in the coming years there will certainly be more ships venturing into Arctic waters – between 2006 and 2007, for example, the number of cruise ships docking in Greenland increased from 157 to 222 – but talk of trans-Arctic maritime routes is very speculative.

However, it is quite possible that several different types of commercial carriers could start to use the trans-Arctic trade routes for longer summer periods. In particular, metal ores and timber could be moved from the ports of northern Europe along the Northern Sea Route if more ice-class ships are built and can be chartered on demand. A great deal of oil and gas, perhaps as much as 330,000 barrels every day, could also be shipped along the route from the Russian port at Varandey to Western or perhaps Eastern markets.

In the coming years, it is likely that a great deal of research will be done to weigh the commercial risks of using such trade routes against their benefits, such as the drastically shorter distances they offer.

Implications for international shipping

Governments and businessmen have long been aware of just how much an Arctic Bridge might have to offer them. In 1957, they had watched with great interest as three icebreakers of the US coast guard became the first ships to cross the Northwest Passage, covering 4,500 miles of semi-charted water in 64 days. Twelve years later a number of Western oil companies sent a specially reinforced super tanker, the *Manhattan*, through the Passage to get a more accurate idea of whether it was a viable route for moving Alaskan oil from one side of the world to another. The purpose of the mission, as one of the organizers argued, was 'to gather scientific and engineering data for guidance in building a fleet of super tanker icebreakers that may turn these desert waters into teeming sea lanes'.

Such high hopes were cruelly dashed, however. The *Manhattan* was stuck in the ice no less than 25 times, and on each occasion an accompanying icebreaker had to pull it free. Not surprisingly, its sponsors decided that the route was just too difficult and expensive to use and opted to build a pipeline in Alaska instead.[8]

Others shared their scepticism. In 1993, Moscow commissioned a special research study with Norway and Japan to carefully explore the viability of using the Northern Sea Route, but its findings, published 6 years later, were very disappointing. Although the route had obvious advantages, ran the report of the International Northern Sea Route Programme, they were heavily outweighed by the sheer cost of building and operating ice-strengthened vessels, which would have to be used even if a Russian icebreaker travelled in front. Assuming these icebreakers would be available, the ships would have to be particularly small in order to get through the shallow straits in the New Siberian Islands and to keep strictly within the path cut by the Russian icebreakers. Such small ships would only be capable of carrying relatively small cargoes and were therefore far less commercially viable than their much bigger counterparts that made their way through the Suez Canal. The report also argued that, in such extreme conditions, ships would be completely incapable of keeping to schedule, particularly if Russian icebreaker assistance should prove to be unreliable.

If, at some future point, the ice does retreat sufficiently, the implications for international shipping would certainly be staggering. Sailing between London and Tokyo, for example, currently involves going through the Suez Canal, but ships could instead cross the Arctic Bridge, moving either eastwards over the Northern Sea Route, or else sail the Atlantic and go through the Northwest Passage, to reduce the journey by some 3,500 miles and, if they avoid traversing the Panama Canal, by as much as 5,500 miles. Overall, these new routes would cut the length of some of these journeys by as much as one-third. Key markets, such as Japan, China, India and South Korea, would become far more accessible while Alaskan oil could be moved to refineries, as the *Manhattan* tried to prove decades earlier, by tanker. 'Shipping along the Northern Sea Route will cut sailing distances from Bremen to Shanghai by as much as 3,200 nautical miles', as Niels Stolberg, the head of a big German shipping company, Beluga, has emphasized.[9] Using this route, or the Northwest Passage, to reach Far Eastern consumers 'would slash our costs by half' if it ever became a reality, says a representative of a British company, Angus & Ross, that is currently excavating Greenland's mineral deposits.[10]

Reducing the journey length of international freight has all sorts of implications that are vital in the world of commerce. Most obviously it allows carriers to cut their fuel costs, which imposed a particularly heavy burden during the drastic increase in the price of crude oil between 2003 and 2007, and to reduce emissions of carbon dioxide. It also keeps to a minimum the cost of chartering large container ships, which are leased on a daily basis and command high premiums, especially when trade is booming and the market is tight.[11] Ships would also avoid paying large sums of money to use the Panama and Suez Canals, either because they could avoid these waterways altogether or because alternative routes would give the canals competition, forcing them to reduce their transit fees. This may prove particularly important over the next few years because the Panama Canal is currently undergoing a hugely expensive upgrade, costing around $7 billion by the time it is due to be completed in 2014, and some analysts estimate that transit fees will have to rise perhaps fourfold to pay for the improvements.

Altogether this means that a large container ship could slash its costs if it uses the Northwest Passage or Northern Sea Route, saving exporters billions of dollars a year. The savings would be even greater for the so-called 'megaships', the huge vessels that, since they were first built in the late 1990s, have been unable to fit through the Panama and Suez Canals and so currently sail around the Cape of Good Hope and Cape Horn.

There are numerous other Arctic possibilities. Some experts even think that, when enough ice has melted, a new route could eventually be opened that runs straight over the North Pole. Such a route, which would probably go between Iceland and Alaska's Dutch Harbor, would connect newly built shipping 'megaports' in the North Atlantic with those in the Pacific and radiate outward to other ports in a hub-and-spoke system.[12] But this looks an even more remote prospect than the opening of a sea route through the Northwest Passage, and may well never happen at all.

Distant though it is, the prospect of an Arctic Bridge has raised eyebrows because of the growing importance of two key markets, both of which would become much more accessible to European and American cargos when it opens. Of course Japan has long been a huge market as well as a key exporter, but it is only in recent years, mainly since the mid-1990s, that the economies of both China and India have surged dramatically ahead, expanding by between 10 per cent and 15 per cent every year. China, in particular, is a key exporter, and its goods could be shipped to Western markets much more quickly along the Northwest Passage. But as prosperity and standards of living soar and populations continue to rise, both countries also have booming domestic markets that the outside world is also keen to reach.

Any such Arctic Bridge would also offer international shipping two distinct advantages over existing routes. One is the avoidance of an old scourge that, centuries after it was stamped out, has recently returned to haunt some stretches of coast.

Piracy

From their bases along the coasts of Somalia, heavily armed and well-organized pirates have, in recent years, proved highly adept at seizing international freight as it moves through the Gulf of Aden and off the coasts of East Africa, and demanding high ransoms in exchange for both the crew and the cargo. In the course of 2008, a multinational task force that included warships from NATO members and from the United States Fifth Fleet had started to patrol the region, but met with only limited success. Having already staged more than 80 single attacks off the Gulf of Aden in the preceding few months, the pirates still managed to pull off two highly audacious coups within the space of just weeks. At the end of September they stormed on board a Ukrainian ship that was carrying 33 tanks and what Defence Minister, Yuri Yekhanurov, called 'a substantial quantity of ammunition'. And in mid-November they seized the attention of the world's media by hijacking a Saudi super tanker, the *Sirius Star*, which was moving a $100 million cargo of crude oil, causing universal panic and outrage by doing so.

The threat of piracy may eventually recede, but for the foreseeable future shipping companies are likely to look further afield to find and explore safer routes, such as the Northwest Passage. Within a week of the seizure of the *Sirius Star*, Europe's biggest ship owner, A. P. Moller-Maersk, announced that it had decided to divert its fleet of 83 tankers along the longer and much more expensive route that goes along the coasts of southern Africa and around the Cape of Good Hope. A Norwegian company, Odfjell, also ordered its 90-strong fleet of chemical tankers to follow the same path, while Frontline Shipping, the world's biggest tanker operator, admitted that it was reconsidering its routes. This would of course drastically increase shipping costs, as well as hugely reduce the transit fees earned by the Egyptian government from maritime traffic passing through the Suez Canal.

So instead of passing through the Suez Canal, European or North African cargo ships that are heading for the Far East could conceivably one day move westwards, crossing the Atlantic and then moving through the Northwest Passage to reach their destination, or else head eastwards along the northern coasts of Russia.

Although any ships that move over the Arctic Bridge would be at risk of being obstructed or damaged by floating icebergs, they would not only be immune to the threat of piracy but also be less vulnerable, in the short term at least, to a nightmare scenario that is increasingly haunting the imagination of international shippers and their insurers. This is the real risk of a collision between container ships or, much worse, between carriers of crude oil or liquefied natural gas. This can pose a serious risk anywhere in the world, and as the next chapter shows it will eventually become a real danger in the Arctic. But because some of the world's key waterways are already very congested, the Arctic Bridge would initially offer shipping companies a good way of reducing their exposure to risk; although it might not be long before sea lanes in the Northwest Passage and the Northern Sea Route become equally overcrowded.

The most important single reason is that global demand for almost every commodity, particularly oil and gas, is expected to grow in parts of the world that are geographically distant from sources of supply: as the populations and economies of China, India and Japan continue to surge, increasing quantities of oil will be shipped, rather than piped, from the producing countries of the Middle East. This is the main reason why, according to some estimates, the number of tankers in service is expected to expand enormously over the next two decades, with their capacity increasing by more than half over the next 20 years.[13]

Shipping companies are keener than ever to avoid some of the world's most congested waters. Perhaps the most notorious are the

Malacca Straits, lying between the Indian Ocean and the South China Sea, through which maritime traffic has to pass to get to and from the Far East. But although the narrowest point of this shipping lane measures just over a mile wide, approximately 60,000 vessels pass through it every year. Overall, about one-third of the world's trade and half of its oil moves through these straits, making them the busiest waterway in the world.

Congestion on this scale makes international shipping highly vulnerable to delays caused by accidents, or indeed to the threat posed by the region's own pirates. 'Congestion and accidents in the Straits can cause major delays, with significant negative repercussions to the whole supply chain and the coastal and marine environment of the three littoral states', as Singapore's Deputy Prime Minister, Shunmugam Jayakumar, has pointed out. 'The threat does not come from navigational risks alone. These straits have traditionally had a high incidence of armed robberies at sea.'[14]

It is easy to see, then, why the prospect of trans-Arctic trade is stirring so much interest in the world of commerce and why over the past few years shipbuilders have started to show much more commitment than ever in building ice-capable ships.[15] The private sector is already investing billions of dollars in a fleet of Arctic tankers. In 2007 there were 262 ice-class ships in service worldwide and another 234 on order, all using cutting-edge technology that can allow ships to sail through some frozen waters without any icebreakers at their side. One such innovation, is a 'double-acting tanker' that steams through open water bow first, but can turn right round when it moves into frozen seas and then use a specially reinforced stern to smash through the ice. Such breakthroughs are making Arctic shipping more cost effective and turning what were once commercially unviable projects into booming business.

Various governments are encouraging this trend. The European Commission, for example, wants to help 'maintain the competitive lead of European shipyards in developing technology required for Arctic conditions', and thinks that that 'the potential to provide specially designed, environment-friendly ships, including icebreakers, is an important asset for the future'. It also wants to 'improve maritime surveillance capabilities in the far north' and is working closely with the European Space Agency to build a polar-orbiting satellite system that can pick up signals from anywhere in the world. 'If successful', the Commission claims, then 'this would allow a better knowledge of ship traffic and mean that emergencies could be responded to more quickly. The Galileo satellite navigation system will also play an important role in the Arctic by providing better and safer navigation, maritime surveillance and emergency response.'[16]

The Canadian government is also keen to see more traffic passing through the Northwest Passage. 'We're not just waiting for the ice to melt', as Ron Lemieux, the Transportation Minister in Canada's Manitoba province, told one British newspaper. Although by 2008 some ships were already being toughened with an extra inch of steel to speed them through the softening ice in Hudson Bay and the wider region, Lemieux was still 'lobbying hard' for 'nuclear icebreakers (that) could keep that port open for twelve months a year'.[17] The Russian government has also declared a strong interest in reopening the Northern Sea Route and commissioning the construction of new icebreakers: on 1 October 2008, when the Kremlin published a document on the future of the Russian economy, it highlighted the importance of the Route and set out a plan to establish a joint control and security system for shipping by the year 2015.

National and commercial interests frequently converge but sometimes also differ considerably.

National interests

Some governments are as keen as businessmen to encourage the opening of an Arctic Bridge, although their enthusiasm is based on different grounds. While industry can keep pace with global competition if goods quickly reach their destination markets and are less vulnerable to disruption by pirates or accidents, governments view this priority not just in terms of profit and loss but also from a different angle. For all governments are painfully aware that civil protests can easily be triggered, anywhere in the world, by massive unemployment and food inflation. Over the past few years, with burgeoning demand in China, India and the rest of the world, they welcome any development that can help their businesses stay competitive, keep commodity prices to a minimum and reduce unemployment at home. This not only allows them to tax company profits but also helps to preserve social stability.

The growing if distant prospect of an Arctic Bridge is all the more appealing in this regard because it has coincided with heightening fears of food riots. The price of foodstuffs has soared in recent years for a number of highly complex reasons, chief among which is the huge, unsustainable rate of population growth in the Third World. Whatever the causes, events in the summer of 2008 realized every government's worst nightmare, as huge numbers of angry and violent protestors the world over took to the streets to demonstrate against dramatic rises in the price of food. In the course of 2009, experts and political leaders continued to warn that 'the food crisis has not gone away' and could soon return with a vengeance, fast 'resuming [its] upward trend' to threaten an impending 'food crunch'.[18] Coupled with a worldwide recession, which in 2009 is already provoking public anger, this presents a potentially ominous development.[19]

This is the one reason why governments have watched the melting of Arctic ice with mixed feelings, dismayed by the prospect of rising sea levels and environmental destruction, but at the same time welcoming the commercial opportunities that it appears to bring. As the EU's Fisheries and Maritime Affairs Commissioner, Joe Borg, told the Arctic Council in 2008, 'as the ice recedes, we are presented with a first-time opportunity to use transport routes such as the Northern Sea Route [and] this would translate into shorter transportation routes and greater trading possibilities with the opening up of new waterways and international trade routes'.[20]

An Arctic Bridge also offers governments some benefits and rewards that are simply not available to businesses, or else are of no real interest to them. So in December 2008 the member states of the EU tentatively agreed to reduce carbon dioxide emissions by as much as 20 per cent, and any reduction in the journey times of international shipping will help them reach these ambitious targets. This, of course, leads to a rather curious situation, for carbon dioxide is melting Arctic ice and thereby creating new routes that will in turn enable countries to reduce their carbon dioxide emissions.

For two neighbouring governments – Russia and Canada – the opening of Arctic sea routes to international shipping could potentially offer a hugely tempting bonanza: the payment of transit fees that would go straight into their coffers.

Transit fees

The Suez Canal illustrates exactly how much money a country can make from an international waterway that passes through its territory. The Egyptian government has long been highly dependent on the revenue drawn from the Canal, which now constitutes the country's third source of foreign exchange earnings, surpassed only by tourism and the remittances sent home by expatriate workers. So in 2007, when a boom in global trade allowed the Egyptian government to hike up prices, its takings from the 20,410 ships that made their way through the Canal amounted to a staggering $5.2 billion. 'Since the first oil crisis in 1973 and the soaring prices, the economic importance of the canal for Egypt never ceased to grow and it has become an irreplaceable source of income', as the economist Samir Radwan told one news agency on the 50th anniversary of the nationalization of the Suez Canal Company.[21] Other governments are well aware of how they can cash in from international trade, particularly from the growth of Asian and Far Eastern economies. Moscow, for example, has been busily promoting an overland trade route known as the North-South Corridor. Using a combination of road, rail and river links, this corridor has the potential to transform intercontinental trade, since it is around 6,000 miles shorter than the Suez Canal route. The Russians estimate that it could handle between 15 and 20 million tons of freight every year, and know just how much money they could earn from transit fees – perhaps as much as $10 billion a year – if the project takes off.

So the debates about the legal status of the Northwest Passage and the Northern Sea Route could have enormous financial implications for Ottawa and Moscow. While no signatory member of the 1982 Convention can levy these transit charges over any section of the territorial sea or an economic zone, the treaty has no bearing over 'internal waters'.[22] So if any section of these seas is judged by the ICJ to be their own 'internal waters', then the Canadian and Russian governments, like Egypt and the Suez Canal or Canada and the St Lawrence Seaway, will have a right to charge transit fees from international shipping.[23] This assumes that there is no 'international strait' that runs through these waters – in which case the 1982 Convention would prohibit the levying of any transit fees – and that the World Trade Organization does not change its rules to wholly prohibit these charges: under the rules of the General Agreement on Tariffs and Trade (GATT), any such fees can only be levied for 'services rendered' to traffic along the way.[24]

The 'Arctic Five' might potentially be able to claim a right to levy a charge from any ships that pass through their economic zones on the grounds of Article 234 of the 1982 Convention, which gives a right to impose 'non-discriminatory laws and regulations for the prevention, reduction and control of marine pollution' in these waters. Russian regulations have always stated that any ships wanting to pass anywhere along the Northern Sea Route must formally apply for access and pay an exorbitant 'icebreaker fee', even if a ship doesn't specifically need to be escorted. In 2009 the Russians were charging $16 per ton of oil cargo – partly to compensate for the low trade volumes moving through the waters – whereas Finland charged Baltic shipping just $1 per ton. This consideration may explain President Gorbachev's apparent enthusiasm for the route. In 1987 he argued that:

across the Arctic runs the shortest sea route from Europe to the Far East, to the Pacific. I think that, depending on how the normalization of international relations goes, we could open the Northern Sea Route to foreign ships under icebreaker escort.[25]

In the meantime, disputes between Canada and the rest of the world over the legal status of these waters are likely to continue. The EU has decreed its strong interest in defending 'the principle of freedom of navigation and the right of innocent passage in the newly opened routes and areas', while emphasizing 'the need to avoid discriminatory practices (in particular in terms of fees, obligatory services, regulations) by any of the Arctic coastal states towards third countries' merchant ships'.[26] Not surprisingly, these sentiments caused dismay and alarm in Ottawa: 'This is really troubling for Canadian interests', as one expert on the region, Rob Huebert, told the local media at the end of 2008.[27]

Strategic importance
But it is not just the prospect of transit fees, no matter how lucrative, that is now heightening the interest of some governments in the Northwest Passage. Even more vital, particularly for the United States and Russia, is the region's crucial strategic significance. As a NATO report on the Arctic argued in January 2009, 'it is a region of enduring strategic importance for NATO, and allied security [and] developments in the High North require careful and ongoing examination'.[28]

Most trade routes have strategic value because anyone who controls them can potentially hold both producers and consumers to ransom. But this is clearly much more true of some routes than others for the simple reason that, in the event of any local disruption, shipping can often simply switch to alternative routes that are longer and more expensive but perfectly navigable. However, the Northwest Passage would not fall into this category; instead, it could become a 'chokepoint' like the Suez and Panama Canals, or the Strait of Hormuz in the Persian Gulf, where any disruption to shipping traffic would cause serious havoc, huge delays and even economic turmoil.

If key waterways like these are disrupted, then almost everyone can lose out. Consumers can suffer from a shortage of resources that might be vital to their economy, just as in 1956 the British premier, Anthony Eden, feared that the Egyptian leader, Gamal Nasser, had his 'finger on our windpipe' as a result of his nationalization of the Suez

Canal Company. But exporters can also suffer equally badly, just as in the early 1950s a British blockade of the refinery at Abadan in the Persian Gulf stopped Iran from exporting oil, starving it of foreign exchange earnings and devastating its economy.

In other words, controlling the Northwest Passage, or at least stopping someone else from doing so, is likely to be a key strategic objective for any country concerned about its national security. Above all, American strategists will harbour no illusions about who might prise control over, or establish a presence in, some section of the Passage if they don't: China. Since the late 1990s or so, the Chinese have adopted what Western defence experts call the 'String of Pearls' strategy, which involves establishing a political or military presence along the sea routes that lead to the oil-producing states of the Middle East. Each of these 'pearls' represents a particular presence, the purpose of which is to provide 'energy security' by guarding the movement of oil tankers in the event of any disruption. So at various sites, such as Gwadar in Pakistan, Chittagong in Bangladesh and Woody Island east of Vietnam, the Chinese have been busily building deep-water ports, shipping container facilities, navy bases and airfields while at the same time establishing strong diplomatic ties with governments.

Lying behind China's strategy is a deep sense of insecurity. The United States' overwhelming presence in the Gulf and close to the Malacca Straits, through which 80 per cent of China's oil imports pass, has made Beijing very fearful that, in the event of any conflict over the future of Taiwan or any other issue, Washington could choke off its oil supply. China is 'looking not only to build a blue-water navy to control the sea lanes, but also to develop undersea mines and missile capabilities to deter the potential disruption of its energy supplies from potential threats, including the US Navy, especially in the case of a conflict with Taiwan', as an internal Pentagon report, published in 2005, pointed out.[29]

It would be completely inconsistent for China to guard its corridor to the Middle East without also making some effort to do the same over any new supply lines that may eventually open along the Northwest Passage. Just as a Chinese company, with close ties to Beijing's communist rulers, holds long-term leases on port facilities at either end of the Panama Canal, so too in the same way could the Beijing regime potentially establish a foothold along some parts of the Northwest Passage, or along the sea lanes that lead to and from oil and natural gas fields. The mere possibility that China could disrupt the flow of shipping traffic through this region, Beijing strategists might argue, would be enough to dissuade the United States from intervening in any confrontation that China has with Taiwan or any other dispute that Beijing regards as its own private affair.

The mutual mistrust between Washington and Beijing is also likely to prompt the United States to find ways of stopping the Chinese from making such moves and to stake out its own claim instead. American strategists might regard the Northwest Passage as offering a form of insurance that would guard them from Beijing's aggression in the event of a future war between the two countries, or at least prevent the Chinese from exerting the same leverage over the United States.

8

The Environmental Challenge

For thousands of years, perhaps even since the advent of the last ice age, a curious ritual has taken place along the banks of many rivers and bays in northern Canada. It is in these areas that, during the weeks of early winter, hundreds of polar bears congregate and wait patiently for the water to freeze before beginning their annual migration and making their way, across the ice, into the frozen wastelands that lie further north. The sea ice is indispensable to these creatures, the world's largest land predators, which use it as a floating platform to catch seals before heading back to their dens where they devour their prey.

But over the past decade or so, the bears have been forced to delay their journey longer than ever while they wait for the ice to freeze. This delay is having a highly adverse effect on their wellbeing, since they are spending less time on the ice and therefore have fewer opportunities of finding any food. As a result their health and fitness is being affected, their birth rates are falling and they are becoming less resilient to disease and to the demands of this harsh climate. Throughout the year they are also being forced to swim huge distances to find the ice cover they need and many are drowning in the process. So at one of their favourite venues, outside the tiny settlement at Churchill on Hudson Bay, where Pat Broe had made such a shrewd investment in 1997, their numbers are thought to have dropped by around one-quarter since the late 1980s.[1]

Throughout the Arctic region, the polar bear is already suffering badly from the general retreat of ice cover, and it is expected to continue doing so as the ice retreats; some meteorologists even predict that the region could have 'Florida summers in forty years'. This is why, over the last few years, the animal has become a symbol not of the Arctic region, but also of the impact of global warming and climate change upon it. Above all, the huge attention and publicity that has been focused on its tragic plight is a reminder that the international scramble to discover and exploit the Arctic's resources will inevitably inflict heavy environmental damage, creating enormous tension between governments, business, the general public, non-governmental organizations and pressure groups. In short, the fate of the Arctic environment is a major issue of international contention and controversy.

Part of the problem is simply that the Arctic is like any other wilderness, untouched and unspoilt by the hand of progress and civilization, but once lost, environmentalists point out, something unique and special can simply never be recovered. Most people feel a pang of sorrow and regret when they see a large, beautiful tree being cut down, or watch a green field being ploughed up and then covered with concrete, and if these feelings are familiar then you are likely to react in the same way when you read about the despoliation of the Arctic. This line of argument can't really be proven or demonstrated with facts and figures, but is instead something that someone either does feel or does not.

To some extent, the exploitation of the Arctic is more likely to stir the passions of environmentalists for the same reasons as any other wilderness area. This is not just because of its vast size, or because it is home to ancient and traditional ways of life, such as those of the Inuits and other indigenous people, and to various rare species of flora and fauna. Instead it is because some of the natural resources that can be found there, or can be moved through it, pose grave environmental risks: so if crude oil, for example, is lifted from the region and then transported away by tanker or pipeline, then the surrounding area is at risk of spillages that could inflict lethal and long-lasting damage. Other forms of economic exploitation can be just as bad: the excavation of resources such as copper, gold or coal often creates large, open pits that can ruin the natural beauty of a much wider area.

While these are dangers that confront any wilderness region where natural resources are being exploited or transported, the Arctic's unusually harsh climate and environment pose particular risks. For anyone who ventures into this region, whether it is an explorer, geologist, naturalist or businessman, has to contend with all manner of difficulties posed not so much by extremely low temperatures, but rather by the impact of climate change on its traditional landscape. For example, as waters continue to get warmer, icebergs are splintering and drifting through the seas, posing a real risk to any shipping or offshore installations that aren't braced up for them.

However, much of the controversy that surrounds the Arctic's environment is focused on the type of damage that any unspoilt region – rather than the Arctic in particular – suffers from when its resources are exploited: green activists point out that the extraction and transportation of natural resources inflicts devastating environmental damage on wildlife, habitats and ways of life.

Environmental damage

To appease pressure groups and public opinion, most international oil companies are generally keen to minimize the environmental damage they cause when they lift oil or natural gas from the ground. Companies like British Petroleum and Royal Dutch Shell, for example, have invested huge sums of money in high-profile media campaigns that are designed to project exactly such an environmentally friendly image. Sometimes they succeed at living up to their promises because modern technology allows them to use minimal infrastructure to extract huge quantities of oil and natural gas while the surrounding countryside looks barely any different: the Snow White complex at Hammerfest in Norway has been built almost entirely underwater, and most of its production facilities have been hidden from the mainland. British firms, in particular, are currently pioneering the development of 'subsea' technology that allows the exploitation of oil and gas not from above the surface, using rigs and platforms, but from under it.[2] At other times, however, the exploitation of petroleum reserves has enormous environmental consequences that no amount of clever marketing or ingenious engineering can disguise.

Drilling in the Beaufort Sea

In recent years the environmental lobby has fought particularly hard to stop offshore drilling on Alaska's North Slope and by the end of 2008 had managed to win its battle, although some international oil companies have promised to keep fighting the wider war and continue pressing their case.

Their chief antagonist in this particular struggle was Royal Dutch Shell, whose geologists feel sure that the offshore waters of the North Slope offer a huge, untapped source of oil. 'The [outer continental shelf] is a potential bonanza for oil and gas, and every day we are not drilling are days we're not going to be producing, and that will materially impact Alaska and the nation', as the company's General Manager in Alaska, Pete Slaiby, later claimed.[3] Another Shell director concurred, arguing that 'we see the Beaufort Sea as a significant basin. It offers a wide diversity of geology and is largely untested'. She added that, in Shell's view, 'North America continues to hold promising

opportunities' and that 'Alaska, because of its large resource potential, is one such area'.[4]

Shell's chance came in 2005, when a United States government
agency, the Minerals Management Service, adopted an aggressive
leasing strategy that was designed to offset the declining output from
Prudhoe Bay. It decided to sell the rights to search for oil in two areas
that were thought to be particularly promising – the Chukchi and
Beaufort Seas – and Shell seized the opportunity, buying a number
of leases in both areas for $2.1 billion and $84 million respectively
and then getting ready to drill three wells at a remote spot, 16 miles
offshore, called Sivulliq.

Environmental groups, such as the Alaska Wilderness League, were
infuriated by the decision. Most of all, they argued, any commercial
activity in these seas – even the arrival of icebreakers, the undertaking
of seismic surveys and the movement of thousands of tons of piping
as well as heavy drilling – posed a real threat to bowhead whales,
which migrate through the Beaufort Sea twice a year. This was bad
enough, they claimed, but it was even more important because the
local Inupiat community hunt the whales and rely on them as a key
source of food. If the whales are driven from the sea, went the argument, then local ways of life would also disappear along with them.

There are a number of other reasons why environmentalists particularly fear offshore drilling. Activists point out that it is not just
the surveying and excavation itself that causes a problem, but also the
enormous logistical effort that is required to sustain these operations.
Hundreds of ships are often required to support underwater drilling,
and their constant movement through a particular area can have
an enormous effect on both local wildlife and indigenous peoples.
Many also argue that investing so much money to search for oil and
then extract it is in any case badly misguided. 'It just feeds a vicious
cycle', argues Athan Manuel, a director at the American pressure
group the Sierra Club, pointing to the way in which oil development
in the Arctic is both a cause and effect of climate change. Much more
important, he argues, is to emphasize energy conservation while
making much greater use of cleaner technologies. 'More drilling is
not the solution', he says. 'We think this is a terrible idea.'[5]

In August 2007, the United States Court of Appeals imposed a
temporary injunction on Shell's offshore drilling, a delay that would
inevitably cost the company huge sums, until it reached its final
verdict. Fifteen months later it made its long-awaited pronounce-
ment and ruled in favour of the environmentalists. The Minerals
Management Service, it argued, had violated American law (the 1970

National Environmental Policy Act) by failing to take a 'hard look' at the impact that offshore drilling would have on both the bowhead whale and the region's indigenous community. 'There remain substantial questions as to whether Shell's plan may cause significant harm to the people and wildlife of the Beaufort Sea region', as the judges argued in the courtroom in San Francisco.

Green campaigners were of course jubilant. 'This is really a signal that Shell's plan was simply too much, too fast and too shoddy', as Peter Clausen, director of the National Resources Defense Council, told one newspaper. He also noted that the decision virtually coincided with the election of a new American president who has always proclaimed his opposition to offshore drilling: 'By this decision, the court has opened the door to a new administration to take a whole new approach, and hopefully a more precautionary approach, to America's Arctic and make sure we don't lose endangered species.'[6]

The Beaufort Sea lies adjacent to Alaska's Arctic National Wildlife Refuge, which is the setting for another, quite distinct, environmental controversy. One of the most contentious issues of American domestic politics in recent years has been the proposal to open this 20 million acre region to drilling. The USGS estimates that the Refuge contains 10.36 billion barrels of oil, and although by the standards of the industry these reserves are not enormous, the fate of the area has nonetheless acquired tremendous symbolic value for both the oil lobby and environmentalists alike. Lobby groups emphasize that this coastal plain is special not just because of its superb natural beauty, but also because it has a vast and varied wildlife population that includes caribou, wolves, polar and grizzly bears, and is the last remaining habitat of the highly traditional Gwich'in Inuits, who call the area 'the sacred place where life begins'. But although in June 2008 President Bush had urged Congress to reverse the ban on offshore drilling in the Refuge, Barack Obama was elected to the White House in November with a much less sympathetic approach to the issue.

The impact of tar sands

Environmentalists have won a temporary victory in their campaign to keep oil companies out of the Beaufort Sea but they are still struggling to protect Canada's Arctic mainland. One such risk emanates from a region that lies south of the Arctic Circle, close to Lake Athabasca in Alberta.

The controversy surrounds a particular type of oil – dense, sticky and mixed with bitumen, sand and clay – that is usually known as tar sands. The Athabasca tar sands deposits are thought to be vast, containing around 175 billion barrels of oil, and not surprisingly their discovery has lured international energy companies such as Shell, which has already invested billions of dollars in extracting them.[7] 'The deposits are huge, potentially even greater than in Saudi Arabia (and) the time is right to exploit them', as Clive Mather, chief executive of Shell Canada, has said.[8] Shell and its partners are already extracting about 150,000 barrels of oil a day and are aiming to expand this output fivefold, while some other companies, such as Suncor and Syncrude, have also entertained ambitions to drastically step up their own involvement in the project. These plans had been put on hold in the spring of 2009, when the profitability of the operations was slashed by the crash in the oil price, but are still likely to resume when economic conditions recover.

The trouble is that these oil deposits can only be lifted if they are dug right out, destroying whatever lies on top. 'Tar sands are the worst kind of source for oil', says James Leaton, a policy adviser on gas and oil for the WWF. 'Extracting oil takes huge amounts of energy and devastates the local environment by destroying the forest and polluting rivers, lakes and the air.'[9] In time, the technology will doubtlessly be developed to avoid this environmental slaughter, but that could be years or even decades away. Until that happens around six barrels of waste are produced for every barrel of oil that is extracted from tar sands, and these wastes, together with a flow of water, sand, fine clay and residual bitumen, are usually stored in vast reservoirs that are dug out of the surrounding area.

The huge environmental impact of tar sands mining operations inevitably affects a very wide area, and many campaigners argue that it is already having a serious impact on rivers and wildlife in the Arctic region and elsewhere. If rivers and waterways in Alberta are contaminated and polluted, they claim, the fallout is felt much further away. As one Canadian pressure group, Environmental Defence, has pointed out, 'all Canadians are impacted by the tar sands, no matter where they live. If you live downstream, your water is being polluted and your fish and wildlife may be dangerous to eat'.[10] But there is one respect in which Alberta's oil sands promise to adversely affect Canada's Arctic much more than any other region. This concerns an issue that has become hotly and bitterly contested in Canada and beyond: the construction of a pipeline that would run all the way from the Mackenzie Basin in the far north to Athabasca in the south.

Pipeline controversies

In order to extract bitumen and then refine what's left over, the production of a barrel of synthetic crude oil from the tar sands always requires huge amounts of heat. This, in turn, depends upon a vast input of energy. To put the point another way, pumping one barrel of oil, or its equivalent, into the site at Athabasca to generate this heat enables the production of just three barrels. This also makes its production very expensive: the cost of producing one barrel is around $30–$40, more than six times the figure of extracting oil from some Middle Eastern wells.

The most usual power source for this task is natural gas, and the oil companies that are developing Alberta know where an excellent source is to be found. Lying northwards, above the Arctic Circle, is the Beaufort-Mackenzie Basin, which is home to vast deposits of natural gas that could be tapped and then piped southwards to feed the energy-hungry project at Athabasca. With the exception of local gas production from the onshore Ikhil field near Inuvik, none of these deposits has as yet been developed, but there are lots of other places that energy companies have been watching with a rapacious eye, even if Shell's drive to exploit the Beaufort Sea has been temporarily checked.

By early 2009, more than 180 exploration wells and around 60 development wells had been drilled in the Beaufort-Mackenzie Basin, resulting in the discovery of more than 50 oil and gas fields. Many of these are located on the mainland, such as the vast Taglu field, which is reckoned to have recoverable natural gas reserves of 2 trillion cubic feet, and the Parsons Lake field, where there are also very large deposits. Some enormous offshore fields have also been located, such as Amauligak, with an estimated 235 million barrels of oil and 1.3 trillion cubic feet of gas reserves. In general, this particular region is reckoned to harbour around 9 trillion cubic feet of recoverable gas and 1 billion barrels of recoverable oil, which is equivalent to about 20 per cent of the total oil potential in all of Canada's frontier basins and 20 per cent of its total gas reserves.

In the eyes of environmentalists, exploiting these deposits would be bad enough, inflicting considerable damage on the natural landscape. But the construction of a pipeline that would then move natural gas to Alberta would deal the region a devastating blow. Building and maintaining any pipeline that stretches 800 miles would require the construction of a whole network of roads and buildings that would completely transform the entire area. This, continues the green lobby, would have immense, tragic and far-reaching consequences for a unique region. This was the main line of argument made in the late 1970s by a Canadian judge, Thomas Berger, who was appointed to consider an earlier proposal to build a pipeline through the same area. In particular, Berger warned that the river valley would become a vast 'energy corridor' covered with feeder pipelines, airports, roads and electric utilities, creating a huge area of urban sprawl.

It is easy to see the environmentalists' argument. The Mackenzie River Basin is a huge area of around 1.4 billion acres of contiguous forest, one that is relatively untouched by modernity (Map 2). It is home to an estimated 360,000 people, a largely indigenous population that is highly dependent on the local myriad of rivers, lakes, deltas and waterways. It is also rich in wildlife and is heavily used by thousands of birds, notably waterfowl, which breed along the Arctic coast and migrate every year across the forest.

Those who argue in favour of building the pipeline claim that other, similar projects have been undertaken before and proved protestors wrong by allowing traditional ways of life to continue and have not seriously impacted on wildlife. In the late 1960s and early 1970s, for example, one of the most bitterly contested issues on Capitol Hill was the construction of a pipeline that would run southwards from the newly discovered oilfields at Prudhoe Bay through the great wilderness region of Alaska. From the moment that proposals were put forward, environmental groups moved quickly to try and block the project, claiming that the plans did not meet the strict demands made by the new National Environmental Policy Act and persuading a federal judge to grant an immediate injunction that stopped any work on the project from proceeding.

Throughout the country the issue was hotly debated, with many people taking the view that America's last great wilderness should be spared the pipeline and preserved intact.

After years of wrangling, the issue was eventually settled in July 1973 after a dramatic vote in Congress, when a debate on the project was deadlocked with 49 senators voting in favour of the pipeline and 49 against. It was the Vice-President, Spiro Agnew, who decided the outcome, casting his vote in favour of the proposed Alaska Pipeline Authorization Act. Work on the pipeline began within months and was completed 4 years later at a cost of $7.7 billion.

But one key difference between the Mackenzie River and Alaskan projects is that the Canadian pipeline is intended to feed the tar sands operation in Athabasca. Environmentalists have a particular loathing for these tar sands not just because their excavation involves destroying so much natural habitat, but also because they also release far more carbon dioxide into the atmosphere than other, lighter forms of oil. This is why some campaigners are not opposed to the construction of a pipeline that would follow an alternative route, diverting natural gas from the Mackenzie River Basin to another destination market. One of America's biggest lobby groups has supported a pipeline that would move the gas through Alaska to reach American consumers. 'The Alaska pipeline would be much longer than the Mackenzie Valley pipelines and carry three times as much gas, but is likely to cause less ecological damage', as the directors of the Sierra Club have argued, and therefore 'may be the lesser environmental evil'. Whereas 'the Mackenzie pipeline . . . would cause greater ecological fragmentation, not to mention harm caused by induced development along the pipeline route' because it crossed through much more intact forest and tundra, 'Alaska gas could conceivably serve to reduce North American greenhouse gas emissions by displacing the use of coal and oil, whereas Mackenzie gas used to produce tar sands oil would result in large increases in Canada's greenhouse gas emissions'.[11]

Tanker traffic

There are various other ways in which the Arctic's natural environment could be imperilled by the gradual encroachment of the outside world. As the previous chapter pointed out, the retreat of sea ice is already opening up the Northwest Passage to international shipping, and this means that a nightmare scenario, one that haunts everyone's imagination, could easily come true. This is the very real threat of an accident involving an oil or natural gas tanker as it passes through the Northwest Passage or along the Northern Sea Route towards its marketplace. Any such accident always inflicts enormous devastation, but its impact would be all the more tragic if it affected what is still, in many places, a wilderness area.

As a previous chapter has pointed out, Arctic waters may be attractive to shipping because in the short or immediate term they are likely to be less congested than other stretches of sea such as the Malacca Straits. But accidents or collisions could still happen for much the same reasons as anywhere else.[12] In the coming decades, the amount of global tanker traffic is expected to increase considerably, creating highly congested shipping lanes in every part of the world.[13] This means that, purely in terms of its weight of traffic, the Arctic's waters could eventually become like the Bosphorus, the straits through which oil and natural gas are ferried as carriers make their way from the wells of the Caspian Sea, move across the Black Sea and then head into the Mediterranean. Every day more than 2,500 vessels, around 30 of which are tankers, pass through these straits, and as a British journalist has pointed out, many of these tankers are 'rustbuckets that shouldn't be at sea, let alone passing right through the middle of a city of 15 million people' and, to make matters much worse, are 'often skippered by drunken incompetents'.[14] There have been a number of very serious accidents here. In 1979 a collision created a massive explosion that rocked Istanbul with a ferocious force, shaking buildings and shattering windows while spilling nearly 100,000 tonnes of burning oil into the sea; similar tragedies could equally unfold in Arctic waters.

One scenario that inspires particular dread is the very real prospect of a terrorist attack on what would be seen as a new and highly tempting target: a tanker carrying liquefied gas. Terrorists generally don't target pipelines because the flow of oil or gas can be quickly cut off, but an explosion on board a liquefied gas tanker would have a disastrous impact. One report, published by an American consultancy, concluded that in a worst case scenario a successful attack on a tanker could result in as many as 8,000 deaths and 20,000 injuries.[15] Most worryingly, these enormous ships could make relatively easy targets for a rocket-propelled grenade or for explosive devices that are detonated by terrorists using a small boat to pull alongside their target. It was just such an audacious attack that Al Qaeda bombers made with considerable success against the USS *Cole* in October 2000.

Another nightmare scenario is the spillage not of crude oil or liquid petroleum but of radioactive waste. In 2001, President Vladimir Putin caused deep alarm among environmentalists by signing a new law that allowed Russia to import nuclear fuel from other countries for storage and reprocessing. From the Kremlin's point of view this seemed like a certain money-spinner, earning up to $15 billion over 10 years at a time when the Russian economy was still depressed. What really bothered environmentalists was not so much that the nuclear waste would be buried on Russian soil, on the island of Novaya Zemlya in the Barents Sea, but that it would move by tanker through Arctic waters to get there. This meant that any spillage would have a devastating environmental impact. 'The trade of toxic waste across national boundaries is a very bad idea. Russia has changed its law to allow the import of waste, we should change ours to forbid its export', as Tony Juniper of Friends of the Earth put it. 'This must not be allowed to happen.'[16]

The people of Alaska certainly have better reason than most to fear what tanker traffic in the Northwest Passage could inflict. For one

of the most devastating oil spills of recent years took place in Prince
William Sound late one night in March 1989, when a giant oil tanker,
the *Exxon Valdez*, struck an underground reef with devastating
effects. Within just 5 hours at least 11 million gallons of crude oil
had been spilled into the water (some pressure groups claim that the
true figure was much higher) and eventually covered around 11,000
square miles of ocean while affecting 1,200 miles of coastline.

The region was a natural wilderness and a habitat for all sorts of
wildlife, including salmon, sea otters, seals and numerous seabirds,
whose populations suffered appallingly from the spillage. And although thousands of local people worked round the clock to clean
up the damage, an independent study by American government
scientists, undertaken in 2007, concluded that nearly two decades
on, the soil on the shoreline still contained at least 26,000 gallons
of oil that 'was disappearing only very slowly, at an annual rate of
around four per cent'.[17] Perhaps the only consolation was that 80 per
cent of the cargo stayed on board the crippled ship, which narrowly
avoided capsizing.

The Arctic's particular dangers

The tragic story of the *Exxon Valdez* is a reminder that, while such
incidents can happen anywhere in the world, the Arctic region poses
particular dangers. For the waters where the accident took place, in
Prince William Sound, have always posed immense challenges for
crews. Much of the year icebergs float freely down the shipping lane
and on the night of the tragedy the ship's captain requested the coast
guard to guide the tanker, helping it to steer a safe journey through
the ice. Undertaking such a hazardous operation in the middle of the
night would have been difficult enough for anyone, but for a crew
that was overtired and led by a captain with a history of alcoholism
it proved impossible, and the tanker struck Bligh Reef just after mid-
night on 24 March 1989.

Accidents are not only much more likely to happen in the Arctic's
supremely challenging natural environment, but are also far more
difficult to respond to. Environmentalists point to all sorts of dangers,
such as a severe shortage of natural light in winter, extreme cold and
high winds that would make it extremely difficult to respond to an
oil spill should it ever happen. 'The Arctic offers the highest level
of ecological sensitivity and the lowest level of capacity to clean up
after an accident', as James Leaton, an adviser to the WWF, has said.
'This combination makes it unacceptable to expose the Arctic to an
unfettered scramble for oil.'[18]

Long distances

The region's very remoteness makes matters even worse. In the case of the *Exxon Valdez*, the Sound was accessible only by helicopter and boat, and this meant that relief agencies were extremely pushed to mount the fast and effective response that they had hoped to. Everything about the local infrastructure was inadequate to meet the immense demands that were placed on it during the emergency.

Even getting to the nearest town, Valdez, was extremely difficult (Map 2). Ordinarily handling only about 10 flights a day, its tiny airstrip had to be specially fitted with a temporary air traffic control tower to manage a sudden, dramatic increase to between 700 and 1,000 daily flights. Larger planes, carrying vital clean-up equipment, were forced to fly much further afield and their deliveries were then put on trucks to undertake an arduous 9-hour journey to the disaster site, although many roads were closed due to bad weather and avalanches. Valdez is, in any case, only small, with a population of just 4,000, and the sudden influx of a huge number of relief workers, officials and reporters made matters very much worse. Besides a desperate shortage of accommodation, it also had a very limited telephone network, and in the days before mobile phones, this meant that urgent calls to the outside world, requesting resources that were vital to the relief effort, simply failed to get through.

Even when equipment and personnel finally did arrive, the spill site was still 2 hours distant by boat. By 13 April the oil covered 1,000 square miles and it took 8–10 hours by boat, at a speed of 10 knots, to travel from one end of the spill to the other. As the official enquiry into the disaster points out, these were just some of the obstacles, since 'staging had to be done on scene from mobile platforms, requiring that equipment be air-dropped or delivered by boat. All of these factors exacerbated the slow delivery of clean-up equipment'. To make matters worse still, 'radio transmissions cannot travel great distances without repeaters in mountainous terrain'.[19]

Similar concerns were raised in the summer of 2008, when the German shipping company, Beluga, announced plans to start sailing along the Northern Sea Route without the assistance of an accompanying icebreaker.[20] Beluga's critics pointed out that accidents and emergencies are much more likely without an icebreaker, and that Russian rescuers would be both distant and unreliable. The Russian authorities responded by announcing plans for what they called a 'Barents Rescue' rehearsal to take place in the summer of 2009. Organized in Varandey, which is a key export terminal for the shipping of Russian oil from the energy-rich Timan-Pechora province,

Moscow proposed that teams from Norway, Finland, Sweden, Canada and the United States would work alongside their Russian counterparts to assist a wrecked tanker threatening the environment of the Nenets Autonomous Okrug.

Environmental groups argue that no oil should be extracted or moved through the Arctic, or any other region, unless detailed contingency plans have first been drawn up. 'The ability to effectively clean up an Arctic marine oil spill is a critical component of the risk equation', argues Dr Neil Hamilton of the WWF's International Arctic Programme. 'The fact that a catastrophic spill might exceed the operating limits of existing oil spill response technologies is a strong argument for a moratorium until the response gap is filled.'[21]

Part of the solution to the threat of oil spills, argue organizations like the WWF, is to impose much more stringent regulations and monitoring of shipping lanes in the Arctic, and elsewhere. In particular, the WWF is currently lobbying for the Barents Sea to be designated by the International Maritime Organization as a special zone known as a 'Particularly Sensitive Sea Area' (PSSA). All shipping has to take particular care when passing through any stretch of water that is assigned this status, and it gives neighbouring coastal countries special rights to decide on the location of shipping lanes as well as new powers of traffic surveillance. The organization also wants shipping lanes to be moved much further away from the coast than they are at present – it advocates a minimum 50-mile distance instead of the present 12 – and wants to establish some 'petroleum free zones' in the vicinity of areas that are deemed to be environmentally particularly sensitive.

But the Arctic's environment is also highly challenging not because it is generally so remote and its climate so extreme but because of the speed with which it is changing as a result of global warming. Climate change is opening the region up to the outside world but it is also creating all sorts of special risks and dangers.

The impact of climate change
One such risk is that an iceberg could move at unstoppable speed towards an oil rig or any other offshore installation. As the Arctic's waters get warmer, icebergs are melting and splintering into smaller, floating segments that could collide with rigs and ships and cause immense damage. And any drilling operations that take place too close to the Arctic ice pack could also suffer the same brutal fate as the ships of some of the region's early explorers. Constantly shifting, but in a direction that is difficult to predict, these often vast ice sheets

still pose real challenges to anyone who ventures into the region, and could easily damage or even crush rigs and platforms.

This means that many of the offshore rigs that international oil companies hope to construct in Arctic waters are at least as vulnerable to the challenges of the local climate as tankers like the *Exxon Valdez*. In a worst-case scenario, any collision could damage the drilling equipment and cause a spillage that would have a disastrous impact on the environment, quite apart from having serious economic repercussions. This nearly happened at the end of 2006, when violent storms sank a large Swedish cargo ship in the North Sea and broke an oil rig away from its tow, setting it adrift off the coast of Norway.[22] As one North Sea oil executive told a British researcher, 'we've had our third "once-in-a-hundred-years" storm so far this year'.[23]

A stark reminder of just how big this ice, and the threat it poses, can be came in the summer of 2007 when a vast section of ice, measuring 11 miles in length and 3 across, broke free of Ellesmere Island and floated hundreds of miles downstream. Scientists were concerned that this vast segment, which they called Ayles Ice Island, was heading straight for oil and gas installations in the Beaufort Sea and were relieved when, at the end of August, it finally became stuck among the rocks, barrier and reefs of the Queen Elizabeth Islands and remained there.

Environmentalists fear that Russia's Shtokman field, which is due to be developed by a consortium of international energy companies, is already at particular risk.[24] Lying 300 miles from the mainland and within the Arctic Circle, it is quite possible that any rigs could be damaged by icebergs, weighing up to 1 million tons and drifting at speeds of up to 12 feet every minute, and even by floating ice that can quite easily move several times faster.

The energy industry is trying to minimize these risks in a variety of ways, not least by using drill ships with double hulls and rigs made out of specially reinforced steel that is less brittle than the variety ordinarily used for such underwater operations. Whereas steel usually breaks at temperatures below 20 degrees Fahrenheit, these newly designed rigs would be much more resilient. 'They're made horrendously strong', as Alan Spackman, director of Offshore Technical and Regulatory Affairs for the International Association for Drilling Contractors, has said. 'The common rigs working in the Gulf of Mexico wouldn't survive.'[25]

Climate change is also presenting various other risks to both off and onshore infrastructure. In the Arctic, and elsewhere, some scientists say that a reduction in sea ice is creating larger stretches of open water, which increases the size and speed of the ocean's waves. This not only poses a risk to offshore rigs, but is also accelerating the erosion of coastal areas where much of the infrastructure that is used to exploit oil and natural gas would be located.[26] What makes things even worse is that storms are already becoming increasingly violent while sea levels are starting to rise, posing a particular risk to the stability of these offshore installations. 'There will be a rise in the frequency and the strength of storms at sea', as Joan Eamer, a manager at the UN's Global Resource Information Database, has pointed out.[27] The *Arctic Climate Impact Assessment* also emphasizes that 'in some regions', such as the Labrador, Norwegian, Bering and Beaufort Seas, 'an increase in storm activity is likely' and that 'climate change is projected to result in more frequent and intense storms accompanied by stronger winds'.[28]

One place that is already at risk from just this sort of environmental threat is a Russian oil storage facility that has been built on a barrier island at Varandey. Although much of this coastline is relatively unthreatened by erosion, the site is proving highly vulnerable to the damage inflicted by storms and sudden surges of ocean waves, and scientists feel that the reduction in sea ice and rising sea levels will aggravate this problem. At Tuktoyaktuk, which is the major port in the western Canadian Arctic and the only permanent settlement on the shores of the Beaufort Sea, the coastline is already being badly eroded by stronger waves, forcing a good many people to abandon their homes. Successive shoreline protection structures have been rapidly destroyed by storms and strong waves, and further efforts to reinforce the coastline will become increasingly expensive but probably prove just as futile, eventually making the site completely uninhabitable.

Minimizing the impact of these changes will require considerable ingenuity on the part of architects and engineers. In the case of the oil industry in particular, offshore platforms will have to be specially redesigned to withstand the increasingly forceful impact of ocean waves, while both governments and industry will need highly effective contingency plans to keep the region linked to the outside world. As the authors of the *Arctic Climate Impact Assessment* write:

> *Increasing storm frequencies are very likely to increase closure periods of wind-exposed roads, highways, railroads, and airports, and are likely to affect industries and other human activities dependent on transportation. For example, an increase in the frequency of closed roads is very likely*

to have an impact on the fishing industry in Norway where immediate
transport of fresh fish to the European market is essential.[29]

The permafrost thaws

Making matters even worse is the speed with which the permafrost
– the layer of ice that runs deep, often very deep, underground – is
melting.[30] This is already having huge implications for every type
of building and structure that either relies on the permafrost for
structural support, or else has been designed and built to withstand extremely cold temperatures, but is quite unsuited for milder
conditions.

Throughout the Arctic region, almost every type of structure, ranging from houses and factories to bridges, dikes, erosion protection
structures, open pit mines, roads, airfields and pipelines, is at some
risk from the thawing of the permafrost. In Siberia, nearly 50 per
cent of all buildings are estimated to be in poor condition, and one
major oil-producing district, the Khanty-Mansi Autonomous Okrug,
had recorded 1,720 pipeline accidents and spillages in a single year,
contaminating 250 square miles of land. In Alaska, roads as well as
buildings are being badly affected, and the number of days when
temperatures are cold enough to allow the use of ice roads on the
fragile tundra has fallen to just 100 – half its previous figure – since
the early 1970s. And in the Canadian Arctic, international energy
companies are confronting the challenges that the permafrost is posing to the stability of oil and gas reservoirs: the three main fields of
the Mackenzie natural gas project – Parsons, Taglu and Niglintgak
– already lie close to sea level and the melting could be what one
expert simply calls 'a nightmare for engineers'.[31]

Designing new buildings that can cope with the thawing permafrost and trying to alleviate its impact on existing structures certainly
presents an enormous, and in all likelihood, very costly challenge.
As the *Arctic Climate Impact Assessment* puts it succinctly, the phe-
nomenon is 'very likely to change the probability of natural hazard
occurrences. This implies that criteria for the location and design of
infrastructure must be revised to keep risks at defined levels'.[32] In
particular, the permafrost is posing immense challenges to the design
and construction of the energy pipelines that will be built in the Arctic
region over the coming years, and green campaigners are generally
not convinced that there are nearly enough safeguards to prevent
environmental disaster.

Pipelines and the permafrost

On the morning of 2 March 2006, an oilfield worker was driving through a remote Alaskan wilderness, about 650 miles north of the state's biggest town, Anchorage, to make his routine daily inspection of a section of the Trans-Alaskan Pipeline System that runs from Prudhoe Bay, further north (Map 2). Over the preceding few years he had never noticed anything seriously out of the ordinary, but on this particular occasion he was hit by the unmistakably acrid stench of oil.

Almost immediately, the sheer scale of the leakage became apparent, for around 267,000 gallons of crude had escaped from a tiny crack in the pipeline caused by metal corrosion. Undetected for 5 whole days despite regular checks, this leakage had inflicted a devastating environmental blow, while also hammering the share price of the operator, BP, and edging up the global price of crude oil. 'I can confirm it's the largest spill of crude oil on the North Slope that we have record of', Linda Giguere, from Alaska's Department of Environmental Conservation, told one news agency. Environmentalists from the Alaska Wilderness League also said the spill was 'a catastrophe for the environment' and 'a painful reminder of the reality of unchecked oil and gas development across Alaska's North Slope'.

The prospect of a leaking oil or gas pipeline in the Arctic is a particularly appalling one. In such a remote region, days or even weeks could pass before any leakage is noticed, and even in a short space of time its impact on a wilderness area could be devastating. This is one reason why plans to build pipelines through Alaska, northern Canada and other Arctic regions have proved highly controversial.

Thawing permafrost poses different threats to oil and gas pipelines because the two substances are moved in quite different ways. Oil usually passes through pipelines at a relatively high temperature that reduces its viscosity and therefore makes it easier and quicker to pump. But natural gas is often pushed through pipelines at temperatures below freezing in order to increase its density.

The high temperature of piped oil can cause a serious engineering problem when a pipeline has been built below the ground surface, which is seen as a cheaper and more environmentally friendly option. In this scenario, the pipeline easily warms the surrounding soil, aggravating the effects of thawing permafrost and making the ground much less firm than before. So anything on top of the ground might collapse as a result, while the underground pipeline is at serious risk of being undermined, becoming distorted and eventually cracking.

Engineers are struggling to get round this problem in all sorts of ways. They have tried insulating the pipelines to prevent the warm oil from thawing the surrounding permafrost, but found this to be completely impractical. Another possible solution is to elevate the pipeline, supporting it above the surface on a special foundation that stops it from thawing the ground. This is very costly to undertake, but about half of the Trans-Alaska Pipeline System, which stretches 800 miles from Prudhoe Bay to the ice-free port of Valdez in southern Alaska, has been raised in this way. However, the problem with this approach is that the pipeline still ultimately relies on the permafrost layer for structural support, since it rests on a specially built foundation that is embedded in the soil. If the ground beneath starts to subside then the strain on the pipeline's metal will be considerable.

Experts have devised a way of burying the pipeline while chilling the oil to more or less the same temperature as the permafrost. So before it enters the Norman Wells Pipeline, which runs 550 miles through the western Canadian Arctic from the Northwest Territories to Alberta, the oil is initially chilled by a refrigeration system and then stays at these low temperatures as it makes its journey. This approach is not only just as expensive as the various alternatives but also carries just as many risks because, once again, the pipe trench is still dependent on the structure of the underlying permafrost. In some parts of the Norman Wells link, for example, the permafrost has thawed and as a result the pipe has moved, often much more than anyone expected.

Either way, the environmental challenges in the Arctic region are considerable, and they are likely to be a cause of serious tensions and disputes, mainly between governments, lobby groups and the general public, in the years ahead.

Part 3
The Contestants

9

Russia and the Arctic

The dramatic flag-planting ceremony that Sagalevich and Chilingarov conducted at the bottom of the Arctic Ocean in August 2007 seemed to express everything about Russia, or rather its foreign policy, which its critics most detest. From their viewpoint, Moscow should have been trying to abate international tension over the Arctic region, like any responsible government, but instead had carried out a reckless and provocative gesture that unnecessarily inflamed disagreements and controversies. The exercise, in other words, was viewed as being characteristic of a reckless and brutal country, one that would think little of using military force to make its claim in the Arctic, or in any other part of the world where it thinks its national interests are at stake.

During the summer of 2008, events in parts of the former Soviet Union reinforced this impression of a Russian government that has, in the words of one of its critics, 'a contemptuous disregard for Western norms' and even less concern for 'the suffering of civilians'.[1] In the early hours of 8 August, Russian tanks rolled southwards through the Roki Tunnel, storming their way not just through South Ossetia but well beyond, moving deep into the republic of Georgia. Within a matter of hours, Moscow's aircraft and artillery had started to pound several places, reportedly dropping cluster bombs in the very centre of the city of Gori and forcing tens of thousands of people to flee their homes.[2] Reports also filtered through that they had targeted a crucial oil pipeline, supplying Western Europe, and that Russian soldiers had been responsible for all manner of atrocities and outrages against innocent Georgian civilians.

By the time President Medvedev halted military operations on 12 August, Russia's image abroad, like parts of Georgia and South Ossetia, had been badly battered. In Oslo, for example, some politicians openly expressed fears that Norway was vulnerable to a Russian onslaught on a comparable scale. The leader of the conservative party,

Erna Solberg, saw the campaign as evidence of aspirations that could eventually pose a threat to Norwegian territory in the Arctic, while a member of Parliament, Per Ove Width, did 'not exclude the possibility of a direct attack on Norway' by a country 'that uses force first, diplomacy later'.[3] And a representative of the right-leaning progress party also told one newspaper that a conflict between Norway and Russia could develop as a result of disputes over fishing rights or the exploitation of oil and gas reserves.

Of course, the truth about what really happened in Georgia was much more complicated than it was often portrayed and perceived to be. Within a few months, Georgia's claims that it was acting defensively against unprovoked Russian aggression had been called into serious question by the accounts given by independent military observers.[4] And in the same way, accusations that the Russian government is particularly likely to cause trouble in the Arctic are just as ungrounded. Although incidents like the flag-planting ceremony can and already have fuelled international mistrust, thereby creating an atmosphere in which war could break out, it would not be in Russia's national interest to even risk conflict in the Arctic unless it really had to.

Russia does have a strong interest in the Arctic and has good reasons to carve out as much territory as it can from disputed areas and from the frozen area of high seas that lies in the far north. This is why it has long regarded the Arctic as a region of national concern. The Soviet scholar, Lakhtine, noted that Russian leaders had staked a claim there as early as 1821, when the Czar had issued a ukase (an imperial order) over the waters of the Bering Sea.[5] The strength of this interest partly reflects the fact that 20 per cent of the country lies above the Arctic Circle, which is home to almost 2 million Russian citizens, and it has six major rivers that feed the Arctic Ocean, while the seven other Arctic countries have just one or two. And if the North Pole is subdivided into 18 different segments that are then apportioned to each adjacent country on the basis of how much Arctic territory they own, then roughly eight of these segments would be assigned to Russia. But Canada would have only four and Denmark two, while Norway, Sweden, and the United States would merit just one each.

Russia is certainly watching developments in the Arctic closely because of the likely presence of oil and gas in the region. Speaking at a security council meeting in Moscow in September 2008, for example, President Medvedev emphasized the importance of the region's hydrocarbons: 'According to estimates by experts', he pointed out, 'the Arctic shelf may have about one quarter of the world's shelf hydrocarbon reserves, and the use of these reserves is a guarantee of Russia's overall energy security.' This means that the region 'has a strategic significance for our country' and 'resolving long-term tasks of developing the state, and its competitiveness on the global market, is directly tied to its development'. Medvedev urged speedy passage of a law to determine Russia's southern Arctic zone and added that the 'marking of the external border of the continental shelf is a long-term goal'. He continued by arguing that 'our first and main task is to turn the Arctic into a resource base for Russia in the twenty-first century (and) using these resources will guarantee energy security for Russia as a whole'.[6]

But although this makes the region very important and interesting to Moscow, it is not likely to be the cause of conflict. The most important single reason is that any new discoveries of oil or gas in the Arctic's High North, or even within Russia's existing national borders, would completely fail to solve the dilemmas that confront its energy industry. On the contrary, using force would make these dilemmas even more difficult to solve by scaring off foreign investors.

Russia's energy challenge

Russia does not stand in dire need of finding large-scale deposits of natural resources. Pumping out around 10 million barrels of oil every day and exporting around three-quarters of this amount, its output is currently surpassed only by Saudi Arabia. And it also has enormous untapped reserves, although estimates of the size of these deposits vary considerably. Analysts at BP estimate that it has around 80 billion barrels, giving it the world's seventh-biggest oil reserves, while a 2008 survey by the highly respected *Oil and Gas Journal* put the figure at closer to 60 billion barrels, most of which are located in Western Siberia, between the Ural Mountains and the Central Siberian Plateau. But many leading figures in the industry think that there could really be much more to unearth, perhaps as much as 100 billion more barrels, which would make it 'the biggest exploration prize in the world', in the words of Robert Dudley, the head of BP's joint venture with its Russian partner, TNK.[7]

Russia's problem is not the size of its existing reserves, but its ability to exploit them. It is true that for many years the dramatic, even stunning, rise of Russia's oil industry seemed to pay fitting testimony to the country's potential as a key global producer. Badly neglected during the political turmoil of the early 1990s, as the Soviet Union crumbled and fell apart, and then suffering badly from the depressed barrel price of the mid-1990s, the oil sector recovered sharply in 1999 and for the next few years its story was one of virtually unchecked growth. Companies like Yukos, Rozneft and Sibneft posted extraordinary profits and their share price soared as their pumps worked furiously hard to keep pace with the mounting strength of global demand.

However, by early 2008, things suddenly began to look less rosy for the Kremlin, even though the market price of crude oil was at this time starting to spiral to new heights. The business world was shaken in early April, when the International Energy Agency (IEA) announced that Russia's output had fallen for the first time in a decade. Having peaked in the first quarter of 2007, ran the IEA report, national production had started to tail off, already dipping slightly and looking likely to continue falling in the years ahead.

Even senior officials in Moscow had to admit that something was going seriously wrong. In an interview with an American newspaper, the president of Lukoil doubted whether output could continue to increase, while business analysts said that the growth experienced in recent years could 'no longer be taken for granted'.[8] Other officials, such as the natural resources minister, Yuri Trutnev, spoke even more directly. 'Two years ago, we said the growth rate was falling, and we said this was bad for Russia, remember?' he asked in televised remarks after a government meeting in Moscow. 'But now we're saying the production rate is falling this year. This is not a bogeyman, unfortunately, this is real.'[9]

Scarcely could any spectre haunt the Kremlin so chillingly as the threat of diminishing oil revenues. The energy sector accounts for half of Russia's national income and 65 per cent of its foreign exchange earnings, and any shortfall would devastate its economy. Without these earnings, the country would run short of the foreign currency that services its external debt and run low on the emergency reserves that it has used in recent years to form an emergency economic 'stabilization fund'. In short, Russia's drastic economic growth since the late 1990s has been built by oil at a time when the market price of crude was climbing, just as since late 2008 analysts have expected its economy to contract sharply as a result of the drastic fall in barrel price.

There are a number of reasons why this output is deteriorating, but chief among them is the fact that the Russian government has regulated the industry very poorly. Desperate to make as much as money as it can from its prize commodity, the government levies a punitively high export duty, taking more than half the proceeds of any barrel that fetches a market price of more than $25. When all the other charges are taken into account – a variety of corporate, payroll and production taxes – then industry insiders complain that the state is taking as much as 92 per cent of profits made by international ventures such as TNK-BP. So the output from TNK-BP's fields in Russia, for example, accounts for one-fifth of BP's overall global production, but only one-tenth of its profits, and its officials have long argued that the oil industry is confronted by rising costs that will make many investments in Russia quite unprofitable unless the tax regime is drastically changed.

The government does offer oil companies some limited tax breaks, but these have made things worse rather than better because they only apply to production from older fields, and this has given oil firms an incentive to concentrate on squeezing as much oil as they can out of wells that are already in a state of decline. For a time, this approach helped to pump up production levels, since some old fields that had fallen into ruin after the collapse of the Soviet Union were revived relatively easily and cheaply. Using new pumps, and applying some basic engineering techniques to increase the flow of oil, a number of private firms were able to raise Russia's production from 6 million barrels every day to almost 10 million, and output jumped by 12 per cent in 2003 alone. But by 2008 this short-term strategy had started to yield rapidly diminishing returns as these older fields reached their natural limit: the reservoirs in the two largest producing regions, at Khanty-Mansi Autonomous Okrug in the west of Siberia and in the Volga-Urals, which together account for about two-thirds of the country's overall production, were both showing signs of exhaustion.

Solving this energy challenge should be relatively simple for a country with such voluminous quantities of petroleum as Russia. What is needed is a huge input of foreign investment, skills and expertise to exploit new fields in remote provinces, such as eastern Siberia and the Sakhalin region, and offshore. Russian companies have always been able to pump out oil from their existing wells, just as they did so successfully in the 1980s, by which time most of their main producing fields were discovered. But they completely lack expertise in two crucial areas. One is making the most of existing fields, squeezing everything they can out of them by using the latest, highly sophisticated methods of enhanced 'tertiary' recovery. The other is offshore drilling, particularly in deep waters. In both cases, it is Western companies – oil majors like BP, Total, Statoil and ExxonMobil, as well as minor service organizations like Schlumberger and Halliburton – that lead the way.

If Russia is to maintain its output in the years ahead, then it will have to exploit new fields and employ foreign expertise to do so.

But this will mean investing far more money into the wells than it is accustomed to because new fields, particularly those that lie offshore, require much more sophisticated technology and higher investment, which drives up production costs. This, in turn, means that profit margins fall, which is all the more painful if the price of crude oil crashes to the lows it achieved in 1986, 1998 and the early months of 2009.

These profit margins are generally likely to be much lower if Russian oil companies are forced to enlist the support of their foreign counterparts, which of course need to claw back the huge costs associated with developing a new oilfield. Above all, Moscow fears exploitation because it lost out so badly in the 1990s. This was partly because the privatization of its oil industry created a number of fabulously wealthy oligarchs who moved their assets abroad instead of investing in new wells and technology. But it was also because at this time Western companies like Shell, ExxonMobil and Total signed 'production sharing agreements' to develop oil and gas fields that Russia now claims were totally unfair. In the eyes of the Russian authorities, these deals demonstrate how foreign, particularly Western, energy companies are likely to exploit them, even when they have been invited there to work.

But this hostility is not just about money and profit margins, but also about national pride and security. Most countries dislike having to admit that they are dependent on foreign expertise to exploit their own resources and this is why most producers – notably those of the Middle East – have their own national oil companies that try to compete with Western 'Big Oil'. 'Can you imagine a politician in France saying I need help from the UK because they have expertise', as the president of Total, Christophe de Margerie, has said.[10]

For a country that has felt so humiliated in recent years by its loss of status since the heyday of the Soviet Union, national prestige is a big consideration. But it is also about security: if the production of its key export is dependent on foreign sources of assistance, then Moscow would feel vulnerable to threats and blackmail in the event of any national emergency. This is one reason why, in April 2008, Moscow introduced a new law that places severe restrictions on the foreign ownership of any company that operates oil and gas fields, as well as any other site 'of federal significance'.

Acquiring more reserves in the Arctic, or anywhere else, would solve none of these underlying challenges that confront Russia's own oil industry. Russia does not lack reserves of oil but the ability to exploit them, and any resources in the High North would be even more difficult to exploit than many of those that it already has in its possession. The same is equally true of its natural gas.

Natural gas

Russia's natural gas sector is just as beset with challenges and just as likely to remain dependent on foreign expertise as its oil sector. The giant energy company Gazprom, which monopolizes natural gas production, is trying to increase its annual output by around 1 trillion cubic feet before the year 2011 but faces insuperable hurdles doing so because Russia's five largest producing fields are depleting rapidly and are expected to decline by nearly twice that figure over the same period of time.[11] Overall, the IEA reckons that Russia will need to invest 11 billion dollars every year until 2030 if it is to meet European demand. Without this investment its output is likely to continue to decline much more dramatically than it has in recent years.[12]

In the Arctic and beyond, Gazprom and other Russian companies are certainly doing their best to develop new fields on their own rather than admitting with a sense of humiliation that they have to rely on the outside world. So after completing a round of exploratory drilling in September 2006, Gazprom announced that it would exploit the massive Shtokman field on its own, unassisted by foreign companies, and that it will be able to get the field up and running by 2013–15. Extracting any of its gas has always looked a formidable task, since Shtokman lies a long way out in the Barents Sea and would present even the most sophisticated energy company with daunting engineering challenges. Many experts were not surprised when, less than a year later, Gazprom softened its position and announced that foreign companies would be allowed to participate after all, and would be rewarded not with a flat fee, but with a share in the profits.

Russia's other challenge is not just to keep producing natural gas at minimum cost but to keep it flowing to its customers at the most profitable price. Every producer of gas wants to achieve 'security of demand', keeping its customers happy so that they don't start looking around for alternative suppliers, while at the same time charging as much as they reasonably can from them. If they keep their customers, then gas producers not only have a guaranteed source of income but a form of strategic leverage as well. So for a country that is as obsessed with its national security as Russia, gas pipelines offer a very effective insurance policy against foreign attack: threaten us and you will freeze. This is why Moscow's official energy policy states that 'energy security is the most important element in Russia's national security'.[13]

Both of these considerations come into play in the context of Russia's dealings with neighbours in the former Soviet Union. Russia supplies these countries with natural gas but has imposed particularly dramatic price increases on the two states, Ukraine and Georgia, which have tried to challenge its influence and break out of its political orbit. So when in January 2006 Gazprom dramatically raised the price that Ukraine pays for gas, its 'market adjustment' coincided not just with parliamentary elections in Ukraine, but rather with the pursuit of a much more pro-Western foreign policy, including a publicly announced determination to join NATO, by President Victor Yushchenko. But at the same time Russia is very reluctant to cut off gas supplies to any consumer. Its brief interruption of exports to Ukraine, which also affected parts of Europe, proved counter-productive, as the British government looked further afield, notably to Norway and Algeria, for its supplies. Poland also considered building nuclear power plants and a natural gas terminal on the Baltic, while the European Commission drew up plans for a new energy 'supergrid' to protect Europe from Russian blackmail.[14]

Russia and the Arctic's natural resources

There are a number of reasons why the Russians should want to win control over the region's resources. Moscow might just want to stop anyone else from getting hold of the Arctic's oil and gas. Another country, they fear, might use its own more sophisticated technology and know-how to exploit the region's resources and then use the proceeds to dwarf Russia's own assets and conceivably even threaten it. The Russians, in any case, aren't sure when they will develop the skills to exploit the Arctic's natural assets: a decade or two hence it is quite possible that their own energy companies will have narrowed the technological gap and be able to exploit these newly discovered fields themselves with relative ease.

Moscow also knows that if it acquires new territory in a region that is considered to be so rich in natural resources then its bargaining power over foreign companies and governments will be dramatically enhanced. No one wants to argue over one issue, the Russian authorities might reason, if they could lose out over another. So BP or any other Western oil major won't want to create a fuss over the terms of their existing contracts in Russia if, at some future point, they might lose out when newly discovered Arctic reserves are eventually auctioned. So even if commercial quantities of oil or gas are never ultimately unearthed in the Arctic region, Russia can still use the mere prospect of their discovery to reward and threaten the outside world.

Using natural resources as a tool of foreign policy is far from uncommon: the Iranians, for example, are adept at using the lure of their own massive energy reserves in a similarly manipulative fashion.

This is just as true of natural gas as it is of oil because Moscow can use the Arctic's natural gas as a means of luring foreign investors: the Shtokman project has long presented a huge prize for international energy companies, such as Chevron and Total, that are anxious to 'book reserves' and please their shareholders at a time when they are being increasingly sidelined by smaller companies and national enterprises. But in the longer term the Arctic's natural gas might also give Russia a means of maintaining its commercial and strategic grip on its European customers. If another country, such as Norway, is able to stake a claim to these resources then key consumers of Russian gas, like Germany, France and Poland, would be able to diversify their supplies.

Another added advantage for the Russians is that Arctic gas could potentially be piped straight to these European consumers without going through any transit country, such as the Ukraine. This is always a huge disadvantage for both consumer and producer, partly because these third parties can charge lucrative fees that make the exporter less competitive, and also because any disagreement between the supplier and the transit country interrupts service to the consumer, just as the brief interruptions to Europe in January 2006 and 2009 were caused by a pricing dispute between Russia and the Ukraine. This is why Gazprom is so keen to construct a new pipeline, Nordstream, which would move Russian gas to Western Europe not overland but across the Baltic Sea.

A conflict over resources?

Nonetheless, if Russia does succeed in carving out a stake in the Arctic's High North and then claiming any natural resources as its own, then its new prize would completely fail to meet the challenges that confront its energy sector. The country does not currently lack the large reserves that the Arctic might perhaps have to offer. But it does totally lack the skills and expertise to extract oil and gas from its existing offshore wells and would also be highly dependent on foreign oil companies to develop any large-scale discoveries in the Arctic region and elsewhere. Acquiring more resources in the Arctic or anywhere else would not necessarily take Russia any further forward than it stands at present.

Above all, although Russia has good reason to want to involve itself in this energy rich area and to claim as much territory as it can, it is most unlikely to want to risk any confrontation. For like almost any other country, it is only likely to enter into a conflict when it really has to. If it genuinely fears an imminent attack by a foreign power, for example, then Moscow would have little choice but to defend itself. But the prospect of acquiring natural resources in disputed parts of the Arctic would certainly not fall into this category simply because Russia's material losses would far outweigh what it could reasonably hope or expect to gain.[15] Even in narrowly military terms, the Kremlin would have to assume that its losses would be considerable and its victory in the field, even against vastly outnumbered enemies, is far from guaranteed. In January 2009, a leading organization, the London-based Institute of Strategic Studies, argued that Russia's armed forces were essentially a 'paper tiger', whose 'shortcomings' were badly exposed by the campaign in Georgia even if some national pride had been restored.[16] In the words of one much respected commentator, this is one reason why 'Russia, contrary to all the feverish talk about its presumed status as a revived superpower, is nothing of the kind'.[17]

Moscow would also forfeit the confidence of desperately needed foreign direct investment, destroying both its wider economy as well as its energy sector in particular. All foreign investors want to put their money down in a stable environment where their initial investment and its returns are relatively safe from any economic calamity that will undermine its value, or from a corrupt and extortionate regime that might take more than its fair share. If there are any such risks lurking in the background, then investors either demand the promise of higher rewards, such as a more generous rate of interest, to compensate or else pull their money out altogether and look elsewhere.

The Russian economy reached a low point in the summer of 1998 when the government effectively became bankrupt, running out of foreign currency and defaulting on its foreign debt repayments. But recovery followed as oil prices rose and by 2005 the major international credit agencies were sufficiently impressed to upgrade Russia's credit rating to investment grade on the basis of its stable economic performance. As a result, foreign banks soon began to lend there quite freely.

It is just such a stable economic environment that Moscow would destroy if it entered into any foreign war unnecessarily. Foreign investors would take immediate flight and it might conceivably take Russia years to rebuild their confidence in the country. In August 2008, Russia's military foray into Georgia had disastrous economic consequences that will make the Kremlin very wary of any repetition. On 8 August, the day of the attack, the stock market in Moscow plunged by nearly 7 per cent, and within a week capital outflow reached a massive $16 billion, suddenly squeezing domestic credit while the rouble plunged. This trauma was soon considerably aggravated by a wider credit crisis that swept the entire developed world, but the war in Georgia certainly shook investors' nerves badly and confirmed all their worst fears. Such intense economic pressures prompted Moscow to try and patch up relations with Washington in early 2009: 'Militarization does not solve problems', as Vladimir Putin told the World Economic Forum in Davos in January 2009.

Of course every country is fearful of the economic fallout of war, but Russia has more reason than most to worry about alienating foreign investors. This is partly because any conflict would reinforce the existing impression that Russia is a rather risky place in which to put money. This impression has already been fostered by a number of other events in recent years. For example, the government has become more intolerant of domestic criticism than at any time since the days of the Soviet Union, a trend that was most obviously exemplified by the murders of the journalist Anna Politkovskaya and the dissident Alexander Litvinenko, or the drafting of a new law, in December 2008, that expands the definition of treason to include critics of the state.[18] In the summer of 2008, it seemed that the whims of a political leader can be more important than any legal institution when Prime Minister Putin made mildly threatening remarks about a steel company, whose share price immediately plummeted.[19]

The Russian authorities can be forgiven if the prospect of any sudden exodus by foreign investors makes them sweat profusely. For this is a country where memories of severe economic crisis are still bitter and recent, and where another similar downturn might push an unforgiving general public too far. The economy reached its nadir during the financial meltdown of 1998, when the government devalued the rouble and in doing so wiped out the life savings of millions of ordinary Russians. But the spectre of not just another economic crisis but a further devaluation would haunt everyone if investors flee the country. At the end of 2008, the rouble dived in value partly because foreign investors were dumping their Russian holdings. The authorities in Moscow were spending the country's foreign reserves to buy up roubles and support the currency's value, but were fast running out of spare money.[20] If this happens, then they would have no option but to let the rouble fall in value, bringing back bitter memories of August 1998 and perhaps forcing the architects of this devaluation to commit political suicide: Vladimir Putin, who became Russia's Prime Minister in 2008, has staked his reputation on avoiding a sharp depreciation of the currency.[21]

The Russians have good reason to fear the exodus of foreign investors not just in their wider economy, but also in their energy sector in particular. This is partly because their own energy companies have built up massive debts, largely by lavish spending on new pipelines and railway links, and therefore need support and cooperation from foreign banks that can help sustain them. For example, in October 2008, the state oil company Rozneft had debts of around \$21 billion, and as the global credit crunch took hold, its creditors suddenly demanded repayment.[22]

It is also because, as the case of the Shtokman field illustrates, they lack the skills, technology and expertise to develop many new fields and to make the most of their existing ones, and they cannot afford to alienate the international companies that can help them to do so. This is why Gazprom has established joint ventures with foreign partners to develop not just Shtokman, but also the South Stream natural gas pipeline to link Southern Europe with Caspian supplies. Oil and natural gas are so vital to the Russian economy that Moscow cannot afford to put future supplies at risk. If output drops then the Russian economy would be starved of foreign exchange and faced with a perhaps unsustainable budget deficit. This was the dire situation that Russia faced at the end of 2008 when its international credit rating was suddenly downgraded by analysts who were scared off by its economic plight.[23]

It is not just the wrath of the markets that Russia would fear in the event of any war, particularly one that it is judged to be guilty of starting. Moscow could also be starved of foreign investment if the United States and the EU impose targeted sanctions not through the UN Security Council (Russia is a permanent member and would probably have Chinese support to veto any such move) but as a unilateral effort. International energy companies such as BP, Shell and Total have shied away from investing in Iranian or Syrian natural resources because Washington has threatened economic retaliation, and the United States could effectively threaten Moscow with similar draconian penalties. In practice, the United States government might be very reluctant to impose such measures, partly because Moscow could threaten its own retaliation – by building closer ties with China, for example – and because American companies could potentially earn huge profits from any involvement there. But the mere threat of any such move would nonetheless be a powerful one. In any event, the

Russians could also be penalized in all sorts of other ways: Moscow's long-held ambition to join the World Trade Organization, for example, has been blocked by the United States since the mid-1990s, but would become even more surreal in the event of any future conflict or confrontation over the Arctic.

This is not to say that Russia's behaviour in the Arctic, or elsewhere, has always been as cautious as this line of economic argument might suggest. On the contrary, the flag-waving expedition to the North Pole in August 2007 or the flights of its warplanes close to the airspace of neighbouring states have all been just as provocative as the flag-waving missions undertaken by Canada and Denmark in Hans Island or the journeys of NATO submarines around the Russian coasts during the Cold War.[24] But to the Russians such actions are quite consistent with an essentially peaceful and peace-loving approach, just as their draconian laws and taxes are seen to be perfectly consistent with their efforts to lure foreign investors. These seemingly contradictory impulses need to be seen in the light of the traditions of a country that is both an inseparable part of the outside world but at the same time quite separated. The Russian mind, as its great biographer once wrote, is torn between recognizing its dependence upon the outside world on the one hand and feeling a world apart on the other.[25]

Far from being an ominous sign of hostile intent, it is in any case much more likely that Moscow has undertaken some of its seemingly provocative actions at least as much to impress domestic audiences as to send a signal to the watching world. For example, the flag-planting expedition to the seabed of the Arctic Ocean took place just seven months before the Russian presidential election, which was held in March 2008. President Putin was doubtlessly well aware that the expedition would allow him to play a nationalistic card that would help rally the Russian people behind him and make a big difference to the electoral chances of his preferred successor, Dmitri Medvedev.

The true risk of conflict in the Arctic region is really very different. For the strength of Russia's strategic interest is much more likely to provoke Moscow into a confrontation over the region than the presence of natural resources such as oil and gas, if they are there in any meaningful quantities at all.

Russian national security

Invaded three times by Western powers in the space of less than 150 years, with many millions of its citizens dead as a result, Russia is arguably one of the most peace-loving nations in the world. But it is also one of the most fearful, harbouring immense mistrust of any foreign power that might potentially pose a threat to its national security.

Fear of naval attack

In the eyes of Russian strategists, the retreat of the Arctic's ice potentially offers a would-be aggressor a gateway through which to attack. American or Chinese warships could hypothetically launch an assault in the east, through the Bering Strait, or from the west, using bases in Greenland, Iceland and Norway to sail towards the Russian mainland through seas that have historically always been thick with pack ice. A worst-case scenario would be a multiple simultaneous attack from several directions, something that the Russians have feared for centuries. These assaults could come from the west, in the same spirit as Napoleon, Tsar William and Hitler; from the east, following the same path that the Mongol-ruled Tatar cavalry hordes had taken around the year 1240, devastating the country and subjecting it to their overlordship until roughly 1480; and through central Asia in the south, where the forces of the once mighty Ottoman Empire had for centuries posed a dire threat.[26]

The strength of these fears emerged during the Cold War. Soviet military experts were convinced that the Bering Strait was vitally important because 'strategists from the Pentagon have always considered Alaska, which lies in the Soviet Union's immediate vicinity, to be an important staging area for launching aggression in this region . . . [it is] the Gibraltar, the eyes and the ears of the Arctic'.[27] Other analysts warned that 'the control of straits and strait zones enables naval forces to manoeuvre rapidly between theatres, and to interdict the movement of [enemy] . . . ships to other areas of sea or ocean'. Their warnings prompted the Kremlin to draw up contingency plans to mine the Bering Strait and the Canadian archipelago in the event of any war with NATO.[28]

There have also been a few occasions when the worst fears of Russian strategists even seemed to be realized. During the political turbulence that followed the revolution of 1917, for example, a number of foreign countries undertook expeditions through the Bering Strait as if to take advantage of the ensuing chaos. In 1924, a team from the United States travelled to the Chukchi Peninsula and put up a sign that seemed to claim part of the region as sovereign American soil.[29] Since then there have also been disputes between Russia and the United States over some of the islands that lie further along the Russian coast. While the British and Canadian governments

both dropped their territorial claims over Wrangel Island in the East
Siberian Sea long ago, in recent years some American press commentators, and even some politicians, have openly urged the United
States government to reactivate old claims not only to this but also
to a number of other islands along the shores of northern Russia,
including Herald, Jeannette and Bennett Islands. All of these were
discovered and formally taken into possession by the United States,
which did not formally surrender its right to them – even if that right
was never pressed – until a maritime boundary agreement was struck
with Russia in 1990.[30] The mere possibility that the United States
had any legal right to press over islands in these seas can only have
inflamed Russia's historic fears of foreign attack.

The Kremlin was equally concerned about the possibility of a
NATO assault from the west. During the Second World War the
Germans had tried and very nearly succeeded in cutting off the Baltic
sea lanes and Allied shipping that sustained the Russian war effort: in
1942, despite the immense difficulty of sailing into ice-laden seas, the
German ship, *Admiral Scheer*, even managed to sail into the Kara Sea
and succeeded in sinking the Russian icebreaker, Sibiryakov. Moscow
was later convinced that its Cold War enemies would prioritize the
elimination of its fleet and attack its northern coasts. Russian plan-
ners always responded quickly to match NATO's efforts to build up
its naval presence in the northern Atlantic and the Norwegian seas,
and in the event of war would probably have tried their utmost to
seize the Svalbard islands on the pretext that the United States had
already broken the ninth article of the Spitsbergen Treaty, which
guarantees the demilitarization of the archipelago.[31] Svalbard would
be particularly important to the Kremlin's defensive strategy because
its possession would allow the Russians to attack any regional enemy
from behind.

One place that both Russian and American strategists are likely
to emphasize in the coming years is Greenland. The east coast of this
vast land mass would make a very convenient staging post both for
any would-be attacker against the Russian mainland and also for a
Russian navy seeking to dominate the northern Atlantic. During the
Cold War Soviet commanders wanted to set up military installations
at the Station Nord runway on the east coast of Greenland in order to
establish an extended protective zone over the Kola Peninsula, where
many important military installations are still based. Its importance
can also be measured by an offer that the Kremlin made to NATO
in 1987: we'll discontinue work on a major radar system in central
Asia, said the Russians, if you agree not to modernize the ballistic

early warning system that is based at the vast American air station at Thule.[32]

Much closer to home is another area that will be a source of particular concern for Russian strategists in the coming years. These are the waters that stretch along its northern shores, through which international shipping may have a right to cross unimpeded. During the Cold War, American submarines sometimes moved into these waters illicitly, carrying out daring intelligence missions during which they penetrated the Sea of Okhotsk and even entered the harbour at Vladivostok. But it is possible that as the ice continues to retreat, maritime traffic will have a right to cross the entire Northern Sea Route. Moscow has always regarded this as a national transport route running, in part, through 'internal waters' that are fully under Russian control and jurisdiction. But other countries could still claim that, like the Northwest Passage, it is really 'an international strait' through which they therefore have a right of 'transit passage', even though this would barely be plausible for the obvious reason that the route has hardly even been previously 'used'.[33] More importantly, they could argue that they have a right of 'innocent passage' through Russia's economic zone as well as freedom of navigation over the high seas that lie beyond. During the Cold War, Moscow implicitly recognized the high seas status of the Kara, Laptev, East Siberian and Chukchi Seas and could not stop foreign ships from moving freely though their waters.

But besides opening up a path towards Russia that a future aggressor can follow, the melting of the Arctic's ice will also offer Moscow some strategic benefits.

Accessibility

On 11 October 1904, a ragbag fleet of 42 ships set sail from the port at Reval in the Baltic Sea. Led by Rear Admiral Zinovi Rozhdestvensky, the 12,000 crew members knew how arduous the forthcoming few months would prove to be as they made their way halfway around the world to engage an enemy whose audacity, speed and fighting skills had taken their fellow Russians in the Far East by complete surprise.

Almost exactly as Rozhdestvensky had planned, it was not until the following summer, after more than 7 months of constant sailing in often atrocious conditions, that he and his men finally caught sight of the Japanese fleet, which launched a devastating onslaught against them on 27 May. The scale of the Russian defeat was perhaps hardly surprising given the distances they had sailed, for they had completed a gruelling 21,000-mile journey that had taken them around the east coast of Africa and the Cape of Good Hope, across the Indian Ocean and then the South China Sea. Another, smaller force led by Admiral Felkerzam had taken a shorter route through the Suez Canal, but even that journey was still lengthy and arduous, exhausting the crew while giving Admiral Togo's fleet ample time to prepare for battle.[34]

It is easy to see why successive rulers of Russia have long been haunted by nightmares about their national security. Most obviously, the country is such a vast landmass that moving men and materials in time of war presents a virtually insurmountable logistical challenge: the distance from St Petersburg to the Far Eastern port of Vladivostok is 6,500 miles, one that covers 11 time zones. But what makes the challenge of defending Russia's Far Eastern territories so much more daunting is not just the distance involved but their accessibility. True, the Russian government had constructed a trans-Siberian railway in the mid-nineteenth century along which a steady stream of soldiers and supplies could flow. But these supplies did not help reinforce the Pacific fleet if it was outnumbered, outgunned or, as in the case of the Russo-Japanese war, completely annihilated. In this scenario, a relief column like the one led by Admiral Rozhdestvensky in 1904–05, would have to undertake, and survive, a long and arduous trek that took them halfway round the world. This was for the simple reason that a much shorter and more direct journey, along the Northern Sea Route, through the Barents Strait and Sea and then southwards into the Sea of Japan, was blocked by ice for most of the year.

In an age of long-range missiles and warplanes, it is of course questionable that moving a fleet from one part of the world to another is of more than peripheral importance. But in the light of such bitter tragedies and national traumas, such as the annihilation of Rozhdestvensky's Baltic Fleet, it is easy to understand why Russian strategists might assign so much importance to the melting of the Arctic's ice. For the opening up of a sea route along its northern coasts and through the Bering Strait makes their Far Eastern territories much easier to defend, just as one of the first goals of a national enemy, in the event of any future war, would be to try and close it off. After the war, in 1905, the Russians started to explore the possibility of establishing a maritime route along their northern coasts and sent out more scientific expeditions to determine the viability: in 1914–15 the explorer Vilkitsky crossed the entire Northeast Passage for the first time, making important hydrographical findings, while at the same time the Russian government built a number of radio-telegraph stations along the way.[35] This was also why, during the Cold War, Soviet naval strategists emphasized that 'since warfare of the future . . . may take on a global scope, various types of naval forces will need to manoeuvre between ocean theatres of military action. The role of straits such as the Bering Sea, the Drake Passage, the straits of the Canadian archipelago and others which have almost never before been utilized in maritime warfare will then be considerably enhanced'.[36]

The true importance of the Arctic Bridge to Russian strategists becomes fully clear in the light of such historic fears. By contrast, relying on the Suez Canal is much more risky. It is not only longer but also highly vulnerable to disruption: the closure of the canal after the Six-Day War in 1967, for example, forced Soviet supplies to North Vietnam to take the long route around Africa. The alternative journey along its northern coasts must now seem all the more important to Moscow at a time when China's economic and political strength has grown so dramatically and its government has started to assert itself on the world stage so emphatically.

These historic fears explain why the Russians are now not only closely monitoring ice levels in the region, gauging how navigable these routes are, but also sending signals to other powers, most obviously the United States, to respect their national interests there. So one of the places that Russian planes fly provocatively close to, 'buzzing' local air defences, is the Bering Strait.[37] The significance of this area emerged in August 2007, when President Putin proclaimed that this old Cold War practice was resuming and the Kremlin announced that 12 strategic bombers, all giant Tupolev 95 aircraft, would practise firing cruise missiles during a show-of-strength exercise over the Arctic. Revealingly, some of the bombers took off in the vicinity of the Bering Strait and then encircled the region, as if warning Washington and Ottawa to respect Russia's interest in the region rather than building up their military presence close to hand.

Russia's traditional fears of foreign attack help to explain not only its interest in developing a Northern Sea Route, while proclaiming it to be 'situated within its inland seas, territorial sea or exclusive economic zone', and warning other powers to keep their distance, but also in carving out new territories in the Arctic region.[38] If Moscow can prove that its continental shelf extends beyond the 200-mile limit of its existing economic zone, then it can stake its claim over an area that, at some future point, another country, perhaps hostile to Russia, might be able to illicitly seize for itself. This would realize the worst fears of Kremlin strategists, who in this situation would have yet another frontline – a northern naval front – with which to contend.

The depth of these strategic concerns became clear from an editorial that was written in *Pravda* in 2005:

> *It has recently transpired that the US administration plans to launch an extensive invasion in the Arctic region . . . the USA particularly plans to build airbases in Alaska while US oil giants intend to develop the Arctic shelf. To mask the intrusion and make it look like a peaceful initiative, the USA would be ready to render humanitarian assistance to Russia to improve the living standard of "the impoverished northern nations of Russia" . . . it is obvious that the development of the USA's new objective in the Arctic region will be conducted within the scope of the nation's ambition to dominate the world. This intention is officially registered in the US National Security Strategy. The document entitles Washington to possess all necessary resources to influence the situation in all key regions of the globe. The Arctic has become one of such regions.*[39]

And when in January 2009, NATO released a short report on the Arctic, the Russian newspaper *Rossiiskaya Gazeta* claimed that the region was all set to become the setting for Western military adventurism. 'It is clear that without the military component, the foreign policy strategy of the alliance will not succeed', as journalist Yevgeney Shestakov wrote. 'If it does not happen now, it will definitely happen in the near future.'[40]

A danger of conflict

Serious diplomatic tensions could arise if foreign ships try to exercise their 'right of innocent passage' by moving unescorted and without Moscow's permission through seas that Russia has long regarded as its own 'internal waters'. Given their strategic importance to Moscow, the melting of the Arctic's waters could create a danger of conflict if vessels also sail through areas of high seas, or Russia's territorial sea and exclusive economic zones, at a time or in a way that fuels mistrust between capitals, convincing the Kremlin that it faces an imminent assault and prompting it to launch a pre-emptive attack.[41]

If NATO warships had made their way through Russia's territorial sea and along the Northern Sea Route during the Cuban Missile Crisis in 1962, then the Kremlin could easily have assumed the worst. Perhaps the most extreme Cold War example of the consequences of such mistrust is the nuclear catastrophe that nearly took place in November 1983, when Soviet chiefs became convinced that NATO was about to launch an attack on the Warsaw Pact and stood on the very verge of pressing the button.

There are at least two different interpretations of the 1982 Convention that might come into conflict. The Russians could argue that if any ship moves through the 'territorial seas' that surround its coastline then they are entitled to have prior notice. This was one argument pitched by Moscow in 1965, when the American ship, *Northwind*, tried to make its way through the Vilkitsy Strait, which is less than 24 miles across at its narrowest point and therefore forces a ship to pass within 'territorial sea', which extends up to 12 miles from the coast.[42] Under Article 234 of the 1982 Convention, which currently gives all of the 'Arctic Five' stronger powers over any ships passing 'within the limits of the exclusive economic zone', this would be a very valid claim. But if the ice continues to retreat along the Northern Sea Route, then it would not be covered by this article, which only applies to 'ice-covered areas'.[43] But the Russians could also claim that the Northern Sea Route sometimes traverses its 'internal waters' and they are therefore entitled to bar foreign ships from passing altogether if they so wish.

If Moscow does win its legal battle to declare some of these seas as its own 'internal waters', then Washington might try to counter argue that they were previously 'used for international navigation', as the 1982 Convention demands, and are therefore a 'strait' through which foreign ships have a right of 'transit passage'.[44] This would really have a very dubious, probably non-existent, legal basis, but it is possible to imagine a United States administration with unilateralist leanings taking its own independent view. In such a hypothetical scenario, Washington lawyers could perhaps point to a number of missions that American submarines made to the region during the Cold War. Some of these journeys were made secretly while others were quite open. The USS *Queenfish*, for example, was sent to the Siberian continental shelf in 1970 to test satellite navigation in shallow waters, while other scientific experiments were conducted under the ice of the Chuckchi Sea in 1958.[45] Since starting a special research programme in 1951, the United States also despatched manned drifting stations to 'navigate' the Arctic.[46]

Other risks could include American attempts to use submarines to test Russian defences, or to gather other intelligence. It is possible that, during the Cold War, both the USS *Skate* and *Nautilus* made their way through Soviet waters en route to and from the North Pole to undertake missions like these. (Details of their precise paths have never been released.) Decades on, the Russians certainly remain highly sensitive about the security of some of their northern shipyards, and sometimes still accuse foreign intelligence services of trying to infiltrate them.[47]

There could also be strong disagreements, or misunderstandings, between Russia and other countries over what constitutes a 'warship', whose innocent passage through areas of Russia's territorial sea has long been disputed by Moscow. The passage of the *Edisto*, *Eastwind* and *Northwind* along the Northern Sea Route was made all the more controversial because, under Soviet domestic law, icebreakers were classified as warships.[48] In the same way, the heightened presence of Russian ships traversing the Bering Strait and making their way through the Canadian archipelago to guard their borders in the Far East could seriously alarm the Americans, convincing Washington that Russia has some agenda to dominate this strategically vital and resource-rich area.

Environmental controversies

Besides the region's strategic importance and natural resources, another source of tension between Russia and the outside world over the Arctic is likely to be its treatment of the environment. In the years ahead Moscow is likely to exchange bitter words not just with other governments but also with pressure groups, non-governmental organizations and public opinion.

Of the eight Arctic countries, Russia has by far the worst environmental record. Pressure groups like Greenpeace point to its particularly dire legacy in the Barents and Kara Seas, both of which were once among the world's cleanest and most undisturbed waters, boasting a very large number of seabirds, bountiful fisheries and communities of diverse and rare marine mammals. But over the past few decades, the Barents Sea, in particular, has been used as an unofficial dumping group for the spent fuel of the nuclear-powered vessels of the Northern Fleet, while anything left over has been put into storage facilities that are completely inadequate for the task.

Anyone who visits Andreeva Bay, which lies halfway between the Russian town of Severomorsk and the Norwegian border, can see at first hand just how much damage this practice has inflicted. This is the site of a huge nuclear waste facility where in recent years tons of highly radioactive waste with large amounts of uranium have been slowly leaking out of the crumbling concrete bunkers and the rusting containers that are supposed to keep it safe and secure. In recent years the local fish population has been virtually killed off by radioactive leaks, while on the mainland both the soil and the groundwater are also badly contaminated. Nobody, not even the officials in charge, suggests that the site is safe. 'The current storage facilities are in poor condition', as a local official told the BBC.[49] Not surprisingly, this situation has shocked and enraged both local people and pressure groups. 'This is the biggest environmental threat facing the Murmansk region today', as Andrei Zolotkov, director of a local green group, Bellona, has said. 'The amount of radioactivity is equivalent to 93 submarine reactors or comparable with Chernobyl.'

Environmentalists are worried that, as Russia steps up its efforts to exploit the Arctic's natural resources, the Barents Sea will be at particular risk of suffering damage on a far greater scale. This is because it is already being used as a corridor through which oil and gas from western Siberia and the Timan-Pechora Basin are being moved, and as new fields come on stream, so too will tanker traffic, and the risk of an accident in the Barents Sea increases proportionately. In 2004, some 12 million tons of oil were shipped from northwest Russia through the Arctic waters of the Barents Sea and down towards Europe along the Norwegian coastline. Such cargo is expected to increase dramatically and by 2010 could amount to as much as 200 million tons every year. 'Several years ago you would hardly see a Russian tanker passing our coast', recalls Ole Berglund, a fisherman from Norway's Lofoten Islands, an archipelago that lies north of the Arctic Circle. 'Now you can spot them daily, heading to markets in Europe and North America.'[50]

In particular, lobby groups regard the newly constructed oil export terminal near Varandey, which opened in the summer of 2008, as a possible threat to the Arctic environment. Located 15 miles off the coast, it can handle around a quarter-million barrels every day and will eventually be connected to land-based facilities by a pipeline that would cause a massive spillage in the event of any accident. Other proposals are causing just as much alarm, including plans to build a liquefied gas plant and an oil export terminal in the Murmansk region, on the coast of the Barents Sea, that would handle between 2 and 3 million barrels of oil every day. In early 2009, the feasibility of both of these proposals was being closely considered.

Lobby groups argue that the number and gravity of spillages in the region has been seriously underreported. 'The oil industry's claim that it can prevent any negative environmental impact from their activities is false', says one campaigner. 'Since 1990 there have been more than 2,500 acute oil spills on the Norwegian shelf. Searching, drilling and transporting oil is inherently risky and the consequences for people and nature are likely to be disastrous.'[51]

It is possible that Russia will defuse international criticism of its environmental record by working more closely with some of the organizations that have been set up in recent years to promote dialogue and cooperation. The Barents Euro-Arctic Council, for example, was established in 1993 as a venue where its members – Denmark, Finland, Iceland, Norway, Russia, Sweden and the European Commission – could meet to discuss precisely these ends. An associated body, the Barents Regional Council, has even more members, which include representatives of three indigenous peoples, the Sami, the Nenets and the Vespians. Both organizations are concerned, in different ways, with protecting the environment, and strive to bring their various members together to achieve this end. In the late summer of 2008, the Russians drew up plans in conjunction with these organizations to hold a large-scale exercise to rehearse the impact of any major oil spillage in the region.[52]

10

America's Arctic Destiny?

In the summer of 2004, residents of a tiny Inuit village in a remote part of Greenland began to notice signs of imminent developments at a nearby air base, located a few miles away. There was more traffic than usual, both within the perimeter and along the roads outside, and security was suddenly being beefed up, as if in preparation for some special event. Among the 60 or so residents of Igaliku, rumours quickly began to spread that some high-level visitor was about to fly in.

The rumours added an even stronger sense of mystery to a place that is, by any standards, supremely intriguing. Located in a wilderness region in the far north-west of the island, the giant air base at Thule has always been closely guarded (and the subject of constant speculation) ever since the Americans had moved into the area in 1953, giving local Inuits just a few weeks' notice to leave their traditional lands and resettle elsewhere. In the intervening years, it had been at the frontline of the Cold War and the setting for numerous top-secret flights and deployments that the Danish, Greenlandic and American authorities had always done their best to hush up. For example, there were numerous allegations of a cover-up when, in January 1968, a B52 bomber carrying four nuclear weapons had crashed a short distance away, creating a big explosion that fragmented the nuclear payload and spread plutonium all over the surrounding ice. Officially there were supposed to be no nuclear weapons at Thule, but the Danish Prime Minister had probably been secretly informed by Washington and then tried to stop Parliament from finding out.

In those summer weeks of 2004, the suspicions of local people were confirmed when, on 6 August, the American Secretary of State, Colin Powell, flew in from Washington and met the Danish Foreign Minister, Per Stig Moeller, to sign a new deal about the base's future. Under the agreement, the radar installations at Thule air base would

164

be upgraded so that the site could, at some future moment, play a key role in Washington's New Missile Defense System – better known as 'the Son of Star Wars'– that would allow the Americans to track incoming ballistic missiles with an advanced radar system and then use sea-based interceptors to destroy them. The Danish and Greenlandic authorities had still not given Washington permission to deploy missile interceptors there, but for the moment they were prepared to take things a stage further forward and let the United States military upgrade its installations.

From a strategic point of view, it is easy to see why Washington has long been so keen to maintain a military presence at Thule and today remains committed to retaining and upgrading it. This is partly because, in the eyes of United States strategists, Greenland appears perilously close to their own shores, and if it fell into the clutches of a hostile power then it could be used as a staging post for attacks on the American mainland and, crucially, on Atlantic shipping. This was why, during the Second World War, President Roosevelt struck an agreement with the exiled Danish government 'to assist Greenland in the maintenance of its present status'. Washington would have a right to establish a military presence on its territory, ran this 1941 agreement, because 'defense of Greenland against attack by a non-American power is essential to the preservation of the peace and security of the American Continent and is a subject of vital concern to the United States of America'.[1]

During the Cold War, Pentagon strategists were also quick to realize that, in the event of any conflict, the quickest route for their long-range bombers to reach Moscow and other targets in the northern Soviet Union was to fly straight over the North Pole, and that Thule lies at the exact halfway point. So in 1951 a further deal was signed between the United States and Denmark that gave Washington a right to 'make use of facilities in Greenland' and 'take necessary and appropriate measures' on behalf of the newly formed North Atlantic Treaty Organization. And more than half a century later, the island retains this crucial strategic role for the United States: in the words of John Holum, the Undersecretary of State for Arms Control and International Security Affairs in the Clinton administration, 'the Thule Radar is very important to the New Missile Defense System, to warn and track. It is our eyes and ears. The radar will track missiles, for instance, from Iraq and the Middle East'.[2]

For many local people, America's strong interest and presence in Greenland has long been ominous. Aqqaluk Lynge, the head of the Inuit Circumpolar Council, is concerned that, if or when Greenland

eventually becomes independent from Denmark, it will become a
tempting target for Washington. 'We are afraid that the United States
will take over Greenland if the Danes get out', he told one journalist.
'If Americans can take Iraq, then why not Greenland?'[3] Lynge also
points out that the United States did not hesitate to push local people
aside at Thule in the early 1950s when it decided that its own national
interests were at stake. 'The existing military infrastructure in our
Inuit homeland was installed during the Cold War without consulting
Inuit', he says, 'because both former superpowers treated the Arctic as
an uninhabited wasteland, and without recognizing that we actively
use and occupy this land.'[4]

The controversy surrounding Thule exemplifies a much bigger
issue, one that affects the entire Arctic. For there are huge swathes of
this wider region that the United States regards as its own backyard
and where it could regard the deployment of military force as a
legitimate means of pursuing its national interest. These aggressive
tactics might perhaps reflect an interest in the region's untapped
natural resources at a time when fears about future shortages are
growing, but they are much more likely to be based on strategic
considerations: if the United States does not step up its presence
there, American strategists might argue, then another country, such
as China or Russia, probably will.

Some scenarios

There are several scenarios in which the United States could become
embroiled in serious political, and conceivably military, confrontations with other countries over the Arctic region.

The most likely scenario is that Washington could argue that its
continental shelf extends beyond the 200-mile limit of its economic
zone and reaches for up to another 150 miles into the Arctic Ocean
towards the North Pole. In order to make this claim, the United States
would first of all need to become a signatory member of the 1982
Convention and would then have a 10-year period in which to collect
geological data and formally submit a case to the UN Commission on
the Limits of the Continental Shelf. But if the American government
does eventually pursue this course and then finds that its submission
is rejected, then it is possible to imagine it blatantly disregarding any
such ruling and perhaps making its own unilateral declaration of
ownership over the region. Because no other country would have any
formal claim over the same stretch of 'high seas', which lie so close to
its existing territorial waters, Washington might calculate that such
a move would arouse only limited protest.

A politically more risky and controversial move would be to stake a claim over an area of 'high seas' that neither America nor any other country could legally claim as its own because it falls beyond the maximum 350-mile limit of their outer continental shelves. So there is one large stretch of the Arctic Ocean that is currently due to be administered by the International Seabed Authority (ISA) because it is classified, under the 1982 Convention, as part of 'the Area' that lies 'beyond the limits of national jurisdiction'.[5]

Much more audacious, however, would be for the United States to make some unilateral declaration of ownership over waters that another country has unsuccessfully claimed form part of its own outer continental shelf, having found its advances spurned by the United Nations Commission. In 2001, Russia unsuccessfully claimed that its continental shelf reached beyond the 200-mile limit and was told to resubmit its bid with more convincing geological data. But if its case had been rejected outright, then this additional region, of up to 150 miles, would, strictly speaking, have remained an 'area of high seas' unless another had claimed it.

The most extreme, and unlikely, scenario is that the United States, or any other country, could use force to seize land or control waters that belong to another in the same way that American military forces invaded Iraq in 2003, as Aqqaluk Lynge referred to, or Argentina attacked the Falkland Islands in 1982. Earlier invasions had been undertaken when the United States looked for an excuse to use military force, or even actively created one. American involvement in Vietnam was justified on the grounds of a staged attack on United States warships in the Gulf of Tonkin, which was then wrongly blamed on the Hanoi regime, while prior to the onset of war in 2003, intelligence on Iraq was allegedly 'skewered' in an attempt to prove the presence of Weapons of Mass Destruction. 'Even established facts were ignored if they did not fit in with this intuitive sense, this semi-divine power to select the right', as an American secretary of state had once sighed of his president.[6]

In the same spirit, it is plausible to argue that the United States could search for an excuse to stake a claim over the sovereign territory of another country in the Arctic, such as Greenland, or over its waters. An outright invasion, comparable to the attack of 2003, may be very unlikely. But using a pretext to despatch a large military presence in a country that already has close ties with Washington might sometimes make much more practical politics, just as in 1990 the United States deployed a large contingent of forces to Saudi Arabia, after it was threatened by Saddam Hussein's invasion of Kuwait.[7]

This approach, which was also used by Great Britain at the height of its imperial powers, or the Soviet Union over Afghanistan and Eastern Europe, allows one country to retain its nominal independence even though in practice another exerts a great deal of influence.[8]

Hints of a unilateralist approach towards the Arctic region, unfazed by the constraints of international law, had been dropped in a White House document that was released just days before President Bush stepped down from office in January 2009.[9] 'The United States has broad and fundamental national security interests in the Arctic region and is prepared to operate either independently or in conjunction with other states to safeguard these interests', ran the text.[10]

An American tradition

How likely are such scenarios to come true in the Arctic over the coming decades, as the region's ice melts and governments from the world over look north? Viewed in terms of American history, the answer is 'very likely'. This is because the national story of America, more so than almost any other country, is a story of expansion and acquisition. Just as it began and evolved in this way, so too over the coming decades could the United States view the Arctic in the same terms.

The first chapter of American expansion and acquisition began as the first settlers pushed their way out of the colonies, seizing the land of the native American inhabitants and killing large numbers of them, either by driving them off the land or else simply exterminating them, often with near-genocidal ferocity.[11] As later generations looked further afield, the emerging American nation then seized land from the Spanish, from whose grasp they prised Puerto Rico and the Philippines; from the Mexicans, during the war of 1847–48; and then from the inhabitants of large numbers of Pacific islands. These expansionary energies were also directed against the far west, where the settlers captured huge areas of land in the 13 years that followed the death of Abraham Lincoln in 1865, and then in the far north, when William H. Seward, the Secretary of State under both Lincoln and Andrew Johnson, succeeded in purchasing Alaska from Russia in 1867. Seward also wanted to take French Guyana and Western Hemisphere British Columbia but was frustrated. 'Give me fifty, forty, thirty more years of life', he informed a Boston audience in 1867, 'and I will engage to give you possession of the American continent and control of the world.'

Just as in recent years the United States has followed the same expansionary tradition by turning its attention to the Middle East, so too in the years ahead could it turn north to the Arctic. Much closer to hand than other potential targets and wholly without the large, rabidly anti-American indigenous population found in the Arab street and elsewhere, the lure of its large natural resources might pose an irresistible temptation. But another reason for its interest when, in the years ahead, the Arctic's ice melts, is a motive that has sometimes been difficult to distinguish from its territorial acquisitiveness. This is a strong, even exaggerated, sense of its own strategic vulnerability.

In other words, there have been times when Washington has seized places not just out of interest in their natural resources but because they are also deemed to pose a potential threat to American national security. The Vietnam War is perhaps the most obvious single example of just how exaggerated this sense can be, for events in a remote, poverty-stricken land, tens of thousands of miles away from the American mainland, were deemed to pose a dire national threat that justified enormous personal sacrifice. A decade after President Kennedy had properly started American involvement in South-East Asia, President Nixon and his key adviser, Henry Kissinger, were equally convinced that the outcome of an election in as far away a place as Chile 'poses for us one of the most serious challenges ever faced in this hemisphere', one that would 'influence developments as far away as Italy' and which now presented 'the most historic and difficult foreign affairs decision' for the White House. As a leading historian of the era has written, this 'apocalyptic' perspective on such distant events 'might fairly be described as nothing more than paranoia'.[12]

Finally, Washington's attitude to the Arctic region is likely to be shaped by what is termed 'American exceptionalism': the idea that America, being both historically unique and morally exemplary, is therefore not subject to the same legal or moral restraints as other countries. This attitude, which has already spawned a huge literature, probably has its origins in the distinctive theology that the early settlers brought from England, one that emphasized the unique role of 'Providence', or what President Theodore Roosevelt called 'Manifest Destiny', in the affairs of not mankind in general but the American colonies in particular.[13]

Whatever its roots, the underlying attitude has been evident in all sorts of ways. The decision to spurn the International Criminal Court, or the 'unilateralism' of a Bush administration that was willing to attack Iraq without a clear UN mandate and ignore the Kyoto Treaty on global warming, are obvious examples. And traits of the same mindset were arguably discernible in President Harry S. Truman's landmark declaration that the United States would no longer respect a doctrine that had underpinned international law since the seventeenth century: the doctrine of 'freedom of the high seas'. Instead, argued Truman in 1945, America would have jurisdiction over all resources that were found on its continental shelf.[14]

So it is plausible to argue that, at some future point, Washington could be tempted to use military force in the Arctic region on the grounds that it stands above the 1982 Convention on the Law of the Sea. By the spring of 2009 the United States has still not signed this treaty, although President Bush had endorsed it in April 2007, as it very slowly made its way before the Senate. In April 2009 Secretary of State Hillary Clinton also announced that she and President Obama were 'committed' to its ratification. But until that happens the Convention provides even less restraint on the world's most powerful country than the United Nations Charter, which Washington signed in 1945, but still effectively overrode, taking a very liberal interpretation of the right of self-defence, when it attacked Iraq in 2003.[15]

A sense of American 'exceptionalism' is one reason why the 1982 Convention has never been ratified by Congress, even though President Clinton signed it in 1994. Although it is increasingly supported in Washington, a powerful and vociferous alliance of politicians, academics and pressure groups have always opposed it on the grounds that it runs contrary to the American national interest. Its ratification, they argue, would curtail the freedom of the United States Navy, undermine America's maritime interests and pose a serious challenge to its national sovereignty. Of course this may be equally true of other countries but the United States is different, they claim, because it is the world's policeman and its policies and actions simply can't be compared with those of others. Some of the loudest and most determined of these unilateralists, who have blocked the Convention's path on Capitol Hill, have been leading figures, like the late Jesse Helms, the long-time chairman of the highly influential Foreign Relations Committee, and Senator James L. Malone, who once worked as President Reagan's special representative for Law of the Sea negotiations and who subsequently continued to strongly oppose its ratification. Another critic is Professor Jeremy Rabkin, who has emphasized that disputes under the treaty are decided not by an American court but by a Hamburg-based tribunal.[16] So although the signatory states are exempt from the Convention in times of war, Rabkin points out that the tribunal judges have the freedom to decide what is, and what is not, 'military activity' and therefore perhaps act against America's best interests.[17]

There are other important reasons, besides an underlying sense of 'American exceptionalism', why the Convention has never been ratified in Washington. In particular, some senators instinctively dislike the description of 'high seas' as 'the common heritage of mankind', a phrase that they regard as having strongly Marxist connotations even though it appears to have been coined in a speech by President Richard Nixon.[18] But perhaps the most important single sticking point has been the section that deals with 'the Area of high seas that lies beyond the limits of national jurisdiction'. For one particular article of the treaty – Article 140 – states that any 'activities' of any country in these high seas should be undertaken 'for the benefit of mankind as a whole' and the proceeds of, for example, mineral or petroleum exploitation should then be 'equitably shared' by the ISA. But although these clauses were renegotiated in 1994, the treaty still never even got close to ratification in Washington.

By the spring of 2009, the United States still had not become a signatory member of the 1982 Convention, although in his closing days of office President Bush had urged Congress to endorse it. His presidential directive of January 2009 argued that 'the Senate should act favorably on US accession to the UN Convention on the Law of the Sea promptly, to protect and advance US interests, including the maritime mobility of our Armed forces worldwide. It will secure US sovereign rights over extensive marine areas, including the valuable natural resources they contain'.

The lure of the Arctic

Why, then, should these three distinctive historical traits – territorial acquisitiveness, a strong sense of strategic vulnerability and a feeling of 'exceptionalism' – prompt American eyes to turn northwards, to the Arctic, over the coming decades rather than in any other direction? Part of the answer is that the region is thought to have so much oil and gas, but a more important consideration is its hugely important strategic location.

Energy security

If the Arctic region does have the very large reserves of oil that some analysts hope, then it would offer a long-term, guaranteed source of supply. This would guard against the risk of any disruption to the flow of imported oil that could create a sudden price spike. If the American government could claim any Arctic regions, beyond Alaska, as its own, then it might calculate that it would no longer be at the mercy of any foreign governments that could cut their production of crude oil and thereby force up the price of a barrel in global markets.

There are two reasons in particular why Washington would want to find 'energy security' in the years ahead. One is that America's own indigenous sources of supply have reached a plateau, and in the case of Alaska in particular, are fast dwindling.[19] Output from the vast site at Prudhoe Bay reached a height in the late 1980s but has since been declining steadily and now stands at less than one-third of its peak output. This steady deterioration has happened even though a number of new Alaskan fields, such as the Northstar and Alpine reservoirs, have started to come on stream, and is likely to become even worse because the chances of any really significant new discoveries being made – not just in Alaska but anywhere on the American mainland – are considered to be remote. Overall, American domestic production of crude oil is expected to increase slightly in the years ahead, buttressed mainly by discoveries in the Gulf of Mexico, before levelling off and then starting to steadily decline.[20]

At the same time that America's own production has been steadying, it has become increasingly dependent on imported oil, which now comprises around two-thirds of the nation's domestic oil consumption. This is causing serious concern in Washington, where it is usually viewed as America's strategic 'Achilles heel': not only do oil exporters become rich at America's expense, runs the argument, but they can potentially exert considerable political leverage over US policy. President Bush mentioned the issue in his 2006 State of the Union speech, when he warned that America was 'addicted to oil' that was often imported from unstable parts of the world, notably the Middle East, and vowed to take countermeasures. The same cause was subsequently championed by Barack Obama well before he was elected president in November 2008, and he has promised to make this a key policy. 'A clear goal as president', he has proclaimed, is that 'in ten years we will finally end our dependence on oil in the Middle East'. This is vital, he argued, because 'unstable, undemocratic governments [can] wield undue influence over America's national security'.[21] Predictions that the country's foreign oil dependency will fall from 60 per cent to 50 per cent in 2015, before rising again slightly to 54 per cent in 2030, have not therefore been much cause for comfort in Washington.[22]

Viewed in these terms, the Arctic becomes important not just because it is thought to harbour large reserves of oil and gas but also because some of the most promising areas, such as those that lie off the shores of Canada or Greenland, are relatively close to the American mainland. This means that installations, tankers or pipelines can be guarded much more easily as they move crude oil than in the case of, for example, a reservoir in Africa, where around three-quarters of the world's newly discovered oil reserves have been located.

These considerations explain why President Bush's directive, issued in January 2009, emphasized the importance of the region's natural resources. 'Energy development in the Arctic region will play an important role in meeting growing global energy demand', it ran, 'as the area is thought to contain a substantial portion of the world's undiscovered energy resources.' The document did caution, however, that 'the United States seeks to ensure that energy development throughout the Arctic occurs in an environmentally sound manner, taking into account the interests of indigenous and local communities, as well as open and transparent market principles'.

An exaggerated risk

These concerns are far from likely to precipitate any conflict in the Arctic region, or elsewhere. This is partly because, as earlier chapters have already emphasized, it is far from certain that the Arctic region really does have any large quantities of oil, at least in areas that America, or any other country, could realistically hope to claim for itself. And even on the assumption – which is a big assumption – that the Arctic region does have large quantities of commercially recoverable oil, no administration is likely to want to risk war over a commodity whose economic value is likely to dwindle significantly in the years ahead as replacement fuels are pioneered. At the beginning of his presidency, Barack Obama has given a very strong commitment to sponsoring the development of these alternatives to oil, pledging to ensure that by 2012, 10 per cent of America's electricity comes from renewable sources and to invest $150 billion in developing alternative fuels over a 10-year period.

Nor is it really clear why the United States, or any other country, should want to acquire 'energy security' by 'reducing its dependency on foreign supplies'. Any consumer can buy its oil from the open market, bidding for cargoes as tankers make their way around the world, and these sources come from suppliers all over the world, not just from the Middle East or anywhere else in particular. A better government strategy might simply be to give energy companies more financial incentives to find and then exploit new oil fields whose output, when traded on the open market, would reduce the global price of crude. More radically, Washington could prioritize its efforts to heal relations with oil producing countries like Syria, Iran and

Cuba, or at the very least carefully calibrate its policies towards them. In recent years the United States government has heavily sanctioned these countries, threatening draconian penalties against any energy company that involves itself there, starving them of investment and badly curtailing their output.

Even if Washington does, at any point, look to the Arctic as a source of long-term energy security, it would need to ratify the UN Convention on the Law of the Sea to properly exploit the region's resources. But any country that has ratified the Convention is far less likely to behave high-handedly over disputed stretches of sea; for any country to disregard the obligations and procedures of an international treaty it has signed risks exacting a heavy political price, provoking uproar and condemnation from politicians and the general public world over.

Ratification of the Convention would enhance US 'energy security' because it would grant the oil industry much greater freedom and opportunity to explore and develop the resources of American Arctic waters. This is not because the Convention necessarily bestows the United States with sovereign rights over a bigger area of continental shelf than it would otherwise enjoy: Washington remains a signatory party to the 1958 Geneva Convention on the Continental Shelf, which potentially bestows sovereign rights over an even bigger area than the 1982 Convention. In order to claim sovereignty under the 1958 deal, a signatory state has to provide geological evidence of the reach of its continental shelf and demonstrate that the 'depth of the waters admits of the exploitation of the natural resources'.[23] So in one sense, it might conceivably be in American interests to remain a member of the 1958 Convention, because rapid technological advance could bestow sovereign rights over areas of sea that stretch way beyond the theoretical maximum limits – an outer continental shelf covering 291,383 square miles – allowed by the 1982 Convention.

In the United States, supporters of ratification are now pointing to the likely size and scale of America's continental shelf. In particular, the coast guard vessel, *Healy*, has undertaken several sonic-probing missions demonstrating that America's Arctic shelf could potentially be three times the size of California, and almost certainly extends well beyond the 200-mile limit. In the summer of 2007, the National Oceanic and Atmospheric Administration spent $1.2 million sponsoring a journey by the *Healy*, which focused its attentions on a section of the Chukchi Sea, a few hundred miles from the Alaskan coast. 'We found evidence that the foot of the slope was much farther out than we thought', as Larry Mayer, the chief scientist for the expedition, told one newspaper. 'That was the big discovery'. A year later, *Healy* sailed north from Barrow, Alaska, to start another long mission in the Chukchi Cap to bolster American claims.[24]

The reason why US membership of the Convention would enhance American 'energy security' is not that it would necessarily bestow sovereign rights over a larger area of potentially oil-rich territory. Instead, the main reason is that oil companies could feel reasonably sure about the legal status of any waters into which they might want to invest. Once Washington has ratified the Convention it is most unlikely to withdraw because any efforts to do so would almost certainly encounter huge congressional and public opposition. This would mean that the legal status of disputed stretches of sea could be firmly settled. But otherwise oil companies would risk investing huge sums into stretches of water that, before ratification, Washington might regard as its own but which, after ratification, are deemed by the UN Commission to be part of 'the Area' that is administered by the ISA. Administration by the ISA would mean a radically different tax regime – any resources in 'the Area' are judged by the Convention to be 'the common heritage of mankind' and subjected to special taxes – and therefore drastically alter the commercial risks of exploration and development (see Conclusion p. 219).[25]

This is why giants like ExxonMobil, Chevron, and ConocoPhillips have argued in favour of ratification, joining forces, paradoxically, with a number of environmentalist groups whose members argue that ratification would strengthen regulation and control over any drilling that does take place. As the White House document of January 2009 argued, 'defining with certainty the area of the Arctic seabed and subsoil in which the United States may exercise its sovereign rights over natural resources such as oil, natural gas, methane hydrates, minerals, and living marine species is critical to our national interests in energy security, resource management, and environmental protection'.

Washington also knows that if it wants to criticize what other countries are doing in the region, then its case would sound much more convincing and plausible if it has first signed up to the same legal rules. This became clear in September 2007, when Deputy Secretary of State, John Negroponte, spoke before the Senate Committee on Foreign Relations about Russia's geological missions in the Arctic. These expeditions, he argued, 'have focused attention on the resource-related benefits of being a party to the [Law of the Sea] Convention'. He then added, 'currently, as a non-party . . . there is no US commissioner to review the detailed data submitted by other countries on their (continental) shelves'.[26]

Signing the Convention would probably also help Washington's bid to keep the Northwest Passage open as an international strait, rather than as Canada's 'internal waters'. This is because, although it is often opaque, the 1982 Convention specifies and defines these terms more clearly than the customary law that the United States would otherwise have to rely upon.

The United States' strategic interest in the Arctic

Although the possible presence of oil, gas and other natural resources will not be a cause of conflict in the Arctic, the gradual retreat of its ice does nonetheless pose serious dangers. Above all, the United States regards large parts of the region as vital to its own national security, and would be seriously alarmed by the mere possibility of another country establishing or increasing its own presence there.

Most obviously, America has a strategic interest in maintaining the security of both its Alaskan coastline, which at its narrowest point lies just 57 miles across the Bering Strait from Russian territory, and of Canada's shores. Some commentators have claimed that these shores might eventually provide an enemy force with a possible route into the American mainland, but more important is the fact that they are the location not only of existing energy infrastructure but also of vital radar and communication links that are heavily used by the United States military. As George W. Bush's presidential directive of January 2009 summarized, the interests of the United States in the region include 'missile defense and early warning; deployment of sea and air systems for strategic sealift, strategic deterrence, maritime presence, and maritime security operations; and ensuring freedom of navigation and overflight'.

The strength of Washington's concern that these northern coasts are the weakest link of its national defences quickly emerged during the Cold War. In 1955, as part of a joint defence venture between the United States and Canada, construction began on a radar network, known as the Distant Early Warning Line, which stretched for 3,000 miles all the way from Alaska to Greenland. More sophisticated radar designs were soon developed, the most recent being the North Warning System, which monitors the coasts from Northwest Alaska to Newfoundland for any sign of foreign attack.

Since September 2001, Washington has also been concerned about terrorists moving into the American homeland through these soft, northern borders. Again, the January 2009 presidential document argued that 'the United States also has fundamental homeland security interests in preventing terrorist attacks and mitigating those

criminal or hostile acts that could increase the United States' vulnerability to terrorism in the Arctic region'. It continued by saying that
'this requires the United States to assert a more active and influential
national presence to protect its Arctic interests and to project sea
power throughout the region'. Although these fears are probably
baseless – it is likely to be many decades before climatic conditions
make any such infiltration through the High North remotely possible – they do illustrate the strength of America's strategic concern
about the area.

Washington is also concerned that in the event of any future war
its own national security, or the security of its European allies, might
still heavily depend upon the shipment of key supplies across the
Atlantic. Although this is still far less important than it was in the
two world wars, when long-range transport aircraft had still not
been developed, it could still turn out to be economically crucial for
a country that is likely to remain so dependent on importing oil and
natural gas, and which is still the world's largest trading nation. But
these Atlantic shipping lanes are vulnerable to attack from the north,
and an enemy force would find places like Iceland, Greenland and
Norway ideal bases where their fleets could be equipped, supplied,
repaired and rested.

This was why, during the Cold War, American strategists made
detailed proposals to establish an anti-submarine 'barrier', comprised
of carefully coordinated ship movements, which would stretch across
all the waters lying between Greenland, Iceland and the UK and
detect any Soviet submarines that were leaving their bases in the
Baltic and heading for the Atlantic. At the same time, Washington
worked hard to build close alliances not just with Denmark, to gain
a foothold on Greenland, but with Iceland and Norway. In 1951 an
American military base was established at Keflavik, in south-west
Iceland, and the following year the United States and Norway signed
a secret agreement that would give the Strategic Air Command
wartime access to the Norwegian air bases at Gardermoen and Sola.
Three years later the United States finally obtained permission from
Oslo to fly its bombers over the Norwegian mainland.[27]

Along with national prestige, this strategic interest lay behind
Washington's drive to deploy atomic-powered submarines to the
region. In the summer of 1958, the crew of the USS *Skate* broke new
ground by crossing the North Pole underwater, surfacing sporadically
in the course of their 10-day journey in the depths of the Arctic Ocean
and earning a special bravery award from the United States Navy by
doing so. Two years later, the *Skate* set out on a similar voyage and on

this occasion became the first submarine to surface at the Pole, where on 17 March it scattered the ashes of a famous explorer, Hubert Wilkins. At the same time that *Skate* was making its first Arctic mission, another American submarine, *Nautilus*, also broke a new record by crossing the entire Arctic Ocean – nearly 2,000 miles from the Bering Strait to the Greenland Sea – completely submerged.

The real danger

It is the Arctic's strategic location, not the presence of any natural resources, that creates a real risk of future confrontation, or at least of the United States using force in the scenarios discussed above. The retreat of Arctic ice in the years ahead will gradually create larger areas of 'high seas' – or, in the case of the Northwest Passage, a more navigable stretch of 'internal waters' – that ships from all over the world will be able to use. The danger comes when ships from a country that the United States regards as a rival, competitor or enemy assume a stronger presence, even quite innocently, in a way that might be viewed as a potential threat to American national security. So Chinese or Russian warships can not only sail through high seas but also have 'innocent passage' through the territorial sea that lies adjacent to the coast and a right of peaceful 'transit passage' through any strait that is deemed to lie within the internal waters, territorial sea or economic zone of any coastal state.[28] Yet for a country that has historically had such a keen, even exaggerated, sense of its own vulnerability, the prospect of so many foreign ships in its own backyard, or in such a strategically sensitive area, might be very alarming.

Although this danger would exist even if the Arctic has no important natural resources to boast of, the likely presence of oil, gas and minerals might make matters significantly worse. In the coming years it is possible that Chinese or Russian energy companies could establish a presence in a petroleum-rich place like Greenland, causing serious concern in Washington of a wider political alliance or even a military takeover. Just as Beijing has established close links with African countries, Pentagon analysts might reason, so too could it do the same in America's strategic backyard.

These fears would then be aggravated if the Chinese, in particular, do what they have done very effectively elsewhere in the world by using their vast foreign exchange reserves to buy majority stakes in national and international companies. In recent years, Chinese investors have been adept at doing this, particularly in the mining sector, with a view to influencing important commercial decisions. Although this does not necessarily pose any direct strategic threat to the United

States, such moves might well appear to confirm what Washington strategists think they can already see. Foreign governments have been very wary about Chinese overseas investment because they fear, rightly or wrongly, that it could be used for political ends. For example, an investment in Costa Rica in 2007 by China's State Administration of Foreign Exchange appears to have been made on the condition that the government shifted its allegiances from Taiwan to Beijing.[29] And when, in the spring of 2009, the Chinese state-owned metals group invested heavily in the massive Anglo-Australian organization Rio Tinto, some analysts wondered if the Chinese government viewed the deal more as a strategic holding.[30]

The strength of American fears over the possibility of political manipulation by Beijing became clear in 2004, when the Chinese National Overseas Oil Company made a bid to buy the American organization, Unocal. This met with stiff opposition in Congress, where the Californian Representative Richard Pombo stated quite simply that the Chinese bid would have 'disastrous consequences for our economy and national security'.[31] The same fears have been voiced by Brad Setzer of the United States Council for Foreign Relations, who claimed in November 2007 that 'the rise of sovereign wealth funds represents a shift in power from the US to a group of countries that aren't transparent, aren't democracies and aren't necessarily allies'.[32] There was similar unease in Britain in the summer of 2008, when Chinese investors bought a 3 per cent stake in Barclays Bank.[33]

In the months or years ahead it is quite possible that, in commercial terms, the Americans will be completely indifferent to any such Chinese acquisitions and may even welcome it. If the Chinese exploit the Arctic's oil, Washington might reason, then that simply frees up other sources of supply. Oil, it has already been emphasized, is a fungible commodity, and what China or any other consumer takes from one market source simply means that they don't have to take it from another. And if the Chinese develop oil and gas fields in the Arctic, then it would bring more sources of supply onto the market, thereby alleviating rather than creating any imbalance between supply and demand. Because Western energy companies are generally more commercially cautious than their Chinese competitors, Beijing's involvement may allow these new fields to come on stream a lot more quickly than they otherwise would. This is why, during the ongoing credit crunch that began in 2008, world leaders appear to be welcoming a Chinese buying spree. Flush with foreign exchange reserves, China is investing huge sums into foreign companies, offering cash in exchange for guarantees about future supply of key commodities. In

February, the state-owned China Development Bank agreed to lend $10 billion to the Brazilian energy giant Petrobras in exchange for a long-term supply of oil. But these developments were welcomed by the outside world, or at least failed to arouse any protest, because without them future supplies of oil and other resources will be imperilled. 'It's a good thing because a lot of projects have been postponed', as one analyst said. 'Oil companies may now have the money to produce oil. There's going to be more oil produced.'[34]

While in commercial terms Washington might even welcome Beijing's investments in the Arctic region, it is likely to be alarmed by the prospect of a growing physical presence in the region that those commercial investments bring. Whether it is Chinese personnel on the ground, or ships moving to and from key installations, this growing presence in such an important strategic region could arouse America's strong sense of strategic vulnerability.

Judging by the lack of any preparation in the Pentagon, this eventuality still looks a very long way off. In the 1990s, the United States Navy did spend up to $25 million every year on polar research, and in early 2001 warned that its weapons, ships and procedures were completely ill-suited to the extreme climatic conditions of the High North. 'Safe navigation and precision weapons delivery capability', the report stated, 'may be significantly constrained unless these shortfalls are addressed.' But after the attacks on the World Trade Center in September 2001, spending priorities were completely changed and the navy's budget for polar research was suddenly and dramatically slashed.

For the next few years Washington officials appear to have given sparse attention to the issue. In January 2005, the State Department's Bureau of Intelligence and Research held a confidential meeting to consider the implications of a melting Arctic. 'There are likely to be a number of foreign-policy issues that must be addressed by the United States and other nations', the meeting concluded. 'These issues include the availability and potential for exploitation of energy, fisheries and other resources; access to new sea routes; new claims under Law of the Sea; national security; and others.' By this time there had been no executive statement on the Arctic region since 1994 and this report had not even mentioned the retreating ice.[35]

Since then the United States has also remained very short of large icebreakers, which are extremely expensive to build and operate. It currently has only two heavy icebreakers, one of which, the *Polar Star*, was out of service in 2008 and early 2009, while the *Polar Sea* is, like its counterpart, already more than 30 years old. Although the

Healy is used in the Arctic region, mainly on scientific missions, it is not designed to crush the thickest ice. Senior commanders want at least two more icebreakers and point out that the Russians, by contrast, have 18 and Canada, six.

By the summer of 2008, some American military chiefs had certainly started to become seriously concerned by the climatic changes in the Arctic, recognizing the strategic challenges it might pose. In April, the leaders of the Pentagon's Pacific Command, Northern Command and Transportation Command wrote directly to the Joint Chiefs of Staff in Washington and urged them to spend more money and concentrate more attention on the Arctic region. At the same time Admiral Thad W. Allen, the head of the coast guard, also advised a House of Representatives committee that the United States Navy needs more icebreakers to match the Russian capability in the region: 'I am concerned we are watching our nation's ice-breaking capabilities decline', as he told the House Transportation and Infrastructure Committee.[36] Not only is Russia's fleet bigger, he pointed out, but it is also nuclear-powered and better equipped. In particular, the newly commissioned Russian vessel, *50 Let Pobedy* ('50 Years of Victory'), which is the biggest icebreaker in the world, can power its way through more than 9 feet of solid ice without slowing down, whereas any ice thicker than 6.5 feet holds up its strongest American counterpart, the diesel-powered *Polar Sea*. 'We are losing ground in the global competition', as Allen told the committee. Rick Larsen was one of the congressmen who concurred, arguing that 'despite the Coast Guard's best efforts to prepare for future operations in the Arctic region, they do not currently have the assets and the capabilities necessary to perform the most basic of Arctic operations'.

Their pleadings appeared to have reaped some rewards when, in January 2009, President Bush issued a new directive on the Arctic region, the first since 1994.[37] This emphasized that the United States should 'develop greater capabilities and capacity, as necessary, to protect United States air, land, and sea borders in the Arctic region (and) increase Arctic maritime domain awareness in order to protect maritime commerce, critical infrastructure, and key resources'. How quickly President Barack Obama will act upon these recommendations remains to be seen.

11

The Canadians Look North

One afternoon in the late summer of 2002, the miners who were working deep underground in Canada's High North, at a spot lying around 450 miles above the Arctic Circle, finished their final shift. After more than 25 years in service, the mine at Nanisivik was being closed down, partly because the world market for its chief raw materials – zinc and lead – was badly depressed and partly because the site was, in any case, considered by most experts to be relatively exhausted.

Despite the shock of redundancy, some of the 80-strong workforce may have greeted the news of the mine's closure with mixed feelings, perhaps slightly relieved to leave such an austere setting. In this very remote, isolated corner of Baffin Island, the miners had no choice but to live in the confines of a tiny settlement that the operating company had had specially built about 1.5 miles from the excavation site. Contact with the outside world was minimal, although they could often hear planes landing and taking off from a nearby airstrip or see the occasional ship pulling into a distant port. Morale would have been undermined even more by the serious ill health that some of the men suffered, and many of the buildings were so badly contaminated by dust that they were demolished soon after the mine closed.

Unenviable and completely deserted though it was, this remote site suddenly found itself the centre of attention when, 5 years later, the Canadian prime minister, Stephen Harper, announced plans to redevelop the old dock and runway, using them to supply new Arctic patrol vessels. Converting the port into a deepwater facility would cost around C$60 million and upgrading the airstrip, although it had previously been 'jet-capable', was projected to be at least as much.[1] But despite such a high capital outlay, the government was determined to press ahead and wanted to start work in the summer of 2010 with a view to opening the site 2 years later.

The Canadian government regards this high expenditure as a worthwhile investment for one simple reason: Nanisivik is at the eastern entrance of the Northwest Passage and therefore commands a vital strategic location. So if Canada has a strong military presence there, then it can much more easily deter any unwelcome visitors and, if necessary, block them altogether from trying to make their way across its waters.

Canada's armed forces have, of course, long had some presence north of the Arctic Circle, but it has not been much of a presence. Officers of the Royal Canadian Mounted Police had often been despatched to various outlying settlements and regions to reaffirm Ottawa's political authority, and had stepped up their numbers there during the Gold Rush in 1898, when a volunteer force helped to maintain law and order. But there has only been a regular contingent since 1970, when a permanent base was established at Yellowknife in the Northwest Territories for a unit, known as the Rangers, that is drawn almost entirely of Inuits who have a deep knowledge of and close familiarity with local conditions.

Its other Arctic resources are equally sparse. Canada has six icebreakers, but none of these are all-season polar icebreakers, despite the huge areas its Arctic shorelines cover, and its two most powerful vessels, CCGS *Louis St Laurent* and *Terry Fox*, are not powerful or resilient enough to cope with the worst of the Arctic's conditions. They are therefore 'two season' icebreakers that spend the winter months not in the High North but in the somewhat milder climate of the Gulf of St Lawrence. A number of governmental efforts have been made to improve things but to little avail. In 1985, Brian Mulroney's Progressive Conservative government declared that it would build a powerful all-season icebreaker and 12 nuclear-powered submarines but went on to cancel the contracts a few years later. Nearly 20 years on, Ottawa acquired four second-hand, diesel-electric submarines from the Royal Navy that have always been unable to travel completely submerged for more than a few hours, rendering them completely useless under the ice. But as the ice retreats and other Arctic powers appear to flex muscle, Ottawa has suddenly started to turn north and change its priorities.

Signs of this change had first emerged in the run-up to the 2006 federal election, when Harper had promised to spend billions on the construction of icebreakers and on building a new army base in northern Cambridge Bay. The following July his government also announced the construction of between six and eight navy patrol ships that would be sent to guard the Northwest Passage. Building these vessels, which are classified as Polar Class 5 Arctic Offshore Patrol Ships, would not be cheap: they would cost over C$3 billion to construct and another C$4.3 billion to run and maintain over their projected 25-year lifespan, but advocates of the programme argued their corner: 'It is no exaggeration to say that the need to assert our sovereignty and protect our territorial integrity in the north on our terms has never been more urgent', as Harper said at the time. 'Our expectation is over the next twenty-five years you're going to see an increasing range of human activity in that part of the world that you haven't seen in the past hundred years.'[2]

A few weeks later came a further announcement, made just days after the Russian flag-waving ceremony at the bottom of the Arctic Ocean, when international tension over the region suddenly reached new heights and the need to build a stronger military presence seemed so much greater than before. On a tour of the far north, Harper stood next to Gordon O'Connor, his defence minister, and a group of soldiers to make a statement that a new Canadian forces winter fighting school would be built in Resolute Bay, also in the Northwest Passage, and assert that the new facilities would 'tell the world that Canada has a real, growing, long-term presence in the Arctic'. He also emphasized that 'Canada's government understands that the first principle of Arctic sovereignty is use it or lose it, and make no mistake, the government intends to use it', while adding that 'protecting national sovereignty, the integrity of our borders, is the first and foremost responsibility of a national government'.

A source of controversy

It can, of course, be dangerous if any country suddenly steps up its military presence in the Arctic region, or indeed in any other part of the world. Such measures can heighten, as well as reflect, a state of underlying international mistrust, prompting other governments to feel that their own interests are being threatened and to then take countermeasures of their own that aggravate matters even more. But although Canada's interest and military presence in the Arctic is clearly fast-growing, there is no reason to suppose that it in any way heralds a looming confrontation over its natural resources. In the years ahead there will almost certainly be serious disagreements be-tween Ottawa and other governments over the region, notably Russia, the United States and Denmark, but none is likely to be even remotely serious enough to spill over into conflict. If Canada's track record in the Arctic is anything to go by, then some of these tensions could even be concluded in a constructive way, leading to the brokerage of new agreements from which everyone ultimately benefits.

Lying behind these tensions and disagreements will not just be the future of the Arctic's natural resources but a number of other issues, some of which have been the cause of earlier disputes.

National pride

When an American fast-attack submarine, the USS *Charlotte*, pulled into harbour in Norfolk, Virginia at the end of November 2005, its 154 crew members were jubilant. After spending months away at sea, they had managed to sail right under the Arctic ice cap and were very proud of their remarkable feat. 'Conducting an under-ice transit presented both unique challenges and rewards for the *Charlotte* team', proclaimed the captain proudly. 'I am very proud of the men on board who engaged the situation head-on, and I am ecstatic that they were able to experience a North Pole surfacing.' Nicknamed 'Bluenoses' by their colleagues in the United States Navy, most of these sailors also had some great stories to tell: 'I couldn't believe how dark it was at the Pole. It was pitch black and incredibly cold, but it was still really exhilarating', as one sailor put it, 'after all, how many people can say they have been at the North Pole?'[3] Others recounted how they had been able to take a walk on the windswept ice and even play a quick game of football in the bitter temperatures, which sank well below freezing.

Although the United States Navy refused to reveal details of the *Charlotte*'s precise route, the submarine had started its journey from Hawaii and then headed northwards, steering through the Bering Strait and then reaching the Pole on 10 November. But what deeply alarmed the Canadian government and general public was the very real possibility that it had managed to slip unnoticed through what they regarded as their own sovereign seas. After all, the shortest southerly course between Virginia and the North Pole runs past Ellesmere Island, through the Nares Strait and then leads into Canadian waters. Nearly all independent observers were sure that the Americans hadn't even bothered to ask permission: a retired senior officer in Canada's Northern Command told the press that Ottawa usually relied 'on their goodwill to know if they're in our waters or not', adding that 'I don't think they told us a thing: I don't think they told anyone'.[4]

Within hours a political storm had broken out. Prime Minister Paul Martin made public assurances that his government would take the 'necessary measures' to stop American submarines passing through Canadian seas. 'Arctic waters are Canadian waters, and Canadian waters are sovereign waters', he asserted. 'Canada will defend its sovereignty.' But his Conservative critics accused him of being a soft touch, claiming that he had completely 'failed to enforce our sovereignty and increase our security in the north', and that the government was guilty of slashing the defence budget and imperilling the national interest by doing so.

The US ambassador to Canada also entered the ring, accusing politicians on both sides of whipping up a fervent anti-Americanism that was on a 'slippery slope'.[5] Even if the *Charlotte* had gone past Ellesmere Island, ran the Washington line, it had traversed an 'international strait' instead of moving through Canada's 'internal waters'.[6] And under the Law of the Sea, submarines may pass through an international strait without surfacing or even alerting the adjacent coastal state.

This was not the first time that the two countries had clashed over the question of who ruled Arctic waters. In the late summer of 1969, the American ship, the SS *Manhattan*, completed a journey through the Northwest Passage, moving at a slow, even agonizing pace from the Beaufort Sea to Davis Strait.[7] Because this was the first time anyone had sailed the whole way down the Passage since the end of the Second World War, and because only ten such voyages had in any case ever been previously made, the crew were doubtlessly overjoyed at their achievement, even if their sponsors, a number of American oil companies, were disappointed by the amount of time, effort and money the journey had taken.[8] But the passage of the SS *Manhattan* infuriated and outraged many Canadians. Two Inuit hunters even tried to ram home the message by driving their dogsleds into the path of the passing ship, forcing it to make a sudden halt before they were forcibly removed and the *Manhattan* could continue its journey.

In one sense at least, the public and political outcry was hard to understand. Two American submarines were thought to have passed through Canadian waters in the Passage – USS *Seadragon* in August 1960 and USS *Skate* two years later – but their journeys had not sparked any serious diplomatic incident.[9] On this occasion, a representative of the Canadian government had even been on board the *Manhattan* as it made its way, and a Canadian coast guard vessel, *J. A. Macdonald*, had in any case always escorted the ship.

The two American submarines, *Skate* and *Seadragon*, had slipped through these waters quite unnoticed and unnoticeable. But the voyage of the *Manhattan* was made in full glare of the general public, and was seen as a brazen, blatant intrusion into Canada's national waters. This would have been bad enough if any other country was deemed responsible for such an intrusion but for the United States to do so – a country that Canada has long viewed with a certain suspicion and mild hostility – was that much worse. In the full glare of the public eye, the United States was seen to have arrogantly disregarded Canadian sovereignty or, at the very least, Canadian feelings, because although the authorities in Ottawa had been informed of the trip in advance, it seemed that no one had ever approached them to request official permission.

Not surprisingly, the announcement, made soon afterwards, that the *Manhattan* would make another attempt to cross the Northwest Passage inflamed public indignation even more, prompting Prime Minister Trudeau and other government officials to publicly declare that the waters did, despite high-handed American behaviour, belong to Canada. But, as in 2005, Washington refused to admit that it had done anything wrong. In 1969, Canada had never even made any formal assertion of its sovereignty over these waters, which the Americans claimed were 'high seas' under international law.

Sixteen years later, in the summer of 1985, the same controversy broke out when an American icebreaker, the USS *Polar Sea*, made its own voyage from east to west. The scenario was just the same, for once again the organizers failed to request permission from the Canadian authorities to make the journey, even though Ottawa was informed of the plans in advance and arranged for coast guard vessels to accompany the ship as 'invited observers'. Keen to downplay the incident and limit any political damage, the government balked at lodging a formal protest and instead claimed that the voyage 'does not compromise in any way the sovereignty of Canada over our northern waters, or affect the quite legitimate differences of views that exist between Canada and the United States on that question'.[10]

Such careful diplomatic language could not disguise the fact that, as in 1969, there was considerable disagreement between Washington and Ottawa over the status of the Northwest Passage. This strong disagreement persists to this day. 'The longstanding position of the US is that the Northwest Passage is a strait used for international navigation – that's the same position shared by many others in international communities such as the European Union', as the American ambassador to Canada, David Wilkins, told one media organization in 2007. 'No one is questioning sovereignty over the land or over the mineral rights, it's simply an international navigational strait.'[11]

Lying at the very heart of this disagreement is not any concern about the possible presence of oil, gas or minerals in the region, or even about the strategic significance of its location. It is something much simpler, and that is national pride. Of course some countries are more insular and private than others, but all countries resent others meddling in what they regard as their own domestic issues for the same reason that most people resent the same thing. Canada's long-serving prime minister, Pierre Trudeau, once spelt out exactly how important 'national prestige' is as a political consideration, writing in his memoirs that 'it would have been a terrible abdication of Canadian pride and power to say as soon as we did anything the Americans didn't like, "well, we'll try to adjust"'.[12] It was plain that to many Canadians, American actions in the Passage crossed what seemed to be a very clear line.

Exactly when Canadians began to regard these waters as their own is hard to say. By the end of the nineteenth century the Canadian government had acquired all of the territories that belonged to Great Britain; although this included a number of islands, the waters of the Northwest Passage had never been formally ruled from London. But at the beginning of the twentieth century a number of politicians and officials began to make more ambitious claims about how much belonged to Ottawa. In 1907, Senator Pascal Poirier spoke before the Canadian Senate and recommended that Canada should proclaim possession of all the lands and islands lying north of its coast up as far as the Pole, while the expeditions made by explorers like Captain Bernier have to some extent become the stuff of myth.[13] As Stephen Harper has said, Canada's Arctic 'is central to our national identity as a northern nation. It is part of our history'.[14]

Environmental concerns

For many Canadians, the legal status of the Northwest Passage is not just a matter of national pride, one that merges with a wider suspicion and mistrust of American motives. Another big consideration is the fate of the Arctic environment, which could so easily be damaged by an oil spill from just one passing tanker. At times the Canadian government has doubtlessly used this as a convenient fig leaf with which to disguise other motives, but it is nonetheless still an important consideration in its own right.

Canada's concern about the environment became clear in the wake of the *Manhattan*'s voyage in 1969. Although it was not carrying oil at any stage of its journey, the ship was slightly damaged by ice and this prompted Ottawa to introduce the Arctic Waters Pollution Prevention Act as a piece of domestic legislation. Under this law, Canada claimed a right to impose certain safety standards on any vessels passing through waters that reached up to 100 miles off its shores. Unless it was built, navigated and operated according to certain standards, the law decreed, then a ship could be barred from moving through the Passage.

Strictly speaking, the enforcement of this legislation would have been contrary to international law, which at this time did not give rights to a coastal state over any stretch of water beyond the 'territorial sea' that lay immediately adjacent to its shorelines. But Ottawa was in no mood for compromise and warned that it would not necessarily respect any contrary ruling by the International Court of Justice (ICJ).[15] Prime Minister Trudeau claimed that 'we're saying somebody has to preserve this area for mankind until the international law develops. And we are prepared to help it develop by taking steps on our own'.[16] Meanwhile the Minister for External Affairs, Mitchell Sharp, referred to the 'gap' that existed in international environmental law and expressed his ambition to 'deal with a pollution threat of such a magnitude that even the vast seas and oceans of the world may not be able to absorb, dissolve or wash away the discharges deliberately or accidentally poured into them'.[17]

Canada's position on both the environmental protection and the wider legal status of the Northwest Passage was put forward soon after the voyage of the *Polar Sea*, when the minister for external affairs asserted that there are 'straight baselines around the Canadian Arctic archipelago'. This had far-reaching implications because it meant that any seas that fell within those baselines were 'internal waters', and that the surrounding 'territorial sea' covered a proportionately wider area because it could be measured not from the existing baseline, along the mainland, but further out to sea, from the archipelago, instead.

Crucially, this new definition gave the Canadian government much greater powers over all maritime traffic. Since these were 'internal waters', Ottawa could lay down environmental regulations, just as the ministerial statement emphasized that Parliament would bring in 'new legislation to enforce Canadian and criminal laws in the offshore areas enclosed by the straight baselines'.[18] And if any ship refused to toe the line, it could be barred from crossing the Passage altogether, since it generally has no 'right of innocent passage' through internal waters. If, on the other hand, there is an 'international strait' running through these internal waters, then ships from the world over have a right to make 'transit passage' that coastal states have much less power to interrupt.[19]

Some of the initiatives that Canada first introduced in 1970 have subsequently been formally incorporated into international law. So in those places where perennial ice creates exceptional navigational hazards, Article 234 of the 1982 Convention allows coastal states to enforce rules and regulations against maritime pollution throughout the surrounding 200-mile economic zone. But other claims made by Canada have been hotly disputed. For example, the baseline it draws through the Arctic archipelago is highly controversial because the 1982 Convention, or earlier treaties that preceded it, does not give much guidance about how such a line should be drawn.[20] In particular, the United States strongly argues that the Northwest Passage, far from being Canada's 'internal waters', is really a 'strait' that has previously been 'used for international navigation' and through which it therefore has a right of 'transit passage'. It is in this regard that the trips made by the *Charlotte*, *Polar Sea* and *Manhattan* become important: every time any vessel passes along the Northwest Passage, it becomes easier for Washington to make a convincing case that the waters have been 'used' in this way.[21]

Since ratifying the 1982 Convention in 2003, the Canadian government has had the option of enforcing environmental standards on maritime traffic not by declaring the Passage as its 'internal waters' but by appealing to Article 234 instead. So far it has downplayed this option because the legal status of this clause is far from clear: Washington denies that it gives Canada or any other coastal state a right to prevent the transit of a ship that is deemed to pose an environmental danger.

Self-defence and security

Besides harbouring feelings of national pride and of responsibility for its natural environment, the Canadian government is doubtlessly also concerned that, unless it imposes proper safeguards, the Arctic's waters could pose a potential threat to its national security.

Some commentators have argued that terrorists, smugglers and criminals could potentially make their way through these seas, wholly undetected, and then move into the Canadian mainland. Just as in the early 1930s, at the time of prohibition in America, the Canadian government tried to extend its national borders and powers in the archipelago to curb the problem of liquor smuggling, so too in the future might it regard the same waterways as highly vulnerable to infiltration. But climatic conditions in this area are likely to remain extreme for many decades and in the meantime there will be far easier ways for any such enemy force to infiltrate the Canadian or American mainland. Instead the Canadian government is probably more concerned by the possible seizure or destruction of key strategic assets, such as oil and gas installations, by a foreign military force in the event of a national emergency. Even in peacetime, it is possible to imagine foreign vessels or commercial organizations treating as 'high seas' stretches of water that Canada, or any other coastal state, regards as its own outer continental shelf even if its claim has not been formally accepted by the United Nations.[22]

Fears that the Russian military was preparing to establish just such a presence emerged in the early summer of 2008, with the disclosure that Moscow had despatched a fleet of nuclear-powered submarines in the area. The news certainly alarmed some of Canada's allies: 'Four of the five Arctic powers are NATO members, yet NATO seems ill-configured to be able to respond to the sort of activities we have seen from the Russians', as a British minister told one newspaper. 'We need to ensure NATO has the will and the capability to deter Russian activity that contravenes international laws or treaties.'[23]

In any event, the legal status of the Northwest Passage is, once again, extremely important: as noted above, if it is deemed to be an international strait, then it is much harder for the Canadian authorities to stop and refuse entry to a foreign ship that may perhaps have hostile intent. Any vessel that passes through its internal waters, or through its 'territorial sea', can be stopped and searched without difficulty, and if necessary, turned away. In practice this is not always possible because the Canadian coast guard has often been too under-resourced to carry out thorough searches, and in recent years ships have only had to voluntarily declare that they are abiding by the terms of the Arctic Waters Pollution Prevention Act.

A concern for Canada's national security, as well as for its environment, lay behind Stephen Harper's decision, announced in the summer of 2008, to impose a crackdown on maritime traffic. Harper declared that the Canada Shipping Act, initially passed in 2001, would be amended so that all ships within 200 nautical miles would have to report to Canadian authorities, and he hoped that this would send a strong message to the outside world 'as an environmental matter, as a security matter and as an economic matter'.[24] The Prime Minister added that 'we are acting today to protect our environment, improve the security of our waterways and ensure that all northern residents – and, in particular, the Inuit – have a strong say in the future of our Arctic for generations to come'. Harper has also emphasized that 'the first priority of national defence is to assert your sovereign presence on your territory, to be prepared to defend Canadians from threats of all kinds, whether they be major threats of invasion, or simply minor threats of unauthorized surveillance or potential unauthorized economic activity'.[25]

Successive administrations in Ottawa have proclaimed their commitment to strengthening national defences in the High North, even if their critics claim they soon balk at the sheer cost of building or upgrading infrastructure in such an inhospitable area, or of buying highly specialized equipment. In 2000, the government released a document, 'The Northern Dimension of Canada's Foreign Policy', stating its ambition 'to enhance the security and prosperity of . . . northerners, assert and ensure the preservation of Canada's sovereignty in the north, establish the circumpolar region as a vibrant geopolitical entity integrated into a rules-based international system, and to promote the human security of northerners and the sustainable development of the Arctic'. Other governments made similar promises. In a keynote speech in October 2004, Prime Minister Paul Martin announced a 'northern strategy' that would, among other things, 'protect the northern environment and Canada's sovereignty and security'. In April 2005, Ottawa released a foreign policy document that placed much greater emphasis on the Arctic region than the previous paper, published 10 years before.[26]

Natural resources

Like any other government, Ottawa is lured by the prospect of discovering deposits of oil and gas, and is well aware just how valuable the Arctic's natural resources could turn out to be. 'We know from over a century of northern resource exploration that there is gas in the Beaufort, oil in the Eastern Arctic, and gold in the Yukon. There are diamonds in Nunavut and the Northwest Territories, and countless other precious resources buried under the ice, sea and tundra', as Stephen Harper said on the eve of his visit to the region in August 2007. He emphasized how important these reserves could turn out to be: 'Whether it is the thawing of the Northwest Passage or the suspected resource riches under the Arctic seabed, more and more countries are taking an interest in the waterways of the Canadian Arctic.' Harper has also pointed out that exploiting these resources would create a lot of jobs, as well as providing the government with perhaps huge revenues: 'I think in the eyes of many Canadians, what defines us is being a northern nation. The north has tremendous resource potential', as he told one reporter. 'We're seeing a worldwide expansion in demand for mineral resources in particular, so we think it's important to take advantage of those opportunities, find work for people up there.'[27]

Although any government would naturally want to claim title over a region thought to be as energy-rich as the Arctic, Ottawa has more reason than most. While production in Russia, and other countries, is falling essentially because of a crippling lack of investment, Canadians fear that many of their best reserves have already been exploited and are nearing exhaustion. In recent years, the output from the Western Canada Sedimentary Basin has comprised nearly all of the national oil and gas production, but these wells are not expected to keep producing at the current rate for more than another decade. Although the energy industry has tried its utmost to find new deposits and develop new techniques to make the most of existing supplies, they have been unable to halt the downward drift of national reserves. Independent studies predict that the country will be able to meet domestic demand until at least 2030, but given that almost no one expects to make any very large discoveries on the mainland, the Canadian authorities have good reason to be worried, even if the industry does succeed in developing unconventional fuels.

This means that the Arctic's resources could conceivably provide Canada's energy sector with a form of long-term life insurance. But one problem is that the legal status of several places thought to be rich in natural resources is heavily disputed. One section of the Beaufort Sea, for example, that both Canada and the United States claim as their own, is also widely considered to be the home of large quantities of both oil and gas. The area's promise becomes clear from the large quantities of money that energy companies have been prepared to invest there. In July 2007, when Imperial Oil and its sister company, ExxonMobil Canada, bid C$585 million to win a large exploration block in the Beaufort Sea, its spokesmen emphasized that the commitment would not have been made 'if we didn't see some long-term exploration potential'.[28]

Another example is Hans Island, situated in the Nares Strait exactly halfway between Greenland and Canada. That anyone should be particularly interested in what is little more than a large lump of rock, measuring just half a mile wide, is surprising. As one description has put it, wryly, 'amenities are scarce but there is a tiny wooden hut with a cot, stove, two pans and some Tang drink crystals. Surveys indicate that restoring this most northern outdoor toilet is feasible. Vegetation includes red lichen and hardy Arctic moss'.[29] What matters is the possible presence of oil and natural gas off its shores, and when the Canadian firm Dome Petroleum began to undertake some research there, in the late 1970s, interest in the region began to heat up.[30]

The dispute really dates back to 1973, when Denmark and Canada decided to create a maritime border through Nares Strait, running exactly halfway between their territories, but couldn't agree over who should have a right to rule the island. Although they decided to settle the matter at a later date, Dome Petroleum's unexpected interest in the area changed everything. In 1984 a contingent of Canadian troops visited the island, staying long enough to plant their national flag and leave behind a bottle of their native whiskey. A week later the Danes retaliated, despatching a government official, Tom Hoeyem, to hoist up their own national flag, claiming that Canada's had been blown away by the strong Arctic winds, and then left behind a bottle of Denmark's own best brandy.

Hans Island has remained a sticking point between the two countries despite numerous promises to resolve the issue. In the summer of 2005, for example, Canadian Defence Minister Bill Graham briefly visited the island and made some remarks that caused serious annoyance in Copenhagen: 'Our view is that it's part of Canada and we continue to be there, to go there. The Danes go there as well and we are making sure that the Danes know that this is part of the Canadian territory.' He added that 'it's a part of Canada. I'm really glad I went there'.[31] But the Danes were unimpressed and, in a radio interview, a legal expert at the foreign ministry in Copenhagen argued that 'we consider Hans Island to be part of Danish territory and will therefore hand over a complaint about the Canadian minister's unannounced visit'.[32] Canada's Foreign Minister, Pierre Pettigrew, and his Danish counterpart, Per Stig Moeller, met in New York less than 2 months after Graham's flying visit and agreed to resolve the dispute but still seemed no further forward when, soon afterwards, Pettigrew reiterated his belief that Canada has sovereignty over Hans Island.

Future conflict?

The controversy surrounding Hans Island has at times come close to resembling the scenario of a 'resource war' that some analysts have feared. So in the wake of the sharp exchanges that followed Bill Graham's visit in 2005, the Canadian government stoked up tension even more by dispatching the frigate, *Fredericton*, to the region while Denmark sent the ice cutter, *Tulugaq*, and threatened to land soldiers onto the island. 'This is a demonstration of Canada's will to exercise sovereignty over our own backyard', warned Commander Bob Blakely of the Royal Canadian Navy. 'The sea is a highway that's open to everyone. We will allow everybody passage as long as they ask for our consent and comply with our rules: use our resources wisely and don't pollute the fragile northern ecosystem.'[33]

There have been other occasions when the Canadian military has staged a number of exercises that other countries could easily regard as highly provocative. In April 2004, for example, a large group of regular troops and Inuit Rangers staged the longest and northernmost patrolling operation that Canada's armed forces had ever undertaken, travelling between Resolute Bay, which is the site of a research centre on Cornwallis Island, and Alert, an outpost located at the northern end of Ellesmere Island on the Lincoln Sea. Four months later came 'Narwhal 04', which took place on Baffin Island, 1,240 miles south of Hans Island. This 3-week exercise involved about 600 personnel as well as a number of aircraft, helicopters and one frigate, HMCS *Montréal*, and only served to aggravate international tensions even more.

Yet these exercises, like the verbal sparring between the capitals, present an essentially superficial image of tension and hostility. No government can afford to appear indifferent to the fate of any disputed region that might prove to be rich in natural resources, knowing that its perceived passivity is likely to merely encourage its international rivals to stake a claim while presenting its domestic adversaries with a golden opportunity to make stinging political criticism. If it indulges in a certain amount of posturing, a government instead reassures domestic audiences that it is prepared to do its utmost to claim these regions as its own, while also sending an unmistakable signal to rivals that such a matter is taken very seriously.

But this is a long way from using military force for much the same reasons that are also at play elsewhere in the region. For once again the potential rewards of using force are heavily outweighed by the certain risks. The Canadian government is well aware that some disputed regions may not even have any oil or natural gas deposits that are worth fighting for, and some investors, who are spending huge amounts of money combing the area for hidden reserves, admit that they are taking considerable commercial risks. 'Although the Arctic is a high potential, technology-intensive frontier area', as a spokesman for Imperial Oil cautions, it nonetheless represents both a 'high risk ... opportunity to add to our resource base in the Beaufort Sea.'[34]

Even if, in the years ahead, Ottawa does become preoccupied with the need to achieve 'security of supply' at a time of diminishing oil output, it could easily acquire this without using military force at all. Its energy industry is currently collaborating closely with American counterparts to develop the ways in which natural gas is exploited and used. One such company is Unconventional Gas Resources, which has hired a number of engineers and geologists who are highly experienced in this very specialized field. The company's chief executive says his company has 'sophisticated investors' who are keen to emulate and apply methods that, over a number of years, have proved to be very successful in the United States.[35]

In as fully fledged a democracy as Canada, the government cannot readily ignore the concerns of public opinion. While the loud outcry provoked by American actions in the Northwest Passage certainly reveals the strength of national attachment to the region, this would not mean that the Canadian public would support the use of armed force to assert ownership over disputed territory. So if such action was undertaken to acquire natural resources, then it is most unlikely that it would enjoy any real popular support. In August 2008, a poll undertaken by the Canwest News Service suggested that Canadians have serious reservations about resource exploitation in the Arctic: 57 per cent of respondents agreed with the statement that 'the Arctic ecosystem is too fragile for the extraction of natural resources that threatens to destroy the sustainability of the ecosystem, so we should leave it relatively untouched'. Only three in ten of those interviewed thought that Arctic sovereignty should be a 'major priority' for the government, whereas nearly two-thirds thought that reducing carbon dioxide emissions is very important.[36]

In the highly unlikely event that Russia, or any other country, uses force to stake its claim over disputed territory, most Canadians would instead be much more likely to support strong diplomacy with the close support of their allies in NATO. Pitched against a country as economically vulnerable as Russia, such a multilateral effort would be likely to prove far more persuasive than any easy reliance on force. And it is of course far less likely that any of the other countries bordering the Arctic Ocean – Norway, Denmark and the United States – would ever contemplate using military force at all, despite all the acts of showmanship in which they, like most countries, occasionally indulge. The political, economic and military ties between them are simply too strong to be disrupted by a single issue: the tensions between Denmark and Canada in 2004, for example, soon dissipated when the two NATO allies agreed to discuss the dispute at the UN. In the same spirit, for all the tension between them over the issue, the two countries are also working closely together to patrol Arctic coasts.

Canada's legal claim in 2013

Far from being provoked into any resource war by the prospect of an Arctic energy bonanza, the Canadian government is much more likely to step up its legal efforts to settle disputed borders. Issues such as the size of its outer continental shelf in the Arctic Ocean, or the demarcation of national borders in the Beaufort Sea, can then be decisively settled by the UN Commission on Limits of the Continental Shelf and the ICJ, respectively. Of course the judgements of these and other international bodies do not always command universal respect, particularly as the United States is not even a signatory of the 1982 Convention on the Law of the Sea, which established the Commission.[37] But few countries are willing to blatantly disregard international law, knowing that this could carry a heavy political and economic price, and the Canadians also know that winning their legal case would be likely to make any reliance on military force quite unnecessary.

In particular Ottawa is likely to prioritize the geological challenge of demonstrating where two underwater formations – the Lomonosov and Alpha ridges – lie in its offshore waters. Every member of the Convention on the Law of the Sea has to formally submit its case over the limits of its continental shelf within 10 years of signing up, and having joined in 2003, Canada is due to present its own geological arguments no later than 2013. Considerable amounts of time, money and effort are being invested by the Department of Foreign Affairs and International Trade in an attempt to show that Canada's outer continental shelf could be as large as 675,000 square miles.

Leading these efforts are researchers of Natural Resources Canada, who are using the latest technology and methods to get a close look at the shape of the seabed and the thickness of the rock deposits that lie on top. The main technique involves beaming down sound waves that travel through the water and are either reflected by the seafloor, giving experts on the surface a very exact idea of its shape, or else move through underwater rock before they are reflected back to show the sediment thickness. Sometimes this research is undertaken from icebreakers, which are used in late summer, when the ice is thinner, while earlier in the year scientists are flown out and landed on the ice by helicopter, even though this is risky if conditions suddenly change and they become stranded. To obtain the geological evidence they need, the Canadians are also expected to make heavy use of new, state-of-the-art submarines that are due to come into service in 2011.[38]

Some of these surveys have been carried out in close conjunction with a number of other countries. In 2006 Canadian and Danish scientists worked together on a seismic project at the Canadian Forces Station at the settlement of Alert, on Ellesmere Island. Their mutual goal was to determine the course of the Lomonosov Ridge, and despite enduring some atrociously bad weather that forced them to abort nearly all of their planned activities, the joint operation was judged to be a success. Canadian experts are also hoping to work alongside Russian and American counterparts before submitting their case to the UN Commission.

Arctic cooperation

The scientific cooperation that Canada has sometimes undertaken with other Arctic countries is a reminder that, far from being a recipe for conflict and confrontation, the region also offers opportunities for different states to work closer together. This is why, over the past few decades, there have been a good number of bilateral agreements to conserve the region and prevent it from being too heavily exploited.

During the Cold War, for example, the Arctic's distinctive environmental challenges helped to heal international differences and reduce tensions. When discussions between Canadian and Soviet scientists began in 1972, efforts were made to identify areas of common concern in the Arctic region. In 1984 this led to the signing of a formal 'Protocol of Consultation' and, less than a decade later, an 'Agreement on Cooperation in the Arctic and the North'. At the same time the Canadian government was building closer ties with the Americans, and in 1988 the two countries signed an 'Arctic Cooperation Agreement'. Under this deal, they affirmed the need to advance 'their shared interests in Arctic development and security' and 'their understanding of the marine environment', as well as to 'facilitate and develop cooperative measures for navigation by their icebreakers in their respective Arctic waters'.

Although there have been numerous bilateral initiatives and agreements over the Arctic region, there have been far fewer deals between more than two partners. Nonetheless in 1911 a number of countries signed a deal to end the exploitation of fur seals in the Bering Sea, and 9 years later reached a compromise to determine the future of the Svalbard archipelago.[39] In 1973 Canada, Denmark, Norway, the Soviet Union and the United States struck a deal to try to conserve the polar bear, while in 1991 the Arctic Environmental Protection Strategy was signed. And in March 2009 the 'Arctic Five' met in Tromsoe to reaffirm their commitment to preserving the polar bear at a time when it seems under increasing threat.

In other words, the Arctic region can bring people together to confront shared challenges and solve common problems and obstacles, as well as creating and aggravating international tension. In the same cooperative spirit, some of the disagreements over the status of the waters in the Canadian archipelago are likely to be amicably resolved. Because the Canadian coast guard has far greater powers over any ships that make their way through 'internal waters' than a 'strait', United States officials have sometimes admitted that American national security might even be enhanced if they recognize Ottawa's claim. 'We are looking at everything through the terrorism prism', as the then United States ambassador to Canada, Paul Cellucci, said in November 2004. 'Our top priority is to stop the terrorists. So perhaps when this is brought to the table again, we may have to take another look.' And as one leading authority on the region, Professor Michael Byers, has argued, the Canadian government would never deny a request from the United States to allow one of its ships or submarines through the Northwest Passage.[40]

Conversely there may be other moments of serious tension and disagreement between the two capitals, perhaps leading not just to an exchange of harsh words but conceivably inciting popular protests. This is what happened in the early to mid-1980s, for example, when a reluctant Canadian government gave Washington permission to test-fire cruise missiles over its territory, triggering huge demonstrations by the Canadian public.

12

Some Other Arctic Claims

In the summer of 2007, a group of geologists began an arduous journey to a remote, barren part of Spitsbergen Island in the Svalbard archipelago. Their destination was Festningen, an isolated inland area that lies between Is Fjord and the Russian settlement at Barentsburg, where they were planning to take a close look at some of the local rock formations. If they could find enough samples, then they hoped to get a much better idea of the region's geochemistry, mineral composition, fossil content and age, as well as gauging the approximate direction of the Earth's magnetic field during earlier ages.

Making this trip a particular success story was the fact that it was a joint venture by experts from two countries. In the course of the previous year, Norwegian scientists had struck a deal to work closely with their Russian counterparts to map a huge geological area that runs all the way across Svalbard, Franz Josef Land and Novaya Zemlya, stretching across thousands of square miles of land and water. This presented a daunting scientific challenge, reasoned the geologists, and their chances of success would be much enhanced if they pooled their expertise and resources with neighbours and worked closely together.

On a relatively tiny scale, this international joint venture illustrates how the lure of the Arctic's resources might serve to bring different countries together instead of acting as a source of conflict and division. Svalbard acts as a microcosm of this wider spirit of cooperation because 13 countries have permanent research bases there, and experts from every corner of the globe undertake sporadic visits to conduct their own projects. Of course cooperation between some countries, most obviously Russia and the United States, is much less likely than in the case of others, such as Norway, Denmark and Iceland.

The Norwegian challenge

Like Canada and the United States, the Norwegians have every reason to look north and do everything they reasonably can to stake their claim in disputed areas of the Arctic. This is because they too have to resolve a huge and growing tension between what they want to spend and how much they can earn.

Since its discovery in the 1960s, North Sea oil and gas has provided Norway, like the United Kingdom, with vast revenues. Its output began to seep into the global market in the early 1980s, and Norway eventually became the second-largest supplier of natural gas to Europe and the world's fifth-biggest oil exporter, pumping out around 4.5 million barrels every day at the peak of its production in the 1990s. In this time its earnings from the sale of oil and gas have constituted one-third of government revenue, as well as providing jobs for nearly a quarter of a million people who were employed not just in the energy industry but in providing the vital infrastructure – the ships, buildings and essential services – that is needed to support it.

The trouble for the Norwegians is, like many other key oil producers (notably those of the Middle East) they have become heavily dependent on maintaining this high level of output. The proceeds of North Sea oil and gas have allowed them to subsidize benefits and privileges – benefits such as free universal health care and sick and disability allowances – with a generosity that other countries would consider excessive or even unrealistic. This has meant raising public expectations so high that any cutbacks would prove painful not just to those who are used to being recipients, but also to the politicians who are deemed responsible.

Norway seems well prepared to survive the global economic slowdown that began in earnest in the course of 2008. Over the preceding few decades it has acquired the reputation of being one of the best-managed economies in the world, having carefully used its oil revenues to finance its non-oil budget deficit and invested the rest overseas into a 'Global Pension Fund', better known as its 'Oil Fund'. This acts as a form of insurance to guard against harsh economic times, restricting how much the government can spend at home by ensuring that 'over time, the non-oil budget deficit does not exceed the expected real rate of return of the fund, estimated at four per cent'. This allows Norway's leaders to sound upbeat over the prospect of encountering any short-term difficulties. 'We have held back and been restrictive in our use of oil revenues in strong times', as Prime Minister Jens Stoltenberg told one newspaper, 'but we can start to spend more now that we see a downturn coming.'[1]

But although Norway is one of the best-placed governments in the world to spend its way out of an economic downturn, its longer-term outlook appears increasingly doubtful. After enjoying almost 40 years of virtually uninterrupted growth, oil and gas production reached a plateau in 2001, and although it is expected to remain at this level for a few more years, most analysts anticipate a gradual, steady and significant decline after about 2015. 'Between 2009 and 2013 we expect significantly reduced oil production', as Bente Nyland, head of the Norwegian Petroleum Directorate, told a press conference in early 2009.[2] This is essentially because the largest, most productive fields are well past their best (the once giant deposits at Gullfaks and Statfjord, for example, are thought to be largely exhausted) and many others are depleting at an annual rate of between 13 per cent and 40 per cent. At the same time, Norway's economy has failed to diversify away from its dependency on oil and gas exports, and will have little else to depend on besides fishing and tourism when these energy reserves eventually run out.

It is in this context that the Arctic's natural resources become so important for the Norwegian government, which is stepping up its search for undiscovered reserves. One of the most promising areas is believed to be around Lofoten, which lies just above the Arctic Circle on the west coast of the mainland. The Norwegian Petroleum Directorate is currently in the process of arranging surveys in these waters, and also thinks that two-thirds of its undiscovered resources are located in the Norwegian and Barents Seas. 'We are still confident that there are a lot of resources to be found on the Norwegian continental shelf, especially in the deep-water part where we have the new licenses', as Henrik Carlsen, a director of Statoil, the state-owned energy giant, argues. 'We think it is important that the government releases as much as possible, and we want the Lofoten area to be opened.'[3]

The government that was elected to power in September 2005 quickly showed a strong interest in the energy resources that lay north of the Arctic Circle but within its territorial borders. One of the central features of its 'High North' policy has always been to recognize that 'the focus of Norwegian energy policy is thus continuing its historical shift towards the north'. This involves undertaking 'an active licensing policy that takes into account the need to follow up exploration results and the need to open up new areas for exploration'.[4]

Dispute and controversy

Government spokesmen have tried to reassure voters that 'the conditions relating to environmental concerns and fishery interests . . . have been strengthened in some areas . . . and time limitations have been introduced on seismic surveys' conducted by energy companies searching for oil and gas.[5] At the same time, the 'sustainable use of resources' and the setting of 'strict environmental standards' form a central part of the 'High North' policy. But these efforts to discover and then exploit new reserves to replenish the old are certain to stoke bitter conflict among Norway's own politicians and pressure groups that are mindful of their hefty environmental price.

This is partly because many of the areas that energy companies are watching with so much interest are traditional fishing grounds, particularly for cod and herring, and any attempt to explore or drill for oil there would cause serious disruption for fishermen. This is why conservative and right-wing political parties have in recent years opposed any move to surrender more areas of Arctic sea to energy companies. In recent years these parties have taken the side of the fishing industry while the centre-left has been more sympathetic to the oil lobby, and this conflict of interest was an important feature of the campaigns fought in the run-up to the elections of September 2009.

Environmentalists share these concerns and are watching these developments with horror. The seismic scanning of the waters around Lofoten in the summer of 2007 was 'very worrying considering that this is the spawning season for the fish' as well as a bad time for whales and sea birds, argued the leader of one pressure group, who refuses to rule out acts of civil disobedience to stop it from going ahead.[6] Others see it as a threat to the region's natural beauty, particularly when Norway has experienced its fair share of disasters. In December 2007, it suffered its second-worst spill when around 25,000 barrels of oil seeped into water as they were being loaded onto a tanker at an offshore field, Statfjord. Matters would have been much worse if the oil had made its way onto the shores, 100 miles away, as a result of strong winds and prevailing currents. But for environmental campaigners it was quite bad enough. 'This should be the final nail in the coffin of exploration in the north', as a spokesman for the pressure group Bellona told one newspaper. An official at the WWF for Nature in Norway also said exploration areas should be pushed further away from coastlines to prevent similar accidents affecting shores.[7]

While Norway is likely to experience a great deal of antagonism at home, the scope for international dispute, between Oslo and neighbouring governments, is more limited. Mindful of how much oil and gas its surrounding waters could be harbouring, Oslo has certainly pushed its legal case hard to win possession of several disputed areas. Having signed up to the Convention on the Law of the Sea in July 1996, it formally submitted its case to the United Nations 10 years later, just days before its deadline expired. Claiming that its outer continental shelf extends well beyond its 200-mile economic zone, Norway sought to stake its territorial claim by as much as 96,500 square miles. This claim included an area of the Norwegian Sea, known alternatively as the 'Herring Loophole' or the 'Banana Hole' that lies beyond Iceland's economic zone; the Western Nansen Basin, which lies north of the Svalbard archipelago; and the Loophole, the area of high seas that lies in between the economic zones of both Russia and Norway. These claims were accepted in April 2009, when the UN Commission issued its final recommendations on Norway's case. Its decision 'confirms that Norway has substantial rights and responsibilities in maritime areas of some 235,000 square kilometres', a triumphant Jonas Gahr Stoere pronounced.[8]

This is certainly enough to create considerable friction with its neighbours, most obviously the Russians. In addition to the Loophole, Moscow and Oslo are still at loggerheads over the status of the 'Grey Zone', adjacent to the coast, and the waters around Svalbard, where geologists feel reasonably sure significant quantities of oil and natural gas are to be found. The possibility of tension over these areas has already raised eyebrows in Oslo. A Norwegian government White Paper on Arctic policy, published in 2005, warned that these areas had the 'potential for a conflict of interest', while during the reading of the White Paper in the Parliament, the Stortinget, members of the Standing Committee on Foreign Affairs pointed out that:

> one of Norway's main challenges is that we presently have large areas in the north where Norwegian management or sovereignty is disputed, and where many states have no clear position to the Norwegian view.[9]

Disputes with Russia

Among the very few places where such disputes could arise, the most obvious likely arena is the Barents Sea. In August 2008, reports emerged that the Agency on Subsoil Resources (Rosnedra) in Moscow was preparing to undertake extensive geological mapping of Russia's outer continental shelf and had allocated 2.6 billion roubles – far more than in previous years – to do so. While as many as 34 separate areas were due to be surveyed, Moscow proclaimed that it regarded the Arctic's waters as the most important and was set to prioritize mapping in the Barents, Kara and Pechora Seas. However, the Norwegians were concerned that this unexpected move was a sign of much greater Russian interest in Svalbard and could herald trouble. Soon afterwards, in an interview with a Russian journal, Foreign Minister Jonas Gahr Stoere reiterated the long-held Norwegian view that his country was entitled to declare a 200-mile economic zone around the archipelago and that the 1920 treaty only gave Russia a claim over resources found on land and did not apply to the surrounding waters beyond the belt of 'territorial sea'.[10]

Despite Stoere's upbeat tone, a few other developments appear to confirm that Russia's ambitions around the archipelago are growing. Four months after Rosnedra's statement, for example, Artur Chilingarov informed the Duma that a new scientific station in the old mining village of Pyramiden was going to be opened. 'We are going to be all over the Arctic', claimed Chilingarov, 'this is not just science: this is presence in the Arctic.'[11] Shortly before, the Russians had blatantly disregarded a request by the Norwegian governor of Svalbard to hand over a number of historical objects that were kept in a museum in the Russian settlement of Barentsburg. Under local law, all objects found in Svalbard belong to the Norwegian authorities, who in this case were concerned that the objects were not being stored in the special conditions they need. However, the Russians flatly refused, partly because they were increasingly reluctant to recognize Oslo's rights, and partly also because the artefacts were made and used by Russian hunters of the seventeenth century and therefore helped to demonstrate Moscow's long-standing affiliation with the islands.

But as an earlier chapter has mentioned, Moscow cannot afford to alienate the Norwegians, who are a very important potential ally in its bid to develop future energy supplies. The successful launch of the Snow White field near Hammerfest exemplifies all the technical capabilities, and the management skills to organize such a massive project, that the Russians badly need but so sorely lack to develop their own offshore fields. Above all, the Russians know that if they are to realize their goal of supplying the United States, as they originally envisaged, then they would have to liquefy and transport the gas using the very techniques that Statoil is proven to have mastered.

This is why Statoil has always been a frontrunner in the international contest to win contracts to develop the mammoth Shtokman field, and company representatives have held a number of high-profile talks in Moscow with their counterparts from Gazprom to finalize various proposals. Finally, in February 2008, the Norwegian company signed a deal that gave it part ownership of a joint venture with the French giant Total and Gazprom, whose chief, Alexei Miller, publicly praised Statoil's 'long experience, vast resources and advanced technologies which are fundamental to the success of this unique project'.

In general, Norway and Russia have a long history of working together in the Barents Sea, and this means that both have a strong interest in resolving their border disputes amicably. Examples of this close cooperation are numerous and wide-ranging. In August 2000, Norwegian divers and experts had tried desperately hard, if unsuccessfully, to save the lives of 118 sailors on board the stricken Russian submarine *Kursk*, and each of the rescuers were personally thanked by President Putin for their gallant but doomed efforts. And in the summer of 2008, the foreign ministers of both countries opened a new laboratory in Murmansk that Russian and Norwegian scientists were operating together to analyse oil samples and use their findings to help clean up any spillages.[12] Their respective coast guards also constantly share information and pool their limited resources to fight the threat of overfishing: in 2008, the fisheries minister in Oslo, Helga Pedersen, publicly praised the stringent efforts made by the Russian authorities to reduce the overfishing of cod in the Barents Sea, which had been slashed from 80,000 tons in 2006 to around half that figure the following year.

This spirit of cooperation became clear from the Kremlin's 2009 document on national security, which argued that 'Russia has been working hard to find ways of cooperating with Nordic countries, and this has included the implementation . . . of joint projects in the Barents/Euro-Arctic region and the Arctic as a whole (taking) account of the interests of indigenous peoples'.[13] In its 'High North' policy document, the Norwegian government has also strongly reaffirmed its wish to work closely with Moscow: 'A number of the challenges in the High North in areas such as the environment and resource management', it argues, 'can only be solved with Russia's engagement and Norwegian-Russian cooperation.'[14]

In a worst-case scenario, even if tension between the two countries does ever flare up over the Barents Sea, Norway would align itself even more closely with its allies in NATO. It has already worked hard in recent years not only to build strong relations with its traditional military partners but also to stop disputes over the Barents from spoiling them. In 2005, Oslo initiated a dialogue with the United States, Germany, the UK, France and Canada over a number of Arctic-related topics and fought to win broad international support for its legal position over disputed regions. At a press conference Prime Minister Kjell Magne Bondevik emphasized that 'we work to gain understanding for the Norwegian view internationally', while Barents Sea minister, Kim Traavik, stated that disputes over Svalbard would be discussed with what he termed 'our most important partners'.[15] Similar sentiments were made by members of the parliamentary Standing Committee on Foreign Affairs.[16]

Greenland and Iceland

Norway's relations with Russia suggest that the possible presence of large deposits of oil and gas in Arctic waters will create a complicated picture of which cooperation, tension and even a certain level of hostility will each form a part. But this is less true of Norway's relations with its two other Arctic neighbours, Greenland and Iceland, which are likely to remain highly cordial.

Oslo's main source of disagreement with the governments in Copenhagen and Reykjavik has previously focused on a large stretch of water that lies equidistant to the territories of all three countries but beyond the 200-mile limits of their economic zones. This area, which is generally referred to as the 'Herring Loophole' or the 'southern Banana Hole', is important not only because of its extensive fishing stocks but also because it may be where considerable quantities of petroleum are located.

The dispute has been temporarily resolved by an agreement between the three claimants. In September 2006, a few weeks before Norway formally submitted its claim to the UN Commission on the Limits of the Continental Shelf, Foreign Minister Stoere met with his Icelandic and Danish counterparts in New York to sign an agreement not to stand in each other's way when trying to determine how the Banana Hole should be apportioned. The ministers also promised to sign 'three parallel bilateral agreements on the final determination of the boundary lines' at a later stage, when the Commission has had time to consider the limits of the outer continental shelves.[17] 'This is the first time such an agreement has been reached in our region', emphasized Stoere. 'This will provide clarity and predictability with regard to the future exploitation of resources.'[18]

But a problem might arise if both Iceland and Greenland decide to make their own claims to this area, submitting their own case to the UN Commission and arguing that their continental shelves overlap with those of the Norwegians. If in this situation the UN Commission accepts the geological arguments of more than two countries, then reaching bilateral agreements to settle all the overlapping claims could prove very difficult. But Norwegian officials remain optimistic and point out that, just as the three countries cooperated to support Oslo's submission to the UN Commission because it would be in their mutual interest to determine the exact extent of Norway's outer shelf, so too are they likely to continue working together in the same spirit. 'After that it would be up to us to sit down and set the boundaries', as Rolf Einar Fife, the head of the legal department at Norway's Foreign Ministry, told one newspaper.[19]

Like any other country, Iceland has a lot to gain from claiming these and other waters as its own. This is not because it needs to use oil or gas at home. Far from it, Iceland is one of the least oil-dependent countries in the world, since around 90 per cent of its houses are heated with geothermal energy and the vast majority of its electricity is generated by hydropower. Instead it is because its economy is still heavily dependent on the fishing industry, and it could earn huge revenues from auctioning untapped fields of petroleum to the international energy companies that have the expertise and infrastructure that it completely lacks itself.[20] But it would nonetheless be quite unwilling to risk any territorial dispute from getting out of hand, partly because it does not have the means to enter into a fight, or even make any meaningful threats of using force, but also because its own economy is highly vulnerable to capital flight: in the autumn of 2008 it was badly mauled by the global credit crisis and the government was forced to turn to the International Monetary Fund for support.

This is why in 1981 Reykjavik reached an agreement with Oslo to settle the status of an overlapping stretch of water that lies west of the Jan Mayen Islands, which are officially Norwegian territory. Having long quarrelled about exactly where the border should be drawn, the two countries decided that the best solution is to draw a line of demarcation and then each take a share of any resources that the other locates within its border: each state is entitled to take a 25 per cent cut of any hydrocarbon discoveries that the other makes.

These waters have become particularly important in the last few years because many geologists feel that the rocks that lie far beneath share the same geological characteristics as important petroleum-rich areas such as western Norway or eastern Greenland. Experts describe the Jan Mayen Ridge as a piece of continental crust that was stranded in the middle of the north-east Atlantic, millions of years ago, by a massive tectonic plate movement deep under the ground, and claim that the manner of its formation is a cause for optimism. 'Both the Atlantic margin and the Jan Mayen Ridge are world class exploration provinces. There is a well documented correlation of source and reservoir rocks between Norway, Greenland, and the Jan Mayen Ridge', as a director of a Norwegian exploration company argues. And referring to the rare 'supergiant' oil and gas fields, known in the industry as 'elephants', he adds that 'there aren't that many places left where you can do elephant hunting. This is one of them'.[21]

Not surprisingly, the Icelandic authorities are keen to exploit these waters as quickly as they can, and are holding high hopes that the exploration efforts of international companies will strike black gold. 'We have high expectations of finding oil in the Dreki area, since scientific research has indicated that valuable resources may be found there', as Ossur Skarphedinsson, the minister of Industry, Energy, and Tourism for Iceland, has said. The only thing that tempers their optimism is the sheer difficulty of extracting and then moving any oil or gas to market. The most promising waters are not insuperably deep – lying at around 6,000 feet below the surface – but bringing anything to shore would be very difficult and expensive because of a complete lack of any infrastructure in the area.

Despite the clashes between trawlers and the Norwegian coast guard, these controversies are likely to be resolved peacefully, even if they sometimes spark stronger reactions than the Norwegians expect. This is what happened in 1985, when Oslo offered its petroleum industry an opportunity to explore for oil and gas in an area that crossed into Svalbard's 200-mile economic zone. The decision sparked warnings from Moscow and a sharp note of protest from London, prompting Oslo to drop the issue for a few years. In 2003, Icelandic premier David Oddson threatened to bring a case to the International Court of Justice if the 'Norwegian Coast Guard arrests Icelandic vessels fishing herring at Svalbard'. The following year, Magnus Thor Hafsteinsson of the opposition Liberal Party announced that he would raise the issue in Parliament and called for a confrontation with Norway in The Hague.[22]

Denmark's submission to the UN

For much the same reasons, Denmark is just as unlikely as Iceland to want a serious quarrel with Norway over the disputed Banana Hole. The Copenhagen government is due to submit its case to the UN by the end of 2014, exactly 10 years after signing the 1982 Convention, and even if its claims are accepted and an area of overlapping shelf is discovered, it would certainly strike a bilateral agreement in the same amicable spirit as the deal signed by the three countries in September 2006. This means that there is only one other area where Denmark's claimed continental shelf could overlap with that of another country and potentially be a cause of serious tension.

This area lies in the very far north of the Arctic Ocean, close to the North Pole. The Danes say that their outer continental shelf runs beyond the 200-mile economic zone that surrounds the coasts of Greenland and reaches far into the frozen wastelands of the High North. But in one small region, which covers just a few hundred square miles, the claims made by both Copenhagen and Moscow overlap.

The Danes are certainly spending a lot of time, money and effort trying to prove that this outer continental shelf belongs to them (they expect to spend around $42 million between 2004 and 2010) and are working closely with other countries to do so. The Danish mission is supported particularly closely by Canada, with which it shares resources and personnel to explore the Lomonosov Ridge that reaches well into their respective territorial waters, and in June 2005 it signed an agreement to use Canada's North Pole command centre at Alert as its headquarters. During 2009 the research team, known simply as 'Lomrog' ('Lomonosov Ridge off Greenland'), comprised 45 specialists from Canada, Denmark and Sweden who plan to collect bathymetric, gravity and seismic data to map the seabed under the ice. 'The preliminary investigations done so far are very promising', as Helge Sander, Denmark's minister of Science, Technology and Innovation, told one television station. 'There are things suggesting that Denmark could be given the North Pole.'[23]

Although the Danes, like the Russians, are taking this scientific effort very seriously, their overlapping claims are more likely to push them together than pull them apart. The two countries have already worked together to explore this area of shelf, and by early 2009 Lomrog's vessels had been closely escorted by the Russian nuclear icebreaker *50 Let Pobedy* ('50 Years of Victory'). The Russians, as a Danish scientist explained, had simply 'offered the best value. The ship has a Russian crew – they'll do what we ask them'.[24] Russia and Denmark are unlikely to quarrel heavily over this disputed area for the simple reason that its climatic conditions are so severe – and likely to remain so for many decades– and its natural resources are wholly unproven.

Nationalism in Greenland

But while serious international disputes between Iceland, Denmark and Norway over the Arctic's natural resources are very unlikely, there are already serious disagreements closer to home. Not only is there a bitter controversy in Norway between environmentalists and the supporters of the oil lobby but, as an earlier chapter has noted, a growing political conflict over who has a right to rule Greenland.[25]

The disagreements between Greenlanders and the government of Denmark have hitherto been a relatively low-key affair but have the potential to become politically explosive. While successive Danish prime ministers have said that they will not stand in the way of independence if the people desire it, in practice talks over how much freedom they should enjoy, and on what terms, have often proved protracted and at times almost intractable. But the issue has become all the more contentious and difficult over the past few years because Greenland is now thought to harbour huge deposits of oil and natural gas, whose exploitation would offer a Danish, or Greenlandic, government huge revenues.[26] So the political question of whom the reserves and their proceeds belong to is suddenly looming very large indeed.

Although the signs of real political crisis have long been evident to most visitors to Greenland (for some years the Danish flag has been rarely if ever seen in the streets of its capital, Nuuk, whereas the Greenlandic flag is almost everywhere), bitter disagreements are likely to emerge after June 2009, when Greenlanders assume even more powers from Denmark. As a result of a referendum held the previous November, in which more than three-quarters of the population voted in favour of the changes, the people of Greenland take control over the local police, courts and coast guard and are given a greater say in the formation and conduct of foreign policy. And on an island where English, Danish and several dialects of Greenlandic are spoken, the Inuit tongue also becomes the island's official language. Crucially, Greenlanders are also allowed a greater share of revenues from the sale of any oil discovered in the region. 'Taking advantage of what nature has provided us when it comes to non-living resources has become closely related to our political quest for more economic self-sufficiency as well as the opportunity to someday establish our own nation-state', as one Greenlandic minister told an international conference on the Arctic in January 2009.[27]

Disagreements over this issue have previously caused major political storms elsewhere in the world and could in the same way easily ignite tensions between Denmark and Greenland. The vote could whet the appetites of those who favour independence while the lure of a vast quantity of petrodollars is stiffening the resistance of those who oppose it. 'Whether the Greenlanders can take over more political institutions themselves depends heavily on the natural resources. It could well be thirty to forty years', as Per Oerum Joergensen, a

member of Denmark's ruling Conservative party and one of the key
negotiators in Greenland's new autonomy deal, pointed out at the
time.[28] Aleqa Hammond, Minister for Finance and Foreign Affairs in
the home rule government, is equally upbeat: 'If Greenland becomes
economically self-sufficient, then independence becomes a practical
possibility. We know that we have gold and diamonds and oil and
great masses of the cleanest water in the world. It may be closer than
we think.'[29]

The Danes argue that they not only have a strong historic link
with this massive 850,000 square mile landmass but also provide
it with vast annual subsidies of around 3.2 billion Danish kroner
($600 million) that make up half of its domestic budget and bestow
Greenlanders with a very generous welfare system modelled on
Scandinavian lines. So if commercial quantities of oil and gas are
discovered, then they point out that Danish taxpayers should either get
a share of the proceeds or at the very least stop forking out so much
money. 'Greenland can't both earn a bundle on oil and keep its block
grant', as Danish negotiator Frank Jensen told journalists recently.

Resolving the political conflict between the two sides could take
years, and is likely to become even more difficult if, in the years ahead,
the price of oil and gas climbs high and thereby raises the financial
stakes involved. So when commodity prices soared in the summer
of 2008, the dispute became more bitter as both sides dug in their
heels. As Kuupik Kleist, one of two Greenlandic representatives to
the Danish Parliament and a leading member of the negotiations, told
journalists, 'on the Danish side, they have gone from being almost
indifferent about the future of Greenland to being very, very much
focused on not giving up Danish rights on mineral resources'.[30]

The most likely scenario is that Greenland will eventually become
independent but retain close links, both formal and informal, with
Denmark. This is partly because, as Chapter 10 has pointed out,
many Greenlanders harbour a deep-seated mistrust of the United
States and would regard the Danes as their natural political and
diplomatic ally. As Svend Auken, a veteran Danish politician and
former energy minister, has argued, 'in the long run, the ideal would
be for them to be recognized as an independent state in the United
Nations, but in close contact with Denmark', still stamping the image
of the Danish queen on their currency and cooperating closely with
the Danish military. If Greenlanders fail to do this, he adds, then 'they
will be very dependent on the Americans'.[31]

China and the Arctic

One other country that could acquire a very important presence in the Arctic region over the coming years is China, even though its own borders lay thousands of miles south of the Arctic Circle and its government therefore has no unique legal right to any natural resources there. Under the 1982 Convention, which it signed in 1996, China only has the same rights as any other country to navigate 'the Area of high seas' in the Arctic Ocean and exploit its natural resources, which are 'the common heritage of mankind', in conjunction with the rules laid down in the treaty.

Beijing first showed signs of real interest in the region in the summer of 1999, when the *Snow Dragon* (RV *Xuelong*), a polar icebreaker that had been specially designed and built a few years before, took a team of scientists to the Bering and Chukchi Seas to investigate the impact of climate change and look more closely at local geology and fishing conditions. The *Snow Dragon* made other expeditions there in 2003 and 2008 to follow up on its earlier findings. 'An important task is to observe the effects of the polar ice surface changes upon the climate of our country', proclaimed Zhang Haisheng, the chief scientist for the 2008 mission and a leading director of a research institute in Hangzhou, just before he set sail. He and his team would do 'comprehensive research' on local geology and meteorology, and planned to use a helicopter, a yacht and an underwater robot to get the data they needed.

The Chinese have also established a permanent presence in the Arctic, founding a scientific research post, known as the Arctic Yellow River Station, in Ny-Alesund on Spitsbergen. This is just a very small base, which can accommodate no more than about 25 people at any one time, and merely allows Chinese scientists to constantly update their information on the local climate and conditions.

Beijing is of course quick to claim that its ambitions in the region are entirely peaceful and honourable: 'Natural resources in the region belong to all peoples of the world', proclaim the authorities. 'China has the responsibility, duty and the ability to take part in the peaceful exploration and protection of natural resources there.' But despite such assurances, it is tempting to think that darker motives lie behind the rhetoric and that the Chinese government could somehow be tempted to deploy, or risk using, military force to seize the Arctic's natural resources.

What is certainly plausible is that when the Chinese economy recovers from the global economic downturn that began in earnest in 2008, it is likely to grow at a steady, perhaps rapid, rate. This may not match the dramatic expansion that began in the mid- to late 1990s and lasted for more than a decade, during which time its rate of growth, at one stage averaging more than 9 per cent every year, was the highest of any large economy in the world. But it could well be high enough to generate enormous domestic demand for the raw materials of growth – oil, natural gas and minerals – which the the country lacks and has to import. By 2007 China had already become the second-largest oil consumer in the world, superseded only by the United States, and some forecasts predicted that its consumption could easily increase in the years ahead.[32] And while the price of some precious metals, such as iron ore, copper, aluminium, manganese, zinc and lead, had subsided in late 2008, they are widely expected to recover when the Chinese economy picks up and gathers pace.

Some of the more pessimistic observers might be tempted to argue that the Chinese government could potentially adopt a highly aggressive approach to the Arctic. If Beijing is desperate to acquire 'security of supply' that will guarantee a fuel source to power its economy, it is perhaps plausible to claim that Chinese-owned companies could get to work in a disputed or unclaimed area of the Arctic Ocean and threaten military force to guard its operations there. For example, there is one sliver of the seabed in the High North that neither Russia nor Norway claims as part of their outer continental shelves, although it is possible, if highly unlikely, that Denmark will make such a claim. If it belongs to no particular country, this area is due to be administered by the International Seabed Authority as the 'common heritage of mankind', but could then nonetheless plausibly make a tempting target for the Chinese government.

The difficulty with this argument is that any such move by Beijing would be wholly impractical and in all likelihood quite unnecessary. It would be impractical to risk using military force partly because of the enormous distances involved – its armed forces would have extremely long supply lines that would be highly vulnerable to enemy disruption – and because they would in any case have to cross waters or move through international straits, such as the Bering Strait, over which other countries could exert strategic control.

This would also be unnecessary because, like the Russians, Chinese oil and gas companies generally lack the sophisticated technology and expertise of their Western counterparts to develop underwater reserves. Therefore, they are dependent on signing up Western contractors, notably service companies such as Schlumberger and Halliburton, to help them out, which is not only time-consuming but also very expensive. So even if the Arctic does have the resources that some experts claim, and even if they do ever become commercially recoverable, then there are likely to be other parts of the world – notably unexplored areas of the Middle East such as Iraq and offshore Iran, or in Africa and South America – that the Chinese would be likely to find much more fruitful and where their moves would be politically less controversial. There are many Chinese nationals living in Cabinda, the oil-bearing province of Angola, but their presence is little noticed by locals and hardly known about at all anywhere else in the world.

However, there are some parts of the Arctic region, such as Greenland, Russia, and northern Canada, where Chinese oil companies would be in a position to search for and exploit any deposits. They could either bid directly to buy a stake in a field in the same way that in early 2009 Sinochem, the country's fourth-largest oil group, paid Soco International $465 million for a stake in a field in Yemen. Or they could even buy whole oil companies outright, thereby seizing in a single move all the reserves that belong to them, just as in 2004 the American company Unocal was the target of a takeover bid by a state-owned Chinese company.[33] The Chinese oil industry had been quiet in 2007, but activity picked up again the following year when Sinopec, the second-biggest listed oil company on Beijing's stock exchange, purchased Tanganyika Oil, a Canadian company operating in Syria, and was said to be hunting around for more commercial bargains. Sinopec was also rumoured to be in talks with Urals Energy, another company operating in Russia, about a possible takeover.[34]

All these Chinese organizations are nationalized and therefore have a distinct competitive advantage over their privately owned Western rivals. This is because they have access to the vast foreign exchange reserves of the Beijing government, and because they are not susceptible to any short-term pressure from private shareholders, who often demand not a long-term strategy but quick profits that will reap handsome dividends.

This could also help the Chinese companies that are likely to start viewing the Arctic as a highly productive and profitable source of mineral wealth and to gradually increase their commercial presence in the region in order to exploit them. Mirroring their approach to other parts of the world, Chinese mining organizations could start to buy up newly discovered deposits, known in the business as 'early-stage development assets', or else invest in existing mines that have long had a high output. Greenland is one relatively undiscovered place that might strongly tempt these investors, who with the same entrepreneurial spirit have in recent years also struck deals to exploit the newly located reserves of Congo and Zambia. If, on the other hand, the Chinese decide that later-stage assets offer more value, then they might put more emphasis on buying distressed companies in any of the Arctic countries, including Russia. In early 2009, for example, Chinese companies were using their considerable cash resources to purchase mining assets in Canada. 'The Chinese realize there are massive opportunities in the market', as one investor told a British newspaper.[35]

It is quite easy to imagine a situation in which this could eventually lead to international controversy. Elsewhere in the world, most notably in a number of African states, Beijing has not only been able to establish a close commercial relationship with various governments but has also used these ties as a basis upon which to build a much broader political association. The Chinese armed forces, for example, have in recent years closely supported the governments of Congo, Sudan, Zimbabwe and Zambia as part of what President Hu has called 'strategic and mutual friendship' with Africa.[36] So in the event that at some future point Greenland becomes independent from Denmark, it is plausible to argue that the Chinese could, in the same way, acquire a strong commercial and political relationship with its government that other countries, most obviously the United States, might regard as a possible threat.

This is a scenario that could very easily become real, although any tension between Washington and Beijing would not, strictly speaking, reflect any rivalry over resources. Precious and plentiful as Greenland's mineral wealth promises to be, it is no more likely to be the cause of conflict than the resources found in any other part of the world, most notably Africa. Any rivalry between these, and other countries, would be much more likely to prompt them to spend more money and resources finding and exploiting new, untapped deposits than to risk provoking a clash of arms that would be extremely costly and which could easily escalate.

The possibility of disagreement between Beijing and other countries here, as elsewhere, is enhanced by China's tendency to try and skewer the terms of the 1982 Convention. It has previously tried to assert its ownership of the South China Sea, for example, by making exaggerated claims about both how baselines can be drawn around an archipelago and about the geography of its coast in a way that would extend its borders more than 1,000 miles from the Chinese mainland.[37] Any such unilateralist tendency might mean that Beijing is particularly likely to disregard disputed, or even settled, claims made by some countries in the Arctic region, such as Canada's assertion that the waters of the Northwest Passage are 'internal'.

But the United States would certainly be very alarmed to watch the rapidly growing presence of a 'strategic competitor' in what it regards as its own backyard. In other words, even if Greenland, or any other part of the Arctic region, was known to be wholly devoid of any natural resources, then Washington would, in all likelihood, still be seriously concerned about its national security. The same is equally true of the Northwest Passage and the key waterways, such as the Bering Strait, that have such overwhelming strategic significance. If, decades hence, Chinese warships should constantly traverse these sea lanes and effectively impose a permanent military presence in the region as a result, there would be considerable international tension between Beijing and Washington. The presence of natural resources can only accentuate these tensions by bringing even more international maritime traffic into the region.

It became easier to imagine such tensions when, in the spring of 2009, the Chinese government unveiled plans for a big overhaul and expansion of its naval forces. Admiral Wu Shengli said that the plans included a bid to develop a new generation of warships and submarines, as well as fighter aircraft and long-range missiles, and did not rule out the construction of China's first aircraft carrier. The plans were a clear sign that for the first time the republic had ambitions to extend its naval reach far beyond its shores. China has 'expanded' national interests, explained the admiral, and needs to 'boost the ability to fight in regional sea wars' using high-tech weaponry.[38] Some American commentators predict that 'by sometime in the next decade, China's navy will have more warships than the United States', and point out that the writings of Alfred Thayer Mahan, the great American military theorist who argued that the power to protect merchant fleets has always been a determining factor in world history, have become highly influential in Beijing.[39]

The type of incident that could flare up in the Arctic, or elsewhere, had also taken place the previous month, when five Chinese ships shadowed and then manoeuvred dangerously close to a US Navy vessel, the USNS *Impeccable*, in the South China Sea. Although the American ship claimed to be making 'innocent passage' through China's exclusive economic zone, Beijing argued that its presence was 'illegal' because it was undertaking surveillance of a secret Chinese military site. The incident caused a diplomatic spat between the two capitals.

Conclusion: The Future of the Arctic

The picture of tomorrow's Arctic that emerges is complex, rich and varied. In political and military terms, there are likely to be opportunities for, and instances of, cooperation between allied and rival governments that seek to work together to confront all sorts of shared challenges and pursue a wide variety of mutual interests. Some of these will be environmental concerns, such as the need to protect endangered species, preserve ways of life that are under threat, or to prevent and alleviate the damage inflicted by oil spills or tanker collisions. There will also be considerable interplay of scientific expertise, as geologists, meteorologists and other experts from the 'Arctic Eight' and the wider world work together not just to consider the challenge of global warming in general but also to assess its impact on the polar regions in particular. And the immense technical challenge of extracting offshore oil and natural gas will, in the foreseeable future at least, often prompt Russia to act with, not against, other countries such as Norway that do have the necessary know-how.

At the same time, this upbeat picture of international cooperation and harmony is likely to coexist with moments of real tension and mistrust that will certainly lead to heated exchanges of words and fierce scientific debates. For international interest in the Arctic's energy resources is likely to engender a new form of diplomacy of which scientific evidence will form an increasingly important part. The 'Arctic Five', and other coastal states the world over, are already spending considerable sums of money trying to obtain the necessary geological evidence to prove that they have outer continental shelves reaching up to 350 miles from their baselines. These countries are already engaging in debates and arguments that are increasingly specialized in scientific terms, and they are likely to continue doing so in the years ahead.

Even if their claims are initially rejected outright by the UN Commission on the Limits of the Continental Shelf, new findings and opinions may prompt some governments to want to resubmit their case, perhaps impatiently seizing the disputed area for themselves before any judgement is formally delivered in their favour.[1] Others may not wish to resubmit their arguments and prefer to take matters into their own hands, perhaps making a unilateral declaration that the disputed area does belong to them and brandishing scientific 'evidence', perhaps of dubious validity, in their bid to prove it. But the emergence of this new type of diplomacy – which, when blended with geology and scientific expertise could perhaps be termed 'geodiplomacy' – is not in itself likely to lead to war. It merely changes the way in which individual governments express and assert themselves. 'There will be a battle between Canadian and Danish scientists on one side and the Russians on the other', as one expert has said of the Lomonosov Ridge, emphasizing that the task of proving its geological formation is a very challenging one.[2]

But disagreements over resources that are located, or thought to be located, in some regions – such as the waters around the Svalbard archipelago and the Barents Sea – could nonetheless lead to some difficult and tense moments. These might become quite serious enough in diplomatic terms but, fortunately, are likely to fall well short of a full-scale 'resource war': as the book has consistently argued, governments are most unlikely to want to risk losing a war over an area that may have nothing, or very little, to offer them.

At one end of the spectrum, there will be serious diplomatic protests if any country exploits the Arctic's natural resources in areas of 'high seas', but then refuses to acknowledge its obligations under the 1982 Convention. Under Article 140 of this treaty, signatories must recognize that their activities in these areas must be undertaken 'for the benefit of mankind' and acknowledge the right of the International Seabed Authority (ISA) to 'equitably share financial and other benefits derived from activities in "the Area"'. But, given their track record, it is not easy to see countries like China, Russia and the United States easily bowing to the ISA's authority. Each might take liberties with the letter and spirit of the law, dragging their heels to avoid making any payments or perhaps even just ignoring such demands altogether. As an earlier chapter has noted, these provisions have already previously stirred considerable controversy in Washington, and are likely to continue doing so in the years ahead.

Another, relatively innocuous, scenario would be symbolic gestures of the sort that Russia undertook near the North Pole in August 2007. The Russian armed forces have also carried out naval manoeuvres in the midst of Norway's oil and gas platforms in the North Sea,

undertaken aggressive air sorties that have grounded all offshore helicopter flights from nearby Norway, made some mock bombing runs,
and in the course of 2008 were responsible for at least three other, all
relatively unpublicized, incidents.[3] Such actions are of course capable
of causing serious alarm and are also likely to be symptomatic of a
wider, underlying tension.

A more serious situation is what might be termed a 'deadlock'
scenario in which the armed forces of one country deliberately and
proactively undertake a provocative action, which is designed to
assert a legal claim and embarrass the other side, but no shots are
actually fired. An example of such a tense predicament took place in
1969, when the American-owned ship, the *Manhattan*, made its way
in a high-handed manner through waters that Canada claimed as its
own; or in 1967 when Washington openly challenged the Kremlin's
requirement that all foreign ships wanting to pass through its territorial waters should obtain its prior permission.[4] Again, the harassment
of the USNS *Impeccable* in the South China Sea in April 2009 falls
into this category. Confrontations like these can sometimes lead to
war, although careful diplomacy, and the fact that one participant
has a significantly stronger force in the field than the other, is more
likely to defuse the situation. In the same way, it is possible to imagine
Russia dispatching a naval force to Svalbard in the years ahead to
assert its claim to the surrounding waters while at the same time foreign diplomats work hard to find a face-saving formula that prevents
such a situation from getting out of hand.

If such a stand-off does escalate and blows are exchanged, then
any consequent confrontation is not likely to be protracted, unless
of course it merely triggers a much wider conflict that has its own
independent causes of which events and developments in the Arctic are
just a sign or aggravation. The violent exchanges between Icelandic
fishermen and the Norwegian coast guard in 1994 instead give a better
indication of the brief but bitter sequence of events that might unfold
in this situation.[5] Such brief incidents would in all likelihood also be
quickly curtailed by a flurry of diplomacy between rival claimants
that have no real wish to enter into a lasting fight, but nonetheless still
want to be seen, by international and domestic audiences alike, to be
making a particular point and asserting the national interest.

The real risk – and the last of the three scenarios – is that countries
on the Arctic rim will feel threatened by the growing involvement of
foreign countries in a strategically important region. The presence
of any natural resources, real or imagined, merely accentuates this
danger, either increasing the amount of shipping in local waters or,

for example, the number of local companies that are bought out by foreign investors, while also prompting Russia, the United States or any other country to misapprehend the motives of others. Historic fears of foreign invasion could easily surface, prompting one coastal state to make a pre-emptive attack at moments of high tension.

Recognizing these dangers is of course only half the battle. It is also necessary to find ways of defusing tension.

Sharing energy resources

To avoid any disagreements that may arise in areas of disputed land or waters such as the Barents Sea, or the Svalbard archipelago, rival claimants could devise a formula for sharing in a fair and equitable way any energy resources that are discovered there. Trying to determine the exact terms upon which this is done is of course very difficult, but a model might be the agreement that Norway and Iceland struck over the Jan Mayen Islands in 1981. When the two countries were unable to agree upon the exact maritime borders, a conciliation commission established by both governments proposed a compromise deal that gave each party a 25 per cent share of any petroleum discovered on the other's continental shelf in an area covering 12,000 square miles.[6] Another model is an agreement struck in June 2008 between China and Japan over the disputed East China Sea, under which each country agreed to work together to explore and develop gas fields and then share the proceeds. A similar deal might be the best solution to determine the ownership of any natural resources found in the 'Grey Zone', the 'Loophole', the Beaufort Sea and the Svalbard archipelago.

There are all sorts of different variants of the 1981 agreement that might have the makings of lasting agreements in each case, or at the very least, diplomats would have nothing to lose by considering. One possibility is that instead of taking a fixed quarter share of any petroleum, each coastal state could receive a proportion that is determined by the location of any discovery: the closer any reserves lie to the shores of a coastal state, the greater its share of the proceeds. In the very centre of the Grey Zone or the Loophole – however that centre is defined – both Russia and Norway could take an equal share, while a sliding scale based on distance could determine how discoveries in any other area of the disputed seas are apportioned. One advantage with this approach is that it means that different claimants could work together to discover resources instead of having a vested interest in scrambling to get there first.

Such an approach does not represent any radical departure from what coastal states are in any case supposed to do with non-living natural resources that are discovered in the waters of their outer continental shelves. Under Article 82 of the 1982 Convention – a clause that looks likely to be the subject of heated debate and dispute between lots of countries the world over in the coming years – these states are obliged to make 'payments or contributions in respect of the exploitation of non-living reserves' in these waters.[7] The Convention adds that these payments should be made annually and, after 5 years, should start off at 1 per cent 'of the value and volume of production at the site' and should increase by the same amount every subsequent year until they reach a capped rate of 7 per cent.[8] This provision is vital for the simple reason that it reiterates the essential principle that no coastal state can just assume that it has any necessary claim over the sea's resources, beyond those that are found in their immediate vicinity. On the contrary, the further away any such resources are found, the stronger the case that a coastal state should to some degree share them, whether it is with the ISA or with other claimants.[9]

Sharing a fixed percentage of the proceeds of any discovery may also be a better solution than the 'Svalbard formula'. Under the terms of the Spitsbergen Treaty of 1920, each signatory state is only granted 'conditions of equality to the exercise and practice of all maritime, industrial, mining or commercial enterprises both on land'. But the trouble with this approach is that each country not only lacks an incentive to work with others, but also has a vested interest in working quickly, scrambling hard to discover any natural resources before anyone else does. This undermines a considered, level-headed approach and could instead even be conducive to panic. It also means that the bigger states could try to bully the weak: Russia or the United States, for example, could try to use veiled or explicit threats of military force to dissuade others from searching for oil, natural gas or precious metals. Such an arrangement would even allow the Barents Sea, and elsewhere, to become the 'sea of cooperation' that the Norwegian government has called for.[10]

The strategic challenge

As argued in this book, the real risk to international stability posed by the great Arctic thaw is not any scramble for its natural resources so much as the increasing presence – a military, commercial, political and economic presence – of foreign countries in a strategically vital region. Are there any measures that could realistically be taken to reduce and minimize so much mistrust and misunderstanding?

The most obvious such step is to demilitarize as much of the Arctic's waters and territory as possible. In this respect the Svalbard archipelago does offer a helpful and constructive example because the 1920 agreement decreed that the islands should be neutral ground even though Norway, the sovereign state they belong to, has long been a member of NATO. In the same way, agreements could conceivably be struck to bar or restrict the passage of warships through certain highly sensitive waterways, such as the Northwest Passage, or to demilitarize highly strategic islands and locations.

The Northern Sea Route provides one example of how easily such an agreement could be implicitly established. Moscow's historic fears of foreign attack would be considerably eased if it is assured of its right to be given advance notice of any international shipping that makes its way along its northern shores, which it demanded of American icebreakers that moved through these waters in the mid-1960s.[11] Whether all or any of these waters are 'high seas', 'territorial seas' or an 'international strait', foreign governments could still implicitly accept Russia's right to request these special conditions by failing to bring any formal legal challenge before the International Court of Justice in The Hague, or else just by failing to raise any diplomatic protest at such an action. This could also be done with the modest intervention of the International Maritime Organization, which could help determine the course and usage of new shipping lanes.

At the very least, other countries could stifle Russian fears if not by giving advance notice of their maritime movements then by simply observing conditions about how many ships could move along key stretches of water at any one moment and what distance they should keep from each other and from the coasts. For its own part, Russia could ostensibly justify such measures by pointing to the 1982 Convention and arguing that they are necessary 'for the prevention, reduction and control of marine pollution', as one of its provisions allows.[12] Such a tacit agreement would, of course, be a vastly preferable solution to the brokerage of a formal international treaty, a process that, like the drafting of the 1982 Convention on the Law of the Sea, can be extremely protracted and often unrewarding.

Some territories in the region could conceivably become neutral ground in the same way as Finland and Sweden. So in the event that Greenland attains independence from Denmark, both Russia and the United States could perhaps give security guarantees while respecting and recognizing its neutrality. The United States is of course most unlikely to want to close its vast base at Thule, but it could still scale this presence down and recognize the rest of the country as a demilitarized, and certainly as a nuclear-free, zone. Iceland could also remain within NATO, but its government could refuse permission to allow the United States, Russia or any other country to reopen the former air base at Keflavik, or to station any troops on its soil, except at moments of national emergency.

There are a number of other steps – known in the days of the Cold War as 'confidence-building measures' – that could minimize the scope for misunderstanding and prevent any regional arms race from breaking out. Foreign governments could have a right to inspect and observe the military presence of their rivals and should be informed a long time in advance of any exercises due to be undertaken in the region. All these exercises should only involve very small contingents of men and materials. There are also large areas of land and sea where such exercises should be completely prohibited and where any military presence could be significantly scaled down.

Unfortunately, by the late spring of 2009 it seemed most unlikely that either Russia or NATO would undertake any such measures. On the contrary, both seemed more interested in considerably escalating their presence in the Arctic, and in doing so risked creating or aggravating international mistrust. 'I would be the last one to expect military conflict – but there will be a military presence', said NATO Secretary-General Jaap de Hoop Scheffer during a summit in Reykjavik in late January. 'It should be a military presence that is not overdone, and there is a need for political cooperation and economic cooperation.'[13] At the same time Norway has since 2007 been quietly boosting its military ties with Sweden and Finland, negotiating a new treaty to enhance cross-border cooperation, and in spring 2009 undertook a big land, sea and air military exercise in the region. The point is not that such actions are in any way unreasonable – they are arguably just a foreseeable consequence of Russian actions, not least in Georgia in the summer of 2008 – but that they are indicative of a wider regional arms build-up that can potentially be averted.

It would be more advantageous if the armed forces of all of the eight Arctic countries could instead cooperate if not on military exercises then on issues that are a matter of common concern. They could, for example, work together and pool resources to guard stretches of sea more effectively from the threat of overfishing, piracy, smuggling and terrorism, or on particular environmental projects such as alleviating the impact of collisions or averting other disasters at sea. Some such steps had been taken by the early summer of 2009, but these were infrequent and limited in scope.[14]

Areas of 'high seas'

These measures – and others that a number of organizations have called for to protect the environment – could be taken without any serious or radical overhaul of the existing framework of international law.[15] In order to defuse mistrust between nations and to prevent disputed areas in the Arctic region from becoming a future frontline for superpower rivalry, nothing very ambitious is necessarily required. Effective measures can be undertaken much more simply, and as a result, far more quickly without overturning existing structures of local government, such as the Arctic Council, or introducing new legislation. This is true not just of sharing the region's natural resources in an equitable manner, and preventing any confrontation from breaking out, but also of preventing environmental damage. As Joe Borg, the EU's commissioner for Fisheries and Maritime Affairs has argued, 'we don't need to reinvent the wheel to build a governance system for the Arctic. Indeed the structures we need already exist'. The existing framework, continues Borg, merely needs to be properly enforced and some gaps properly filled in: fishing stocks in large areas of the Arctic Ocean are still relatively unprotected, for example, and could potentially be covered by an extension of the Northeast Fisheries Commission.[16]

More difficult, however, is the task of preventing international rivalry and defusing mistrust in those areas that lie beyond outer continental shelves. These regions might turn out to be very small if the claims made by the 'Arctic Five' over the size of their outer continental shelves are accepted, but could be considerable if one or any are rejected in whole or in part.

Some such calls for drastic action have been made, and one academic has argued that:

> we need to create an institution imbued with sovereign powers to develop the massive fuel sources in the Arctic Circle. It would be a far-reaching step, but the stakes warrant a special attempt to take it . . . Existing international law cannot deal with all forthcoming disputes. The sheer number of international bodies that claim some jurisdiction – including the Arctic Council, the Law of the Sea Convention, the United Nations International Maritime Commission – is a recipe for institutional competition, polarisation and delay.[17]

This, continues the argument, justifies the establishment of a new organization 'to which sovereignty is ceded by the nations around the Arctic Circle'.

Hopefully such drastic measures will also prove to be unnecessary. Instead it might prove possible to merely strengthen and clarify the role of the ISA. A new agreement, comparable to the 1959 Antarctic Treaty System, could certainly be struck over these areas of high seas, one that would temporarily resolve such issues as the exploitation of natural resources and the distribution of their proceeds, as well as the demarcation of overlapping continental shelves. As one distinguished international lawyer has argued, 'a relatively short framework treaty addressing some fundamental sovereignty and dispute resolution mechanisms which included a set of overarching regional management principles would provide a sound foundation for the regime'.[18] Conceivably such a treaty could eventually cover the entire Arctic Ocean, not merely areas of high seas and overlapping shelves, although this would of course be very much harder to broker.

Of course any such agreement would far from guarantee a peaceful future for the Arctic region, or stop foreign governments from rushing to stake their claim to its waters and resources. It is hard not to be reminded of the Berlin Conference of 1884, which is the most obvious single example of how such deals can sometimes even prove wholly counterproductive: European countries were racing to claim for themselves the newly discovered lands that lay south of the Sahara, but far from slowing them down, as it was intended to, the conference merely helped to create a 'Scramble for Africa'. All these years later, every effort also needs to be made to avert a latter-day scramble in the world's last great wilderness.

Notes

Introduction

1 United Nations Convention on the Law of the Sea (UNCLOS) (1982), Article 56, (1), (a).

2 UNCLOS (1982), Article 76, (6). A coastal state does not have such unconditional rights over natural resources found in this extended economic zone (EEZ). See Conclusion pp. 222.

3 UNCLOS first came into effect on 16 November 1994, having first been signed on 10 December 1982. Switzerland signed the Convention on 1 May 2009, becoming the 158th state to do so.

4 By April 2009, 22 countries had applied to the UN Commission on the Limits of the Continental Shelf to claim an outer continental shelf (OCS). Just nine claims were made between 2001 and 2007. The total area of OCS that could eventually be claimed by the world's coastal countries could amount to as much as 5.7 million square miles, while the world's EEZs are estimated at 32.3 million. 'The Area' covers around 98.8 million square miles. See Paskal, C. and Lodge, M. (2009), 'A fair deal on seabed wealth: the promise and pitfalls of Article 82 on the outer continental shelf', briefing paper, London: Chatham House.

5 This was the view of Leonid Lobkovksy, deputy head of the Russian Institute of Oceanology, interviewed in the newspaper *Nezavisimaya Gazeta*, 13 August 2007.

6 The Arctic is usually defined as the region that lies north of the Arctic Circle, the circle of latitude that runs 66.56 degrees north latitude. But other criteria include the local climate and ecology, such as the 10-degree July isotherm. This book uses the first and more broadly accepted definition.

7 UNCLOS (1982), Article 76, (8); Annex II.

8 Canwest News Service, 11 November 2008.

9 UNCLOS (1982), Annex II, Article 4.

10 'Developing Europe's Energy Security: Is the Arctic the Future Frontier?', Café Crossfire Debate sponsored by Friends of Europe in association with StatoilHydro, 19 September 2008, Brussels, Belgium.

11 Hassol, S. (2004), *Impacts of a Warming Arctic*. Arctic Climate Impact Assessment, Cambridge and New York, NY: Cambridge University Press. This quote is taken from the Executive Summary.

12 See Chapters 5 and 6.

13 Antarctica Treaty (1959), Article 4.

14 Antarctica Treaty (1959), Article 1.

Chapter 1

1 Some of the other countries that experienced serious unrest were Guinea, Mauritania, Indonesia, the Philippines and Senegal.
2 'Food riots fear after rice price hits a high', *Guardian*, 6 April 2008.
3 *Climate Change and International Security*, S113/08, 14 March 2008, p. 5.
4 'A Cooperative Strategy for 21st Century Seapower', *United States Navy Report*, October 2007.
5 Professor John Beddington, speech to the Sustainable Development UK Conference, London, 19 March 2009.
6 In December 2008 the Russian news agency, RIA Novosti, reported that more than 60 bombers and 15 refuelling planes had taken off from Engels' air base near Saratov. See also Chapter 9, p. 158.
7 'Politicus: assessing Russia's plans with a rare fortitude', *International Herald Tribune*, 1 October 2008.
8 General Sverre Diesen's speech at the Oslo Military Academy, 26 November 2007.
9 Interview with Kathleen Harris. 'Laying claim to Canada's internal waters', Sun Media, 23 February 2007.
10 Interview in *Krasnaya Zvezda (Red Star)*, 24 June 2008; interview in *RIA Novosti*, 11 June 2008.
11 Reported by RIA Novosti, 15 July 2008. See also 'Russian navy resumes Arctic sea patrols', *Ice News*, 26 July 2008. Spitsbergen is the largest island in the Svalbard archipelago, which used to be referred to as 'the Spitsbergen archipelago'. The Norwegians replaced the Dutch word 'Spitsbergen' with the ancient Norse 'Svalbard' in 1920.
12 'Russian National Security Strategy until 2020', 25 December 2008. This draft text was approved by the National Security Council in Moscow on 20 February 2009.
13 The document, entitled 'Principles for Russian Politics in the Arctic in the Period to 2020 and in a Further Perspective', was published on the website of Russia's Security Council on 27 March 2009.
14 Article 51 of the UN Charter 1945 states that a member state has 'the inherent right of individual or collective self-defence if an armed attack occurs . . . until the Security Council has taken measures necessary to maintain international peace and security'.
15 Deudney, D. and Ikenberry, G. J. (2009), 'The myth of the autocratic revival', *Foreign Affairs*, 88, (1), 87–8.
16 See Chapter 12, pp. 209–10.
17 UNCLOS (1982), Part XI. In particular, Article 136 states that 'the Area and its resources are the common heritage of mankind'.
18 In his *History of the Peloponnesian War*, Thucydides famously explained war as the outcome of 'fear', as well as ambition and advantage.
19 See below Chapter 4, pp. 54–5, Chapter 11, pp. 193–4.
20 'Russia and NATO look to Arctic co-operation', *Jane's Defence Weekly*, 3 April 2009.
21 The Ilulissat Declaration. Proceedings of the Arctic Ocean Conference. 2008, 27–9 May 2008; Ilulissat, Greenland; Denmark: Danish Ministry of Foreign Affairs. In March 2009 the United States remained a non-signatory state of the 1982 Convention. See Chapter 10.
22 Interview in RIA Novosti, 18 April 2008.

23 The collision took place in 1990. See Franckx, E. (1993), *Maritime Claims in the Arctic: Canadian and Russian Perspectives*. Dordrecht and London: Martinus Nijhoff.
24 Russian attempts to base missiles in Cuba led to the Missile Crisis of 1962. Recent NATO plans to station parts of the Missile Defense Shield in Poland have provoked a very strong reaction in the Kremlin.
25 See Chapter 10, pp. 178–9.
26 The Mary River iron ore deposits on Baffin Island are producing high-grade iron ore with a content of 67 per cent. During the 2008 season 120,000 tonnes of bulk cargo was shipped from the mine to European mills.
27 The meeting of Russia's National Security Council, Franz Josef Land, 15 September 2008.
28 *Arctic Marine Shipping Assessment*, 29 April 2009. Arctic Council, Tromsoe, Norway, p. 73.
29 In 2007, the Canadian Coast Guard (CCG) recorded 132 voyages through Arctic waters, compared with 63 the previous year. The CCG does, however, include the Hudson Bay as part of its Arctic operational area, even though it is technically south of the Arctic Circle. On the Russian use of the National Sea Route see Chapter 7, p. 106–8.
30 Jaap de Hoop Scheffer, 'Speech on security prospects in the High North'. NATO conference; 2009, 29 January; Reykjavik, Iceland.
31 National Security Presidential Decision Directive/NSPD 6, January 2009.
32 'Global Trends 2025: A Transformed World', *Central Intelligence Agency Report*, November 2008, pp. 32, 49.
33 'Russia's role in rescuing Iceland', *BBC News*, 13 November 2008. (Quoting an editorial in *Barents Observer*.)

Chapter 2

1 Kolbert, E. (2005), 'The climate of man', *The New Yorker*, 25 April.
2 Kolbert, E. (2005), 'The climate of man'.
3 Professor Charles Harris of Cardiff University, quoted in 'Earth's permafrost starts to squelch'. *BBC News*, 29 December 2004.
4 'Climate change could doom Alaska's tundra', news report by the College of Engineering, Oregon State University, 5 August 2004. This article quoted Professor Bachelet's speech to the annual meeting of the Ecological Society of America held at Portland, Oregon, 1–4 August.
5 Hagedorn, F. (2008), 'Expanding forests and changing growth forms of Siberian larch at the Polar Urals treeline during the 20th century'. *Global Change Biology*, 14 (7), 1581–91.
6 The report, originally published in *Geophysical Research Letters*, was published in *Globe and Mail*, Ottawa, Canada, 22 November 2002.
7 'Arctic sea ice shrinks as temperatures rise', press release, National Snow and Ice Data Center, University of Colorado, 3 October 2006.
8 'Islands emerge as Arctic ice shrinks to record low', Reuters, 21 August 2007.
9 'Arctic ice is thinner than ever according to new evidence from explorer', *Daily Telegraph*, 17 April 2009.
10 'Mammoth sale of fossil ivory helps nomadic herders', *Guardian*, 2 March 2005.
11 'Arctic becomes Tourism hot spot, but is that cool?', *Wall Street Journal*, 24 September 2007.

12 Address by Ginny Fay, Director of DCED Division of Tourism, to 7th Annual Ecotourism in Alaska Conference, 3 February 2000, Anchorage, AK.
13 'Global warming is killing us too, say Inuit', *Guardian*, 11 December 2003.
14 Speech of Mr Per Bethelsen, Greenland's Minister for Finance and Foreign Affairs, Arctic Frontiers Conference, 19 January 2009, Tromsoe, Norway.
15 The 'albedo effect' is also mentioned in Chapter 2, p. 33.
16 Mark Serreze, quoted in 'Arctic ice "disappearing quickly"', *BBC News*, 28 September 2005.
17 'The methane time bomb', *Independent*, 23 September 2008.
18 Reported in the Arctic Blog by *BBC Newsnight*'s science editor, Susan Watts, 27 August 2008.

Chapter 3

1 Quoted in Officer, C. and Page, J. (2001), *A Fabulous Kingdom: The Exploration of the Arctic*. Oxford and New York, NY: Oxford University Press, p. 45. For a general history of Arctic exploration see Berton, P. (1988), *The Arctic Grail: The Quest for the Northwest Passage and the North Pole 1818–1909*. New York: Viking.
2 Parry, W. E. (1824), *Journal of a Voyage for the Discovery of the North-West Passage from the Atlantic to the Pacific*. London: John Murray.
3 Kane, E. (1857), *Arctic Explorations: The Second Grinnell Expedition in Search of Sir John Franklin, 1853, '54, '55*, Childs and Peterson: Philadelphia, p. 124.
4 The Northeast Passage is distinct from the Northern Sea Route (NSR) because it begins and ends in high seas; whereas the NSR is regarded, by the Russians at least, purely as a national transport route.
5 Bomann-Larsen, T. (2006), *Roald Amundsen*. Stroud: Sutton Publishing, p. 308.

Chapter 4

1 'Islands emerge from the melting Arctic ice', Reuters, 21 August 2007.
2 Under international law, acts of discovery only confer inchoate title. Further acts of occupation and administration are required. See The Netherlands v United States of America, 4 April 1928, 2 RIIA 829.
3 An obvious example is the long-running dispute between the Russian government and BP's joint venture with TNK.
4 Ross, M. L. (2008), 'Blood barrels: why oil wealth fuels conflict', *Foreign Affairs*, 87, (3), 2–8.
5 Shlaim, A. (1995), *War and Peace in the Middle East: A Concise History*. London and New York, NY: Penguin Books, p. 133.
6 'The recognition of Kuwait by Iraq, which had followed the 1963 coup was half-hearted, and Kuwait had to bribe the Iraqis to obtain it anyway'. Aburish, S. K. (2000), *Saddam Hussein: The Politics of Revenge*. London: Bloomsbury, p. 73.
7 Introduction pp. 3–4.
8 The argument of 'ice as land' was adopted by Canadian lawyers in the 1960s. See Reid, R. (1974), 'The Canadian claim to sovereignty over the waters of the arctic', *Canadian Yearbook of International Law*, Vol. 12, p. 119.

9 Burkhanov, V. F. (1957), *Soviet Arctic Research*. Translated by E. R. Hope. Ottawa, ON: Defence Research Board of Canada.

10 UNCLOS (1982), Article 234.

11 UNCLOS (1982), Article 87.

12 The Treaty Concerning Spitsbergen (Svalbard) came into effect in 1925.

13 1867 Convention Ceding Alaska between Russia and the United States, 134 Consolidated Treaty Series (ConTS) 331.

14 Rt Hon Joe Clark (1995), *Statement on Sovereignty*, 10 September. See generally Griffiths, F. (1987), *Politics of the Northwest Passage*. Kingston, ON: McGill-Queens University Press, pp. 269–73.

15 Statement of Pierre Trudeau to the House of Commons, 15 May 1969.

16 The political tensions over this and other Arctic matters are discussed further in Chapter 11.

17 UNCLOS (1982), Article 2, (1).

18 UNCLOS (1982), Articles 2, (1); 8, (1).

19 UNCLOS (1982), Articles 2, 3.

20 UNCLOS (1982), Article 25.

21 UNCLOS (1982), Articles 86, 87. The 'contiguous zone' is contiguous to the territorial sea and may extend for a further 12 miles from the baseline of the coastal state under Article 33.

22 UNCLOS (1982), Part IV, Article 47, *et seq.*

23 The 'Anglo-Norwegian Fisheries Case', United Kingdom v Norway (1951), ICJ Reports 116.

24 UNCLOS (1982), Article 38 (1). A 'strait' can exist through internal waters, territorial sea, a contiguous zone or exclusive economic zone (EEZ).

25 The invention of the category of 'transit passage' in UNCLOS represented a compromise between the competing claims made by coastal states and naval powers. Coastal states wanted maritime traffic moving through any strait to only have 'innocent passage' whereas other countries wanted freedom of navigation. 'Transit passage' represented a halfway measure, giving coastal states powers to impose restrictions on ships, but not as sweeping as they would enjoy on ships making 'innocent passage'.

26 Its claims are specified under section 7 of the Oceans Act 1996.

27 The International Court of Justice recognized a claim of 'historic waters' in a landmark ruling, 'Anglo-Norwegian Fisheries Case' (1951), ICJ Reports 116.

28 So in 1970 the US State Department responded to Canadian claims over the Northwest Passage by stating that 'international law provides no basis for these proposed unilateral extensions of jurisdiction on the high seas, and the United States can neither accept or acquiesce in the assertion of such jurisdiction'. See Rothwell, D. R. (1996), *The Polar Regions and the Development of International Law*. Cambridge: Cambridge University Press, p. 195.

29 United Kingdom v Albania (1949), ICJ Reports 3, 'The Corfu Channel Case'.

30 UNCLOS (1982), Article 3.

31 Nunavut Land Claims Agreement Act, S.C. 1993, c. 29.

32 National Security Presidential Decision Directive/NSPD 66, January 2009.

33 Section 1.2 of 'Regulations for Navigation of the Seaways of the Northern Sea Route', reprinted in Franckx, E. (1993), *Maritime Claims in the*

Arctic, Appendix 1, p. 315. See generally Rothwell, D. R. (1996), *The Polar Regions and the Development of International Law*. Cambridge: Cambridge University Press, pp. 201–12.

34 Brigham, L. W. (1991), *The Soviet Maritime Arctic*. London: Belhaven Press, pp. 216–17.

35 Russia's claim that it had a right to impose restrictions on maritime traffic in territorial sea was later incorporated in the Administration of the Northern Sea Route 1971.

36 The crucial passage of the Soviet message ran: 'The Vilkitsky Strait is within USSR territorial waters. Therefore sailing of any foreign navy ships in the strait is subject to regulations of safety of USSR frontiers. For passing the strait according to the above regulations military ships must obtain preliminary permission of USSR government through diplomatic channels one month before expected date of passing.'

37 UNCLOS (1982), Article 15.

38 See Chapter 5.

39 Message from the Danish ambassador, Embassy of Denmark, Ottawa, ON, 28 July 2005.

40 The Permanent Court of International Justice (PCIJ), dissolved in 1946, was the forerunner of the International Court of Justice.

41 See Chapter 1, p. 20, Chapter 11, pp. 193–4.

42 The 19,475 square nautical miles (nm) of the Grey Zone are comprised of 12,070 square nm of overlapping EEZ, 6,558 square nm of undisputed Norwegian EEZ and 817 square nm of undisputed Russian EEZ.

43 Treaty concerning the Archipelago of Spitsbergen, and Protocol, Paris, 9 February 1920.

44 This 'territorial sea' was previously 3 nautical miles, although by the 1960s a growing number of countries were claiming that the distance was 12 miles instead. In 1957, Norway proclaimed a 3-mile territorial sea around Svalbard. A government report argued that this was to 'lay the formal foundation to claim unrestricted Norwegian jurisdiction over the seabed . . . around Svalbard except for the areas within the 4-mile limits, which would be subject to Svalbard Treaty provisions'. In 2004, Norway expanded the territorial sea borders around Svalbard from 3 to 12 miles.

45 See Chapter 6, pp. 101.

46 House of Lords Debates, Volume 477, 2 July 1986.

47 The British position was that the Norwegians did not need to be invited because their legal case over Svalbard was already clear. This is based on the author's telephone interview with a Western diplomat, 3 February 2009.

48 1978 Agreement on the Interim Practical Agreement for Fishing in an Adjoining Area in the Barents Sea, 11 January 1978.

49 See Chapter 12.

50 UNCLOS (1982), Article 83.

51 Tunisia v Libyan Arab Jamahiriya 1982, ICJ Rep. 18; Libya v Malta 1985, ICJ 13; The North Sea Continental Shelf Cases 1969, ICJ Rep. 3.

52 Tunisia v Libyan Arab Jamahiriya 1982, ICJ Rep. 18.

53 Bernier, J. E. (1939), *Master Mariner and Arctic Explorer*. Ottawa, ON: Le Droit, p. 128.

54 According to the 1926 decree, the USSR 'proclaims as territories all lands and islands already discovered or discovered in the future which at the

time of publication of this decree are not recognized . . . as territories of any foreign state and which lie in the Arctic Ocean north of the shores of Union of Soviet Socialist Republics . . . up to the North Pole'.
55 Norway made its submission to the UN Commission on 27 November 2006; Denmark is due to make its own submission by 2014.

Chapter 5

1 Mouawad, J. (2008), 'Oil survey says Arctic has riches', *International Herald Tribune*, 24 July.
2 In its *World Petroleum Assessment* (DDS-60), published in 2000, the USGS had estimated the world's total undiscovered reserves of both oil and natural gas. Excluding the US, the volumes were estimated to be 649 billion barrels of oil and 4,669 trillion cubic feet of gas.
3 'Circum-Arctic Resource Appraisal: Estimates of Undiscovered Oil and Gas North of the Arctic Circle', USGS Fact Sheet 3049, 2008.
4 '90 billion barrels of oil and 1,670 trillion cubic feet of natural gas assessed in the Arctic', USGS, press release, 23 July 2008.
5 Yergin, D. (1991), *The Prize: The Epic Quest for Oil, Money and Power*. New York, NY: Simon & Schuster, pp. 608, 627.
6 Quoted in 'Iran wields oil embargo threat', *BBC News*, 5 April 2002.
7 See 'Oil's Trouble Spots', *Briefing by the Council on Foreign Relations*, 5 January 2009.
8 'Brown calls for end to the power of OPEC', *Guardian*, 20 May 2008.
9 'Peak oil' has spawned a huge bibliography. An example is Simmons, M. (2005), *Twilight in the Desert: The Coming Saudi Oil Shock and the World Economy*. London and New York, NT: John Wiley & Sons.
10 'Global oil supply will peak in 2020, says energy agency', *Guardian*, 15 December 2008. In its 2007 *World Energy Outlook*, the IEA predicted an annual 3.7 per cent rate of decline, but a year later increased this to 6.7 per cent.
11 Shaxson, N. (2007), *Poisoned Wells: The Dirty Politics of African Oil*. London and New York, NY: Palgrave Macmillan, p. 16.
12 Quoted in Marcel, V. (2006), *Oil Titans: National Oil Companies in the Middle East*. Chatham House, London, and Brookings Institution, Washington DC, p. 133.
13 Debate organized by the Friends of Europe, 19 September 2008. See also the news report of 22 September 2008, 'EU energy chief backs Arctic drilling'. Available at: http://www.euractiv.com/en/environment/eu-energy-chief-backs-arctic-drilling/article-175601
14 'The European Union and the Arctic Region', Communication from the Commission to the European Parliament and the Council, Brussels, Belgium, 20 November 2008, p. 6.
15 Mouawad, J. (2008), 'Oil survey says Arctic has riches', *International Herald Tribune*, 24 July.
16 The figures were West Siberia (3.69 bn barrels of oil), Arctic Alaska (29.96 bn), East Barents Sea (7.4 bn), East Greenland Rift (8.9 bn), Yenisey-Khatanaga (5.58 bn), Amerasia (9.72 bn), West Greenland-East Canada (7.24 bn) and Laptev Sea (3.11 bn).
17 In addition to East Greenland and West Greenland, the USGS estimated that Greenland's northern shores have 1.34 bn of oil.
18 See Chapter 12.

19 'Iceland to offer offshore drilling licenses in race for Arctic's oil', *The Times*, 21 August 2008.
20 The Amerasia Basin extends from Ellesmere Island to the East Siberian Sea. It includes the Bering Strait and Beaufort Sea. The border between Canada and the United States in the Beaufort Sea is disputed, but this is a disagreement between two NATO allies. See also Chapter 4, p. 54 and Chapter 11, p. 193.
21 See Chapter 4, p. 54.
22 See also Chapter 1, pp. 19–21 and Chapter 11, pp. 194–7.
23 See in general Chapter 4 above.
24 'Searching for oil in the Barents Sea', news item on the website of the Research Council of Norway, 28 February 2007.
25 'Climate change may spark conflict with Russia EU told', *Guardian*, 10 March 2008.
26 See Chapter 12.
27 'Russia and Norway Wrestle Over Barents Sea', German Press Agency, 26 June 2006.
28 Ryashin, V. (2005), 'Norway, Russia to restart Barents dispute talks', *Dow Jones Commodities News*, 13 October.
29 Kristian Atland, a researcher at the Norwegian Defence Research Establishment.
30 See in general the author's article: 'Defying the Experts', *International Herald Tribune*, 20 May 2008; and book (2008), *The Oil Hunters: Exploration and Espionage in the Middle East 1880–1939*. London and New York, NY: Continuum.
31 'How much oil do we really have?' *BBC News*, 15 July 2005.
32 'Circum-Arctic Resource Appraisal: Estimates of Undiscovered Oil and Gas North of the Arctic Circle', USGS Fact Sheet 3049, 2008, p. 1.
33 Quoted in '90 billion barrels' by Alan Bailey, *Petroleum News*, 24 July 2008.
34 'Assessment of undiscovered oil and gas resources of the East Greenland Rift Basins province', USGS Fact Sheet 3077, 2007, August.
35 *The Future of the Arctic: A New Dawn for Exploration* was published on 1 November 2006. These remarks were made at a press conference at Houston, USA, and reported in 'Wood Mackenzie downgrades Arctic as energy supply source', *Oil and Gas Financial Journal*, 11 November 2006.
36 'Searching for oil in the Barents Sea'.
37 Author's interview with Dr Rob Mandley, 29 December 2008.
38 See Chapter 9, pp. 149–52.
39 Quoted in '90 billion barrels' by Alan Bailey, *Petroleum News*, 24 July 2008.
40 Circum-Arctic Resource Appraisal: Estimates of Undiscovered Oil and Gas North of the Arctic Circle. USGS Fact Sheet 3049, 2008, p. 1.
41 Author's interview with Dr Rob Mandley.
42 See Andrew Latham's article, 'World's Arctic basins pose array of unique work opportunities', *Oil and Gas Journal*, 13 November 2006.
43 See Chapter 8, pp. 132–4.
44 'Devon Energy has no plans yet for Arctic oil find', *Financial Post*, 17 October 2007.
45 Willy De Backer quoted in the EU-Statoil conference, 'Developing Europe's Energy Security: Is the Arctic the Future Frontier?', 19 September 2008.

46 'Iraq accuses Kuwait of slant drilling and stealing 300,000 barrels of oil daily', Agence France Presse, 17 September 2000.

Chapter 6

1 *International Energy Outlook 2008*, United States Energy Information Administration.
2 Gazprom's exact earnings for 2006–07 were 873.4 billion roubles.
3 See Chapter 12, pp. 201–2.
4 The USGS put this figure at around 84 per cent.
5 The Wood Mackenzie-Fugro Robertson survey estimated that natural gas constitutes 85 per cent of existing discoveries and 74 per cent of undiscovered reserves.
6 'StatoilHydro strikes gas in Barents Sea', *International Herald Tribune*, 1 November 2008.
7 'Study points to major source of natural gas in Alaska', *Washington Post*, 12 November 2008; 'US estimates 85.4 Tcf in Alaska natural gas hydrates', Reuters, 12 November 2008.
8 'Gas trove lurks in Russo-Norwegian "grey zone"', *Scandinavian Oil and Gas Magazine*, 12 June 2008.
9 Author's interview with Andrew Latham, 29 December 2008.
10 'The European Union and the Arctic Region', Communication from the Commission to the European Parliament and Council, p. 6; Andrew Latham of Wood Mackenzie, quoted in *Oil and Gas Financial Journal*, 11 November 2006.
11 See Chapter 3 of the *International Energy Outlook*, 2008.
12 EU Energy Commissioner, Andris Piebalgs, warned Russia on 3 January that 'I don't think making the EU a hostage is the proper way'.
13 'The European Union and the Arctic Region'. COM (2008). Communication from the Commission to the European Parliament and the Council, 763, 20 November, p. 6.
14 'The Arctic Energy Agenda', a roundtable of representatives of the EU, United States, Norway and Russia, Kirkenes, 7 July 2005.
15 'Developing Europe's Energy Security: Is the Arctic the Future Frontier?', Café Crossfire Debate sponsored by Friends of Europe in association with StatoilHydro, 19 September 2008, Brussels, Belgium.
16 'Russian bid to control world's gas prices', *Sunday Telegraph*, 28 December 2008.
17 China accounted for more than 50 per cent of the growth in world consumption of industrial metals from 2002 to 2005.
18 'Greenland's melting glaciers spur mining', *Wall Street Journal*, 17 July 2007.
19 Author's interview with De Beers spokesman, Toronto, ON, 22 January 2008.
20 'The Raw Materials Initiative – Meeting Our Critical Needs for Growth and Jobs in Europe'. COM (2008), 4 November 2008.
21 See Chapter 4, pp. 55–8.
22 Oceanography and Climate Research Group (2006), *Climate and Fish: How does climate affect our fish resources?* Bergen, Norway: Institute of Marine Research.
23 Hassol, S., *Impacts of a Warming Arctic*. Cambridge and New York, NY: Cambridge University Press pp. 433, 507.
24 'The Arctic Ocean and Climate Change: A Scenario for the US Navy',

United States Arctic Research Commission Special Publication No. 02–1, 2002.

25 'As polar ice turns to water, dreams of treasure abound', *New York Times,* 10 October 2005.

26 'The European Union and the Arctic Region', Communication from the Commission to the European Parliament and the Council, COM (2008), 763, 20 November 2008, p. 7.

27 The European Union and the Arctic Region. Report by the EU Commission, Brussels, COM (2008), 763, 20 November 2008, p. 3.

28 Speech at Arctic Frontiers Conference, 19 January 2009. See also 'The European Union and the Arctic Region', Communication from the Commission to the European Parliament and the Council, 20 November 2008, pp. 7–8.

29 In 2008 the UN estimated that about 50 per cent of fish stocks are fully utilized and another 25 per cent are overfished. This leaves just 25 per cent with some potential for increased fish harvests.

30 'The Barents Sea Cod: the last of the large cod stocks', *World Wildlife Fund Norway Report,* 10 May 2004.

31 See William Dunlop's article 'Straddling stocks in the Barents Sea Loophole', *IBRU Boundary and Security Bulletin,* Winter 1996–97.

32 On the growing global demand for fish in the Far East and beyond see 'Japan faces up to the prospect of "peak fish"'. *Financial Times,* 28 January 2009.

33 In May 2008, for example, several boat captains and ship owners in Murmansk wrote jointly to Prime Minister Putin asking for a more secure presence after Norwegian authorities asked the patrol vessel Mikula to leave the port at Barentsburg on Spitsbergen. Reported by the Norwegian paper *Fiskeribladet,* 20 May 2008.

34 'Novaya Zemlya opening up?' *Barents Observer,* 19 May 2008.

Chapter 7

1 'Arctic riches coming out of the cold', *International Herald Tribune,* 10 October 2005.

2 The Russian carriers use the port at Dudinka.

3 'Russian ship crosses "Arctic bridge" to Manitoba', *Globe and Mail,* 18 October 2007.

4 'Naval operations in an ice-free Arctic', a symposium held 17–18 April 2001, Washington DC, reported by the Office of Naval Research, Naval Ice Center, Oceanographer of the Navy and the Arctic Research Commission; 'Arctic Marine Transport Workshop', a conference held at the Scott Polar Research Institute, Cambridge UK, by the Institute of the North, US Arctic Research Commission and International Arctic Science Committee, 28–30 September 2004.

5 *Arctic Climate Impact Assessment,* p. 925.

6 See Chapters 4, pp. 52–3 and 9, pp. 159–61; Butler, W. E. (1971), *The Soviet Union and the Law of the Sea.* Baltimore, MD: John Hopkins Press, p. 116.

7 *Arctic Marine Shipping Assessment,* 29 April 2009, pp. 27, 30, 35.

8 See Chapter 11, pp. 186–7.

9 'Trailblazer Beluga', *Tradewinds,* 5 September 2008.

10 Author's interview with Tim Daffern, Director of Mining and

Exploration at Angus & Ross, 16 December 2008. See also Chapter 6, pp. 92–3.

11 In 2007 the cost of leasing a large container ship was $26,000 per day.

12 See the article by Borgerson, S. G. (2008), 'Arctic meltdown: the economic and security implications of global warming', *Foreign Affairs*, 87, (2), 63–77.

13 From 376 million dwt to 553 million dwt in the year 2030, according to OPEC's *World Oil Outlook*, 2008, p. 177.

14 'Malaysia, Indonesia and Singapore set up cooperative mechanism', *Channel News Asia*, 4 September 2007.

15 Ships that have any chance at all of contacting ice are 'ice-strengthened' or 'ice-capable', while an ordinary ship with no strengthening will not risk touching the ice at all. There is no actual universal definition of what needs to be done to a ship to be 'officially ice-strengthened' and it can be applied to all manner of ships, whether supply ships, tankers, container ships, warships etc. Commonly ice-strengthened ships can cope with continuous ice about 25–50 inches thick, perhaps by having more power or thicker plating in certain places, as well as an icebreaking bow. To cut through ice any thicker, an 'icebreaker' – with a distinctive design, a strengthened hull and specially reinforced steel in its bow and stern – is required.

16 'The European Union and the Arctic Region'. Communication from the Commission to the European Parliament and Council, COM (2008), 763, 20 November 2008, p. 8.

17 'How climate change sparked a Canadian gold rush', *The Times*, 17 February 2008.

18 Moon, B. K. and Zapatero, R. (2009), 'Our forgotten crisis', *International Herald Tribune*, 25 January; Evans, A. (2009), 'The feeding of the nine billion: global food security for the 21st century'. *Chatham House Report*, 26 January.

19 See Chapter 1, p. 13.

20 'The Arctic: a matter of concern to us all'. Speech at the conference 'Common Concern for the Arctic', Ilulissat, Greenland, 9 September 2008.

21 '50 years on, Egypt cashing in on Suez nationalisation', Agence France Presse, 23 July 2006.

22 UNCLOS (1982), Article 26, (1).

23 Egypt's right to levy transit fees was laid down and clarified in the Suez Canal Convention in 1888.

24 UNCLOS (1982), Article 44. Article V (3) of the General Agreement on Tariffs and Trade (GATT) prohibits transit fees 'except charges for transportation or those commensurate with administrative expenses by transit or with the cost of services rendered' which shall be 'reasonable' ;Article V (4).

25 Translated from Pravda and reprinted in Armstrong, T. E. (1988), 'Soviet proposals for the Arctic: a policy declaration by Mr Gorbachev', *Polar Record*, 24, (148), 68–9.

26 'The European Union and the Arctic Region'. Report by the EU Commission, Brussels, COM (2008), 763, 20 November 2008, p. 8.

27 EU report sets up Arctic turf war: expert', Canwest News Service, 22 November 2008.

28 'Security prospects in the High North'. NATO Report, 28–9 January 2009.

29 'China builds up strategic sea lanes', *Washington Times*, 18 January 2005.

Chapter 8

1 'US government sued over failure to protect polar bears', *Guardian*, 10 March 2008; 'Polar bear added to list of threatened species in US', *Voice of America Press Releases and Documents*, 16 May 2008.
2 BP's North Sea renewal strategy forecasts the delivery of 122 wells over the next 5 years, 41 of which will be subsea. See 'BP and Subsea – a combined vision', a presentation by David Campbell, BP's North Sea director and vice president. Available at: http://www.ukooa.co.uk/downloadabledocs/365/3.%20David%20Campbell,%20BP.pdf
3 'Beaufort Sea oil exploration uncertain after court ruling', *KTUU News*, Alaska, 20 November 2008.
4 'Shell awarded Beaufort Sea leases – first step in rebuilding a position in Alaska', press release, Shell, 1 August 2005.
5 Quoted in 'Arctic takes brunt in dirty fight over oil', *Mining Top News*, 20 May 2007.
6 'US court says Shell can't drill near Alaska', *International Herald Tribune*, 21 November 2008.
7 It is estimated that around 175 billion barrels of the Alberta tar sands can be reached with existing technologies and another 135 billion could be tapped with technologies that are still under development.
8 'Shell hit by "dirty" Arctic furore', *The Times*, 20 May 2007.
9 'Shell hit by "dirty" Arctic furore'.
10 Environmental Defence (2008), *Canada's Toxic Tar Sands: The Most Destructive Project on Earth*, report, February, p. 7.
11 'Alaska pipeline "lesser environmental evil" than Mackenzie, says Sierra Club', *Red Orbit Science News*, 2 November 2005.
12 See Chapter 7, pp. 112–13.
13 OPEC's *World Oil Outlook*, 2007, p. 113.
14 'Time bomb on the Bosphorus', *The First Post*, 24 November 2008.
15 'LNG facilities in urban areas: a security risk management analysis', Good Harbor Consulting, May 2005. The risk is also considered in a report by the Council on Foreign Relations 'Liquefied natural gas: a potential terrorist target?' February 2007.
16 'Russian nuclear dump plan attacked by Arctic governor', *Guardian*, 24 May 2002.
17 '18 years on, *Exxon Valdez* oil still pours into Alaska waters', *Guardian*, 2 February 2007.
18 'Oil exploration in Arctic highly risky', *Science Daily*, 31 January 2008.
19 'The *Exxon Valdez* oil spill: a report to the president', National Response Team, May 1989, p. 13.
20 See Chapter 7, p. 110.
21 'Oil spill response challenges in Arctic waters', a report by the World Wildlife Fund, January 2008.
22 'Nordic storm sinks Swedish ship', *BBC News*, 1 November 2006; 'Arctic riches coming out of the cold', *International Herald Tribune*, 10 October 2005.
23 See Paskal, C. (2009), 'The vulnerability of energy infrastructure to environmental change', briefing paper, London: Chatham House, p. 7.

24 See Chapter 6, pp. 85–6.
25 'The Arctic: Oil's last frontier', *CNN Money*, 25 October 2006.
26 *Arctic Climate Impact Assessment*, pp. 921–2.
27 'Global warming opens Arctic seabed to the search for oil and gas', *International Herald Tribune*, 30 October 2007.
28 *Arctic Climate Impact Assessment*, pp. 470, 923.
29 *Arctic Climate Impact Assessment*, p. 920.
30 See Chapter 2, p. 26.
31 'Sovereignty tussles over Arctic territory threaten to impede oil and gas exploration', *Oilweek Magazine*, October 2007.
32 *Arctic Climate Impact Assessment*, pp. 917, 937.

Chapter 9

1 Lucas, E. (2009), *The New Cold War: Putin's Russia and the Threat to the West*. London and New York, NY: Palgrave Macmillan.
2 'Russia accused of dropping cluster bombs on Georgian civilians', *The Times*, 15 August 2008.
3 Reported in an editorial of the *Barents Observer*, 18 August 2008.
4 'Georgia claims on Russia war called into question', *New York Times*, 6 November 2008.
5 Lakhtine, W. (1930), 'Rights over the Arctic', *American Journal of International Law*, 24, (1930), 707.
6 'Medvedev: Arctic resources are key to Russia's future', *Seattle Times*, 18 September 2008.
7 Quoted in 'Russia's Oil Industry: Trouble in the Pipeline', *The Economist*, 8 May 2008.
8 'Russian oil slump stirs supply jitters', *Wall Street Journal*, 15 April 2008; '"Threat" to future of Russian oil', *BBC News*, 15 April 2008.
9 'Russian oil output may fall for first time in decade in 2008', Bloomberg, 27 March 2008.
10 'Oilman with a Total solution', *The Times*, 8 April 2006.
11 Energy Information Administration statistics, 2008. Gazprom produces 84 per cent of Russia's natural gas.
12 Russia's gas production fell by 1.35 per cent in 2007.
13 Quoted in Mankoff, J. (2009), *Eurasian Energy Security*. Report by the Council on Foreign Relations, New York, NY, p. 4.
14 'Poland strives to diversify supplies', *Financial Times*, 5 November 2008; 'Power supergrid plan to protect Europe from Russian threat to choke off energy', *The Times*, 13 November 2008.
15 See Chapter 5, pp. 70–81.
16 'The Military Balance'. IISS, February 2009; 'Russian military a "paper tiger" despite symbolic comeback, says IISS', *The Times*, 28 January 2009. This reiterated the view of the Institute of National Strategy (see 'Experts see decline in Russia's military', *International Herald Tribune*, 13 November 2007). At its peak the USSR spent around 30 per cent of its GDP on defence, around ten times more than Russia spent from 2007 to 2008. During the Georgian campaign Russia lost six planes to Georgia's ill-equipped air defences.
17 Caryl, C. (2009), 'The Russians are coming', *The New York Review of Books*, 56, (2), p. 24.
18 'Russian push on treason raises fears', *International Herald Tribune*, 21 December 2008.

19 Putin accused Mechel, and its main shareholder, Igor Zyuzin, of a number of unfair practices, wiping $5 billion off its capital value and stirring memories of other companies, most notably the energy giant, Yukos, that had also seemed to suffer ruthless persecution by the Russian state.

20 'The Central Bank in Moscow claimed to have spent $87.5 billion buying roubles between September and November 2008', *Financial Times*, 29 December 2008.

21 'Rouble at new low as Russia edges towards devaluation', *The Times* ,19 December 2008.

22 'Russia's oil boom: miracle or mirage', *International Herald Tribune*, 28 October 2008.

23 'Rouble exodus hits credit rating of Russia', *Financial Times*, 9 December 2008.

24 On Hans Island see Chapter 1, p. 20, Chapter 4, pp. 54–5 and Chapter 11, pp. 193–4. During the Cold War, United States and British submarines frequently sailed extremely close to Russia's national waters and sometimes beyond.

25 Hingley, R. (1977), *The Russian Mind*. New York, Charles Scribner, Chapter 3 *passim*.

26 Russia's historic fears of foreign attack are summarised in LeDonne, J. P. (1997), *The Russian Empire and the World 1700–1917*. New York and Oxford: Oxford University Press.

27 Tsvetkov, A. (1985), 'Artika v planakh SShA i NATO' [The Arctic in US and NATO plans], *Zarubezhnoye voyennoye obozreniye* [Foreign military review], 10, (October), p. 8.

28 Morozov, G. and Krivinsky, B. (1982), 'Rol' prolivov v vooruzhennoy bor 'be na more' [The role of straits in maritime warfare], *Morskoy sbornik* [Naval digest], 8, 16–25.

29 The sign read 'Punishment for removing this sign: $250 fine or prison'. Franckx, E. (1993), *Maritime Claims in the Arctic*, p. 142.

30 1990 Agreement between the United States of America and Union of Soviet Socialist Republics on the Maritime Boundary (the Bering Sea Maritime Boundary Agreement).

31 Article 9 of the Spitsbergen Treaty proclaims that the archipelago may 'never be used for warlike purposes'.

32 The Thule air base is described in Chapter 10.

33 See Chapter 4, p. 51.

34 Connaughton, R. (2003), *Rising Sun and Tumbling Bear: Russia's War with Japan*. London: Cassell.

35 Armstrong, T. (1952), *The Northern Sea Route: Soviet Exploration of the North East Passage*. Cambridge: Cambridge University Press, p. 30.

36 Morozov, G. and Krivinsky, B. (1982), 'Rol' prolivov v vooruzhennoy bor 'be na more' [The role of straits in maritime warfare], *Morskoy sbornik* [Naval digest], 8, 16–25.

37 See Chapter 1, p. 15.

38 1991 Regulations for Navigation on the Seaways of the Northern Sea Route.

39 'USA to steal oil-rich Arctic region away from Russia', *Pravda*, 8 December 2005.

40 *Rossiiskaya Gazeta*, 16 January 2009.

41 After the failed attempt by USS *Eastwind* and *Edisto* to cross the Vilkitsky Strait in 1967, a spokesman for the United States Navy pointed out that

'the 1967 expedition has failed in its primary mission, but not without compensating factors. Freedom of the seas in the Arctic outside claimed territorial limits has been tacitly confirmed by the Soviets'. Franckx, E. (1993), *Maritime Claims in the Arctic*, p. 162.

42 See Chapter 4, pp. 50–51.

43 On Article 234 see Chapter 7, p. 116.

44 UNCLOS (1982), Article 37.

45 See McLaren, A. (1985), 'The evolution and potential of the Arctic submarine', in Oceans '85: *Proceedings of the Conference on Ocean Engineering and the Environment*, 12–14 November, San Diego, CA; Pharand, D. (1968), 'Innocent passage in the Arctic', *Canadian Yearbook of International Law*, 6, pp. 3–60.

46 Franckx, E. (1993), *Maritime Claims in the Arctic*, pp. 147–8.

47 For example, in December 2008 Sergey Stepura, head of the Federal Security Service (FSB) Directorate for the Arkhangelsk Oblast, told the news agency RIA Novosti that intelligence services from NATO and the CIA were trying to infiltrate Arkhangelsk Oblast, Nenets Autonomous Okrug and other regions, and that their agents had been 'spotted around sensitive areas'.

48 See in general Rothwell, D. R. (1996), *The Polar Regions and the Development of International Law*, Cambridge: Cambridge University Press, pp. 204–5.

49 All quotes in this paragraph are from the article 'Nuclear waste poses Arctic threat', *BBC News*, 19 October 2006.

50 'A disaster waiting to happen: preparing for oil spills in Norway's Arctic waters', feature story published on the website of the World Wildlife Fund (WWF), 19 January 2006.

51 Dag Nagoda, head of the WWF's Barents Sea Ecoregion Programme, quoted in 'A disaster waiting to happen: preparing for oil spills in Norway's Arctic waters', feature story published on the website of the WWF, 19 January 2006.

52 See Chapter 8, pp. 131–2.

Chapter 10

1 Statement by the Department of State on the US-Danish Agreement on Greenland, 10 April 1941.

2 'Greenland says Russians must have say on U.S. missile shield', Agence France Presse, 23 August 2000.

3 'As a land thaws, so do Greenland's aspirations for independence', *Christian Science Monitor*, 16 October 2007.

4 'As a land thaws, so do Greenland's aspirations for independence', *Christian Science Monitor*.

5 See Chapter 1, p. 18.

6 Robert Lansing of Woodrow Wilson. See Macmillan, M. (2002), *Peacemakers: The Paris Conference of 1919 and its Attempt to End the War.* London: John Murray, p. 18.

7 At a meeting with Saddam Hussein on 25 July 1990, United States Ambassador April Glaspie had assured the Iraqi leader that 'we have no opinion on the Arab-Arab conflicts like your border disagreement with Kuwait'. See Shlaim, A. (1995), *War and Peace in the Middle East: A Concise History.* Oxford: Oxford University Press, pp. 93–4.

8 This was the point of, for example, Great Britain's 1919 Treaty with Persia. See Keddie, N. (2003), *Modern Iran: Roots and Results of Revolution*. Newhaven, CT: Yale University Press.

9 National Security Presidential Decision Directive/NSPD 66, January 2009.

10 National Security Presidential Decision Directive/NSPD 66.

11 In his book *Democracy in America*, Volume 2, Chapter 10, the French writer Alexis de Tocqueville described the means by which the early settlers drove the Red Indians off their native lands. On the slaughter of the Red Indian see generally Brogan, H. (1999), *The Longman History of the United States of America*. London and New York, NY: Longman, pp. 62–9; Reynolds, D. (2009), *America, Empire of Liberty: A New History*. London: Allen Lane.

12 Dallek, R. (2007), *Nixon and Kissinger*. London and New York, NY: Penguin, p. 239.

13 'Manifest Destiny'. See Longley, C. (2002), *Chosen People: The Big Idea that Shapes England and America*. London: Hodder and Stoughton; Clarke, J. C. D. (1994), *The Language of Liberty 1660–1832: Political Discourse and Social Dynamics in the Anglo-American World*. Cambridge and New York: Cambridge University Press; Lipset, S. M. (1996), *American Exceptionalism: A Double-Edged Sword*. London: W. W. Norton & Co.

14 Holmes, S. (2008), 'Breaking the ice: emergent legal issues in arctic sovereignty', *Chicago Journal of International Law*, 9, (1), 323–53.

15 Article 51 of the 1945 UN Charter acknowledges 'the inherent right of individual or collective self-defence if an armed attack occurs against a member of the United Nations'. On 8 November 2002 a second UN Resolution, 1441, decreed that 'Iraq has been and remains in material breach of its obligations under relevant resolutions'. This was used by the US and UK as a justification for the attack that followed 4 months later.

16 UNCLOS, Annex VI, Article 1.

17 UNCLOS, Article 298, (1), (b). Rivkin's views were expressed at a conference, 'The Law of the Sea Treaty: Help or Hindrance?', held by the American Enterprise Institute, July 2007.

18 In 1970, Richard Nixon had proclaimed that 'I am today proposing that all nations adopt as soon as possible a treaty under which they would renounce all national claims over the natural resources of the seabed beyond the point where the high seas reach a depth of 200 metres, and would agree to regard these resources as the common heritage of mankind'. See his 'Statement About United States Oceans Policy', 23 May 1970.

19 The Energy Information Agency's report, *Annual Energy Outlook 2009*, predicts a moderate recovery in the production of Alaskan oil although not to the levels of the 1980s.

20 The *Annual Energy Outlook 2008* report (p. 79) predicted that US oil production will increase slightly from 5.1m b/d in 2006 to a peak of 6.3m b/d in 2018 and then drop gradually to 5.6m b/d by 2030. Alaskan production is expected to wane gradually from 1.8m b/d to less than half that figure by 2030.

21 Remarks of Senator Barack Obama, at Washington DC, 28 February 2006.

22 Energy Information Agency statistics, 2008.

23 Geneva Convention on the Continental Shelf 1958, Article 1.

24 'New seafloor maps may bolster US Arctic claims', Associated Press, 12 February 2008.
25 UNCLOS, Article 140, (2).
26 Written testimony before the Senate Foreign Relations Committee, Washington DC, 27 September 2007.
27 Tunander, O. (1989), *Cold Water Politics: The Maritime Strategy and Geopolitics of the Northern Front*. London: Sage.
28 UNCLOS (1982), Articles 17, 38.
29 'Chinese overseas direct investment and the economic crisis', *The World Today*, Chatham House, London, January 2009, pp. 15–16.
30 'Concern grows as extent of Rio Tinto's concessions to Chinalco is revealed', *The Times*, 14 February 2009.
31 'Washington opposition forces Chinese to withdraw oil offer', *Guardian*, 3 August 2005.
32 Martin, M. F. (2008), 'China's sovereign wealth fund'. *Congressional Research Service Report*, 22 January, p. 5.
33 See, for example, John Kampfner's article, 'The West's great new threat is right at home in the city', *Guardian*, 26 July 2007.
34 'Credit crunch plays into China's shopping plans', *International Herald Tribune*, 20 February 2009.
35 Presidential Decision Directive/NSC-26.
36 'A push to increase icebreakers in the Arctic', *New York Times*, 17 August 2008.
37 National Security Presidential Decision Directive/NSPD 66.

Chapter 11

1 C$ refers to Canadian dollars.
2 'Ottawa buying up to 8 Arctic Patrol ships', *CBC News*, 9 July 2008.
3 United States Navy official website. 'USS *Charlotte* achieves milestone during under-ice transit', 1 December 2005. Available at: http://www.navy. mil/search/display.asp?story_id=21223
4 'US sub may have toured Canadian Arctic zone', *National Post*, 19 December 2005.
5 'Martin offers "necessary measures" in Arctic', CBC TV, 19 December 2005.
6 See Chapter 4, pp. 50–52.
7 See Chapter 7, p. 109.
8 See Chapter 7, p. 109.
9 The story of these early expeditions is told in Calvert, J. (1961), *Surface at the Pole: The Story of the USS Skate*. London: Hutchinson.
10 Joe Clark, Minister for External Affairs, House of Commons, Debates, vol. IV at 6,043, 20 June 1985.
11 Quoted in Kathleen Harris' article 'Laying claim to Canada's internal waters', Sun Media, 23 February 2007.
12 Trudeau, P. E. (1993), *Memoirs*. Toronto, ON: McClelland and Stewart, p. 293.
13 See Chapter 4, p. 60.
14 Official website of the Prime Minister Stephen Harper. 'Prime Minister Stephen Harper announces new Arctic offshore patrol ships', 9 July 2008. Available at: http://pm.gc.ca/eng/media.asp?id=1742
15 Mitchell Sharp, Minister for External Affairs, admitted that Canada was

'not prepared to litigate with other states on vital issues concerning which the law is either inadequate, non-existent or irrelevant to the kind of situation Canada faces, as in the case of the Arctic', House of Commons, Debates, vol. VI at 5,952, 16 April 1970.

16 Trudeau, P. E. (1970), 'Canadian Prime Minister's Remarks on the Proposed Legislation', 9 ILM 600 at 601.

17 House of Commons, Debates, vol. VI at 5,951, 16 April 1970.

18 Statement by Joe Clark to the House of Commons, Debates, vol. V at 6,463, 10 September 1985.

19 There is an important distinction between 'transit' and 'innocent' passage. A coastal state has considerable powers over ships that make 'innocent passage' through its territorial sea or EEZ (UNCLOS (1982), Article 21) but has to treat an international strait in the same way as high seas. Under UNCLOS (1982), Part II Section 2, 'there shall be no suspension of transit passage' by a coastal state (Article 44), although the state can adopt laws and regulations to ensure safety and environmental standards (Article 42).

20 A treaty that preceded UNCLOS (1982) was the Territorial Sea Convention, 1958.

21 UNCLOS (1982), Articles 37, 38; see also Chapter 4, pp. 51–2.

22 See Chapter 1, pp. 17–19.

23 'Russia accused of annexing the Arctic for oil reserves by Canada', *Sunday Telegraph*, 18 May 2008.

24 Official website of the Prime Minister Stephen Harper. 'PM announces Government of Canada will extend jurisdiction over Arctic waters', 27 August 2008. Available at: http://pm.gc.ca/eng/media.asp?category=1&id=2248

25 Interview with Kathleen Harris of Sun Media, 'Laying claim to Canada's internal waters', 23 February 2007.

26 The 2005 governmental document was 'Canada's International Policy Statement: A role of pride and influence in the world', Government of Canada document, Ottawa. Ten years before, the government had published 'Canada in the World: Canadian Foreign Policy Review', Department of Foreign Affairs and International Trade, Ottawa.

27 Interview with Kathleen Harris of Sun Media.

28 'Return to Arctic waters slowly gains momentum', *Calgary Herald*, 7 November 2007.

29 Website of the property company Private Islands Inc. Available at: http://www.privateislandsinc.com/

30 The exaggerated importance of Hans Island is discussed in Chapter 1, p. 20.

31 'Disputing boundaries', *CBC News Online*, 11 October 2005.

32 Interview with Reuters, 25 July 2005.

33 'Canada flexes its muscles in dispute over Arctic wastes', *Daily Telegraph*, 23 August 2005.

34 'Imperial Oil acquires exploration parcel in Beaufort Sea', press release, 19 July 2007.

35 'Canada's Unconventional Revolution', *Petroleum Economist*, January 2008.

36 Ipsos-Reid survey, 18 August 2008.

37 UNCLOS (1982), Annex II, Articles 1–9.

38 See Introduction p. 5.

39 The 1911 Convention for the Preservation and Protection of Fur Seals was

signed by the United States, Great Britain, Russia and Japan. On the 1920 Spitsbergen Treaty see Chapter 4, pp. 55–57, and Chapter 6, p. 101.
40 Professor Michael Byers', speech to the Vancouver Institute, 28 January 2006.

Chapter 12

1 'Norway to dip into $332bn oil fund', *Financial Times*, 14 December 2008.
2 'Norway sees oil production falling 9.7 per cent this year', Bloomberg, 8 January 2009.
3 'Norway: A haven for oil production', *Alexander's Oil and Gas Connections*, 21 July 2004.
4 'The Norwegian Government High North strategy', Norwegian Ministry of Foreign Affairs, 1 December 2006, p. 56.
5 'Norway offers 79 oil/gas exploration blocks', Reuters, 27 June 2008.
6 'Norway proceeds with seismic tests in Lofoten', *Oil and Gas Journal*, 16 June 2008.
7 'Norway oil spill contained, stirs fears for Arctic', Reuters, 14 December 2007.
8 'Extent of Norway's continental shelf in the High North clarified', press release, Norwegian Ministry of Foreign Affairs, 15 April 2009.
9 See Pedersen, T. (2006), 'The Svalbard continental shelf controversy', *Ocean Development and International Law* 37, 3, (4), 339–58.
10 'Norway challenged by Russian plans in Spitsbergen waters', *Barents Observer*, 5 August 2008.
11 'Russia to reopen scientific station on Svalbard', *Barents Observer*, 23 December 2008.
12 'Russia, Norway to jointly fight oil spills', *New Europe*, 16 June 2008.
13 Offical website of the Kremlin. 'Russian Foreign Policy Concept 2008', 12 July 2008. Available at: http://www.kremlin.ru/eng/text/docs/2008/07/204750.shtml
14 'The Norwegian Government High North strategy' (2006), p. 9. This was also the theme of Foreign Minister Stoere's speech in Arkhangelsk, 'Norway and Russia in the High North: common opportunities, common challenges', 21 January 2009.
15 Press conference at Tromsoe, 15 April 2005. See Pedersen, T. (2006), 'The Svalbard continental shelf controversy', 353.
16 On 9 June 2005 the Standing Committee unanimously stated that 'bilateral dialogues with Canada, France, the UK, Germany, the USA and the EU will become very important in time to come' and stressed the need for obtaining 'international understanding for the necessary control and enforcement measures' in the Svalbard zone.
17 Article 9 of the 'Agreed minutes on the Delimitation of the Continental shelf beyond 200 nautical miles between the Faroe Islands, Iceland and Norway in the southern part of the Banana Hole in the Northeast Atlantic'.
18 'Agreement on Continental Shelf in the Norwegian Sea', press release, Norway Mission to the UN, 20 September 2006.
19 'Global warming opens Arctic seabed to the search for oil and gas', *International Herald Tribune*, 30 October 2007.
20 See Chapter 5, pp. 65–6.
21 'Industry experts see future for exploration offshore Iceland', *Alexander's Gas and Oil Connections*, 28 October 2008.

22 Reported by NRK Media, 16 August 2004. See Pedersen, T. (2006), 'The Svalbard continental shelf controversy', 347.
23 'Canada and Denmark join rush to claim Denmark', *Daily Telegraph*, 14 August 2007.
24 'Danish team heads for North Pole', *BBC News*, 13 August 2007.
25 See Chapter 4, p. 58.
26 See Chapter 5.
27 Minister for Finance and Foreign Affairs, Per Berthelsen's speech to the 'Arctic Frontiers' conference, Tromsoe, Norway, 19 January 2009.
28 'Danish doubts over Greenland vote', *BBC News*, 27 November 2008.
29 'As a land thaws, so do Greenland's aspirations for independence', *Christian Science Monitor*.
30 'As a land thaws, so do Greenland's aspirations for independence', *Christian Science Monitor*.
31 'As a land thaws, so do Greenland's aspirations for independence', *Christian Science Monitor*.
32 In 2008, the Energy Information Administration predicted that China's oil consumption will continue to grow during 2009, with daily oil demand reaching 8.4 million barrels. This anticipated growth of over 800,000 bbl/d represents 32 per cent of projected world oil demand growth for the period. However, this estimate was published before the full severity of the global economic depression became clear.
33 For more information on China National Offshore Oil Corporation's bid for Unocal see Chapter 10, p. 179.
34 'Conditions ripe for reshuffle in energy sector', *Financial Times*, 6 January 2009.
35 'China eyes developed mine assets', *Financial Times*, 5 January 2009.
36 'China to boost ties with Zambia', *BBC News*, 3 February 2007.
37 'How the Bush administration should handle China and South China Sea maritime territorial sea', *Heritage Foundation*, 5 September 2001.
38 'Chinese plan to expand navy points to bigger role', *Financial Times*, 17 April 2009.
39 Kaplan, R. D. (2009), 'Center stage for the twenty-first century', *Foreign Affairs*, 88 (2), 16–32.

Conclusion

1 Under UNCLOS (1982), Annex II, Article 8, 'in the case of disagreement by the coastal state with the recommendations of the Commission, the coastal state shall, within a reasonable time, make a revised or new submission to the Commissions'. This also leaves open the possibility of making a further claim if the coastal state claims to have discovered new geological evidence.
2 Professor Frederic Lasserre, quoted in 'Canada says science backs up its Arctic claim', Agence France Presse, 9 August 2008.
3 See Chapter 1, p. 15.
4 See Chapter 4, pp. 52–6, and Chapter 7, p. 116.
5 Another example of just such a scenario was the Yangtze River incident in 1949.
6 See Chapter 12, p. 208.
7 See Paskal, C. and Lodge, M. (2009), 'A fair deal on seabed wealth: the

promise and pitfalls of Article 82 on the outer continental shelf', briefing paper, London: Chatham House.
8 UNCLOS (1982), Article 82, (2).
9 UNCLOS (1982), Article 82, (4).
10 'The Norwegian Government High North strategy', (2006), p. 16.
11 See Chapter 4, pp. 52–3.
12 UNCLOS (1982), Article 234.
13 'Nato chief would put military in Arctic', Associated Press, 30 January 2009.
14 See Chapter 8, pp. 132.
15 The proposals of the World Wildlife Fund to preserve the Arctic's environment are mentioned in Chapter 8, pp. 132.
16 'The European Union's strategy of sustainable management for the Arctic', speech by Dr Joe Borg to the 'Arctic Frontiers' conference, Tromsoe, Norway, 19 January 2009.
17 Jeffrey Garten, 'Create a global authority for Arctic oil and gas', *Financial Times*, 14 August 2008.
18 Rothwell, D. R. (2008), 'The Arctic in international affairs: Time for a new regime', *Brown Journal of World Affairs*, XV, (I), 241–54.

Bibliography

Selected books

Aburish, S. K. (2000), *Saddam Hussein: The Politics of Revenge*. London: Bloomsbury.

Archer, C. (1988), *The Soviet Union and Northern Waters*. London: Routledge.

Armstrong, T. (1952), *The Northern Sea Route: Soviet Exploration of the North East Passage*. Cambridge: Cambridge University Press.

Bernier, J. E. (1939), *Master Mariner and Arctic Explorer*. Ottawa, ON: Le Droit.

Berton, P. (1988), *The Arctic Grail: The Quest for the Northwest Passage and the North Pole 1818–1909*. New York: Viking.

Bomann-Larsen, T. (2006), *Roald Amundsen*. Stroud: Sutton Publishing.

Brigham, L. W. (1991), *The Soviet Maritime Arctic*. London: Belhaven Press.

Brogan, H. (1999), *The Longman History of the United States of America*. London and New York: Longman.

Burkhanov, V. F. (1957), *Soviet Arctic Research*. Translated by E. R. Hope. Ottawa, ON: Defence Research Board of Canada.

Butler, W. E. (1971), *The Soviet Union and the Law of the Sea*. Baltimore, MD: John Hopkins Press.

Calvert, J. (1961), *Surface at the Pole: The Story of the USS Skate*. London: Hutchinson.

Clarke, J. C. D. (1994), *The Language of Liberty 1660–1832: Political Discourse and Social Dynamics in the Anglo-American World*. Cambridge and New York: Cambridge University Press.

Connaughton, R. (2003), *Rising Sun and Tumbling Bear: Russia's War with Japan*. London: Cassell.

Dallek, R. (2007), *Nixon and Kissinger*. London and New York: Penguin.

Dosman, E. J. (1975), *The National Interest: The Politics of Northern Development 1968–75*. Toronto, ON: McClelland and Stewart.

Dosman, E. J. (1989), *Sovereignty and Security in the Arctic*. London: Routledge.

Franckx, E. (1993), *Maritime Claims in the Arctic: Canadian and Russian Perspectives*. Dordrecht and London: Martinus Nijhoff.

Griffiths, F. (1987), *Politics of the Northwest Passage*. Kingston, ON: McGill-Queens University Press.

248

Hassol, S. (2004), *Impacts of a Warming Arctic: Arctic Climate Impact Assessment.* Cambridge and New York: Cambridge University Press.

Hingley, R. (1977), *The Russian Mind.* New York, NY: Charles Scribner.

Howard, R. (2008), *The Oil Hunters: Exploration and Espionage in the Middle East 1880–1939.* London and New York: Continuum.

Keddie, N. (2003), *Modern Iran: Roots and Results of Revolution.* Yale: Yale University Press.

LeDonne, J. P. (1997), *The Russian Empire and the World 1700–1917.* New York and Oxford: Oxford University Press.

Lipset, S. M. (1996), *American Exceptionalism: A Double-Edged Sword.* London: W. W. Norton & Co.

Longley, C. (2002), *Chosen People: The Big Idea that Shapes England and America.* London: Hodder and Stoughton.

Lucas, E. (2009), *The New Cold War: Putin's Russia and the Threat to the West.* London and New York, NY: Palgrave Macmillan.

Macmillan, M. (2002), *Peacemakers: The Paris Conference of 1919 and its Attempt to End the War.* London: John Murray.

Marcel, V. (2006), *Oil Titans: National Oil Companies in the Middle East.* London: Chatham House & Brookings Institution.

Officer, C. and Page, J. (2001), *A Fabulous Kingdom: The Exploration of the Arctic.* Oxford and New York, NY: Oxford University Press.

Parry, W. E. (1824), *Journal of a Voyage for the Discovery of the North-West Passage from the Atlantic to the Pacific.* London: John Murray.

Paskal, C. and Lodge, M. (2009), *A Fair Deal on Seabed Wealth: The Promise and Pitfalls of Article 82 on the Outer Continental Shelf.* London: Chatham House.

Pharand, D. (1988), *Canada's Arctic Waters in International Law.* Cambridge: Cambridge University Press.

Reynolds, D. (2009), *America, Empire of Liberty: A New History.* London: Allen Lane.

Rothwell, D. R. (1988), *Maritime Boundaries and Resource Development: Options for the Beaufort Sea.* Calgary, AB: University of Calgary.

Rothwell, D. R. (1996), *The Polar Regions and the Development of International Law.* Cambridge: Cambridge University Press.

Rothwell, D. R. and Elferink, A. G. (2001), *The Law of the Sea and Polar Maritime Delimitation and Jurisdiction.* The Hague and London: Kluwer Law International.

Shaxson, N. (2007), *Poisoned Wells: The Dirty Politics of African Oil.* London and New York, NY: Palgrave Macmillan.

Shlaim, A. (1995), *War and Peace in the Middle East: A Concise History.* London and New York, NY: Penguin Books.

Simmons, M. (2005), *Twilight in the Desert: The Coming Saudi Oil Shock and the World Economy.* London and New York, NY: John Wiley & Sons.

Trudeau, P. E. (1993), *Memoirs.* Toronto, ON: McClelland and Stewart.

Tunander, O. (1989), *Cold Water Politics: The Maritime Strategy and Geopolitics of the Northern Front.* London: Sage.

Yergin, D. (1991), *The Prize: The Epic Quest for Oil, Money and Power.* New York, NY: Simon & Schuster.

250 *Bibliography*

Journal articles

Armstrong, T. E. (1988), 'Soviet proposals for the Arctic: a policy declaration by Mr Gorbachev', *Polar Record*, 24, (148), 68–9.

Borgerson, S. G. (2008), 'Arctic meltdown: the economic and security implications of global warming', *Foreign Affairs*, 87, (2), 63–77.

Brown, K. (2009), 'Chinese overseas direct investment and the economic crisis', *The World Today*, 65 (1), 15–16.

Churchill, R. R. (1985), 'Maritime delimitation in the Jan Mayen area', *Marine Policy*, 9, 16–38.

Deudney, D. and Ikenberry, G. K. (2009), 'The myth of the autocratic revival', *Foreign Affairs*, 88, (1), 77–93.

Dunlap, W. V. (1997), 'Straddling stocks in the Barents Sea loophole', *International Boundaries Research Unit Boundary and Security Bulletin*, Winter, 4, (4), 79.

Hagedorn, F. (2008),'Expanding forests and changing growth forms of Siberian larch at the Polar Urals treeline during the 20th century', *Global Change Biology*, 14, Issue 7, 1581–91.

Holmes, S. (2008), 'Breaking the ice: emergent legal issues in Arctic sovereignty', *Chicago Journal of International Law*, 9, (1), 323–53.

Kaplan, R. D. (2009), 'Center stage for the twenty-first century', *Foreign Affairs*, 88 (2), 16–32.

Lakhtine, W. (1930), 'Rights over the Arctic', *American Journal of International Law*, 24, 703–17.

Morozov, G. and Krivinsky, B. (1982), 'Rol' prolivov v vooruzhennoy bor 'be na more' [The role of straits in maritime warfare], *Morskoy sbornik* [Naval digest], 8, 16–25.

Pearson, L. B. (1945–46), 'Canada looks down north', *Foreign Affairs*, 24, (4), 638.

Pedersen, T. (2006), 'The Svalbard continental shelf controversy', *Ocean Development and International Law*, 37, (3 and 4), 339–58.

Pharand, D. (1969), 'Innocent passage in the Arctic', *Canadian Yearbook of International Law*, 6, 3–60.

Pharand, D. (1989), 'Canada's sovereignty over the Northwest Passage', *Michigan Journal of International Law*, 10, (2), 653–78.

Reid, R. (1974), 'The Canadian claim to sovereignty over the waters of the Arctic', *Canadian Yearbook of International Law*, 12, (3), 1–136.

Ross, M. L. (2008), 'Blood barrels: why oil wealth fuels conflict', *Foreign Affairs*, 87, (3), 325–61.

Rothwell, D. R. (2008), 'The Arctic in international affairs: time for a new regime', *Brown Journal of World Affairs*, XV, (I), 241–54.

Tsvetkov, A. (1985), 'Arktika v planakh SShA i NATO' [The Arctic in US and NATO Plans], *Zarubezhnoye voyennoye obozreniye* [Foreign military review], 10, 8–24.

Index